Laziness
Does Not
Exist

Laziness Does Not Exist

A Defense of the Exhausted, Exploited, and Overworked

DR. DEVON PRICE

ATRIA BOOKS

New York   London   Toronto   Sydney   New Delhi

ATRIA
BOOKS

An Imprint of Simon & Schuster, Inc.
1230 Avenue of the Americas
New York, NY 10020

First Atria Books hardcover edition January 2021

ATRIA BOOKS and colophon are trademarks of Simon & Schuster, Inc.

For information about special discounts for bulk purchases, please contact Simon &
Schuster Special Sales at 1-866-506-1949 or business@simonandschuster.com.

The Simon & Schuster Speakers Bureau can bring authors to your live event. For more
information, or to book an event, contact the Simon & Schuster Speakers Bureau at
1-866-248-3049 or visit our website at www.simonspeakers.com.

Interior design by Jill Putorti

Manufactured in the United States of America

1 3 5 7 9 10 8 6 4 2

Library of Congress Cataloging-in-Publication Data has been applied for.

ISBN 978-1-9821-4010-6
ISBN 978-1-9821-4013-7 (ebook)

For Kim,
who taught me that if a person's behavior doesn't make sense,
it's because I'm missing a piece of their context

Contents

How I Learned I Wasn't Lazy

I have a reputation as a productive person, but that reputation has cost me a lot. To the rest of the world I've always looked like a put-together, organized, diligent little worker bee. For years, I managed to balance professional success, creative output, and activism without letting anybody in my life down. I never turned work in late. If I said I was going to be at an event, I'd be there. If a friend needed help editing a cover letter for a job application (or moral support as they called their congressional representative about the latest human-rights horror of the moment), I was available. Behind that veneer of energy and dependability, I was a wreck. I'd spend hours alone in the dark, overstimulated and too tired to even read a book. I resented every person I said yes to, even as I couldn't stop overcommitting to them. I was forever spreading myself too thin, dragging myself from obligation to obligation, thinking my lack of energy made me unforgivably "lazy."

I know a lot of people like me. People who work overtime, never turning down additional work for fear of disappointing their boss. They're available to friends and loved ones twenty-four seven, providing an unending stream of support and advice. They care about dozens and dozens of social issues yet always feel guilty about not doing "enough" to address them, because there simply aren't enough hours in the day. These types of people often try to cram every waking moment with activity. After a long day at work, they try to teach themselves Spanish on the Duolingo app on their phone, for example, or they try to learn how to code in Python on sites like Code Academy.

People like this—people like me—are doing everything society has taught us we have to do if we want to be virtuous and deserving of respect. We're committed employees, passionate activists, considerate friends, and perpetual students. We worry about the future. We plan ahead. We try to reduce our anxiety by controlling the things we can control—and we push ourselves to work very, very hard.

Most of us spend the majority of our days feeling tired, overwhelmed, and disappointed in ourselves, certain we've come up short. No matter how much we've accomplished or how hard we've worked, we never believe we've done enough to feel satisfied or at peace. We never think we deserve a break. Through all the burnouts, stress-related illnesses, and sleep-deprived weeks we endure, we remain convinced that having limitations makes us "lazy"—and that laziness is always a bad thing.

This worldview is ruining our lives.

————

For years, I fell into an awful pattern where I'd work nonstop for the first five or six hours of the day, running through as many tasks as possible without any breaks. During those periods, I'd focus so intently on the mountains of e-mails I had to respond to or the papers I had to grade that I would often forget to pause and eat a snack, stretch my legs, or even use the bathroom. Anyone who interrupted me during those cram sessions would get a blank and irritated stare. Once those five hours were over, I'd collapse into a cranky, hungry, emotionally drained heap.

I loved being superefficient like that, plugging away at all the items on my to-do list that had given me anxiety the night before. I could get a truly impressive amount of stuff done during those sprints. But when I worked myself that hard, I'd be completely useless afterward. My afternoons were utterly nonproductive, with me mindlessly scrolling through Instagram or Tumblr for hours. In the evening, all I had energy left to do was flop onto my bed, watch a few YouTube videos, and eat chips in the dark of my apartment.

Eventually, after a few hours of "recharging," I'd start to feel guilty for not using my time in more productive ways. *I should be out with friends*, I'd tell myself. *I should be working on creative projects. I should cook myself a nice, healthy dinner.* I'd start to feel stress about everything I needed to accomplish the next day. And then, the next morning, the cycle of guilt, overwork, and exhaustion would start up all over again.

Even back then, I knew this cycle was bad for me, and yet I found it hard to break out of. As terrible as my exhaustion felt, completing a huge pile of tasks in a couple of hours felt almost equally good. I lived to check things off to-do lists. I would get a rush when somebody would exclaim, "Wow, that was fast!" because I'd e-mailed back sooner than they expected. I would agree to take on more responsibilities than I wanted to handle because I felt a deep need to show I was a diligent, reliable worker. And then, after putting so many tasks on my plate, I would inevitably flame out and become depressed or sick.

For years, I would berate myself for running out of steam. Whenever I didn't push myself to the limit, I felt shame about being stagnant. Whenever I said no to a task at work, I'd worry I wasn't earning my keep. If I failed to help a friend when they needed it or didn't make it to a protest I'd planned to go to or a concert a friend was performing in, I'd feel certain everyone was judging me. I was terrified that anytime I took a break or drew a boundary, I was being *lazy*. After all, there was nothing worse I could be than that. As awful as being tired, overwhelmed, and burned out with no energy for hobbies or friends was, surely being lazy was worse.

———

I learned at an early age to tie my self-worth to how productive I was. I got good grades, and teachers generally thought I was bright, so they encouraged me to work extra hard and take on more opportunities and responsibilities. Whether it was tutoring a struggling peer in civics class or running the arts and crafts table at Bible Camp, adults would constantly ask me to take on extra responsibilities, and I would always say yes. I wanted to be helpful, industrious, and successful. After all, working hard and doing a lot was how you ensured yourself a bright future.

I had my reasons for worrying about the future. My dad grew up in Appalachia, in an old mining town with depleted infrastructure. Job prospects were nonexistent. As an adult, my dad was forever fretting about his financial future. He had cerebral palsy, which made it very difficult for him to write or type, so going to college or getting an office job seemed out of the question to him. Instead, he worked backbreaking manual-labor jobs, knowing his body wouldn't be able to handle them forever. My mom was a dental hygienist, but she suffered from scoliosis, which left her able to work only two or three days per week.

Neither of my parents had university degrees, so their professional options were limited. They desperately wanted me to avoid the same fate, so they taught me to plan, and prepare, and work hard. They signed me up for my school's talented and gifted program as soon as I was eligible. They encouraged me to get a part-time job, to take honors classes, and to participate in extracurriculars like Model UN and speech and debate. They believed that if I worked hard, saved money, and took on many of life's "extra" responsibilities, I could get ahead. I could get into a decent school, earn some financial aid, and forge a successful career for myself— as long as I wasn't lazy. Teachers saw potential in me, and they strongly encouraged this too.

This pressure to achieve my way into stability caused me significant anxiety, but the alternative struck me as far worse. I was already beginning to notice that not all kids were encouraged to thrive the way I was. Some kids were seen as lost causes, because they were disruptive or too slow to master a subject. When those kids were still young, they received some support, and some sympathy. But the longer they struggled, the less patience and compassion they got. Eventually people stopped talking about those students' needs or limitations. Instead, the conversation became about how *lazy* they were. Once someone was deemed lazy, they were much likelier to get yelled at than they were to be helped. If a kid was lazy, there was no fixing it. It was their fault they were missing assignments, failing to grasp hard concepts, and not putting time into anything "productive" after school. Lazy kids didn't have futures. And, the world seemed to be telling me, they deserved what they got.

———

Max also learned to tie her worth to her productivity. Like me, she came from a family that spent multiple generations in poverty in the rural South; like me, she went on to achieve academically and professionally at a high level. And like me, her commitment to overwork started to eat her alive.

Today, Max is a writer at an information technology firm, where she puts together applications and proposals, as well as blog posts about the firm's work. In order to do her job well, Max needs a lot of support from her coworkers. They're supposed to provide her with detailed information on each project, completed application forms, and clean, well-written drafts. Often, though, Max doesn't get that information on time, leaving her scrambling to assemble what she needs herself, while a looming deadline and an impatient boss breathe down her neck. She regularly works eighty- to ninety-hour weeks, and seems constantly to be at her wit's end.

"These proposals have to be perfect, but I can't rely on anyone else to check them carefully enough," Max says. "Every government agency that we work with has different requirements. Sometimes it will be something as specific as requiring that we sign our forms in blue ink, not black. But the people I work with miss this stuff all the time, and my manager doesn't actually manage them. So then I'm in the office from 6:00 a.m. until 10:00 p.m., fixing everybody else's work so we have a chance at getting the contract."

I knew Max had problems with overwork and overcommitment when I heard her complaining, for probably the tenth time, about having logged fifty hours at work in a span of three days. I noticed how frazzled she always seemed to be, how irritation about her job had turned to anger and despair. Her typical workday involves writing and editing proposals for hours, then coming home, ordering takeout, and collapsing in front of the TV. Often, she's so exhausted that she forgets to eat the dinner she's ordered. Her once-beloved hobbies, like witchcraft and embroidery, often go neglected. On weekends she sleeps in until 4:00 p.m., just to recharge her batteries and recover from the stress she endured during the week. She sometimes schedules massages and vacations to help herself decompress, but on a day-to-day basis she's irritable and short-tempered, and often remarks on the joylessness of her life.

I figured Max's intense lifestyle must have damaged her health, so I asked her about it. She said, "This fucking job ruined my health and my personal life. Last year I had an inflamed gallbladder, but I didn't take any time off work because I knew my manager would pick apart my reasons for needing it and guilt me into coming in to the office. By the time I went to the hospital, I was vomiting constantly and had to crawl on my hands and knees to the toilet instead of walking. They opened me up and found out that my gallbladder was completely dead. The surgeon told me it was the most decayed one he'd ever seen, and asked me why I hadn't come to them a month earlier. Then he gave me a big lecture about how I needed to take more sick days at work. I wanted to scream."

When I met Max, we were both aspiring writers, sharing little snippets of stories and essays with each other on Tumblr. The beauty of Max's writing immediately made me want to get to know her better. There was a calmness and sense of perspective in her work back then, which I just don't see in her life these days. She's an intense person (a quality I admire), but her job has made her cranky and brittle. She doesn't have patience for inefficiency or anything that strikes her as foolish. Her temper can flare at something as simple as the pizza delivery person forgetting to bring ranch dressing. She hasn't written a short story in years.

Max knows her work is consuming her life. She can see the toll it's taken on her relationships, her health, and her capacity to enjoy her hobbies. Max is also very aware that she places unfair expectations on herself, and that she shouldn't force herself to regularly work twice as many hours as her job supposedly requires. Still, she doesn't know how to stop.

———

Like Max, I used to work to the point of exhaustion and illness, and had no idea how to make myself stop. Intellectually, I knew I was doing too much, but my fear of missing a deadline or seeming lazy kept me plugging away without breaks. I didn't learn to change my ways until overwork utterly destroyed my health.

It was February of 2014, and I was putting the final touches on my dissertation. I'd known since I was a teenager that I wanted to get a PhD in psychology, and I was finally close to attaining it. I couldn't think about anything else. I spent hours and hours in the lab, analyzing data long after my peers had gone home to their partners and children. I found an apartment two blocks from Loyola University, where I was studying, so I wouldn't waste any time commuting to the office. I spent so much time there that I never bothered to buy furniture for my home or set up a home Internet connection.

Then, about two weeks before I was scheduled to present my dissertation, I caught a nasty case of the flu. I didn't let it slow me down. I trudged into the office every day and stayed late into the night, the same as always, ignoring how sick I felt. I didn't even stop exercising. Since I didn't give myself any time to heal, the flu wouldn't go away. On the day of my dissertation defense, I was still running a fever and shivering in my suit jacket, trying desperately to hide it as I presented the results of my research.

I graduated. The flu was still there. I started applying to jobs. I was still sick. For months, the flu stayed with me. I'd do my best to ignore it all day, for the sake of remaining productive, but every evening I'd start shaking and would feel so weak and faint that I'd have to lie on the ground, wrapped in blankets, until morning. This continued for months. I spent that summer bundled in electric blankets feeling absolutely freezing cold, even on ninety-degree days.

Still, I kept working. I tried to hide from my employer that I was debilitatingly sick. I felt shame over being so frail. I spent all my free time sleeping but berated myself for being so lazy. Doctors couldn't figure out what was wrong with me. I was tested for rheumatoid arthritis, lupus, and mono, but nothing came back positive. Then, a cardiologist found I'd developed a heart murmur, and a hematologist found I had severe anemia, but neither could pinpoint why. I was still sick when winter came, nearly a year after the flu had started.

No medical test or treatment could help me. No doctor could cure the mysterious disease that was plaguing me. The solution, which I finally discovered in November of 2014, was that I needed to rest. *Really* rest—no faking I was fine, no pushing myself to exercise and write and go to work. It was excruciating to sit around doing absolutely nothing. I skipped work meetings and forced myself to relax, because by then I had no other choice. My illness kept getting worse, and denying my body's needs wasn't working. I spent the next two months being completely unproductive: no juggling work and illness, no apologizing for being "lazy" by doing more work than was healthy for me.

Slowly, my energy began to come back. The fever disappeared. My red blood cell count went up. My heart murmur went away. Once I was fully healed, it was time to reenter the world and find a new way to live that wouldn't destroy my body the way my old life did.

———

In the years that followed my illness, I've focused on building a tenable life for myself. I had to learn to budget time into my day for relaxation and recovery. I abandoned my dream of becoming a tenured professor, which would require countless hours of research. Instead, I taught classes part-time as an adjunct, and sought out online teaching options as often as I could. This allowed me to have a more relaxed schedule. I took breaks and defended my free time fiercely. I taught myself, slowly, that I deserved to be comfortable, relaxed, and happy.

That's when a funny thing happened: The more my health and well-being improved, the more I noticed that my students, colleagues, and friends exhibited the same kind of self-punishing attitudes toward work that I once had, and just like me, they were beginning to pay a price for it. I realized that burned-out, sick, overcommitted people were all around me. There was Max, with her eighty- to ninety-hour workweeks; my friend Ed, whose mental health was put in jeopardy by their commitment to the domestic violence hotline they worked for; and my colleague Alyssa, who is forever having to juggle the demands of parenting with the pressures of a full-time research job, all while being judged by her in-laws and neighbors for her child-rearing choices. Then there were dozens and dozens of my students, each of whom had been told at some point in school that they weren't doing enough to get ahead—that they were "lazy," and therefore not deserving of happiness or success.

I realized then that my struggles were part of a much bigger social epidemic, something I'm calling the Laziness Lie. The Laziness Lie is a deep-seated, culturally held belief system that leads many of us to believe the following:

- Deep down I'm lazy and worthless.
- I must work incredibly hard, all the time, to overcome my inner laziness.
- My worth is earned through my productivity.
- Work is the center of life.
- Anyone who isn't accomplished and driven is immoral.

The Laziness Lie is the source of the guilty feeling that we are not "doing enough"; it's also the force that compels us to work ourselves to sickness.

Once I began noticing the Laziness Lie all around me, I used the skills I'd learned as a researcher to delve deep into the history of laziness, as well as the most recent psychological studies about productivity. What I found brought me both massive relief and deep frustration. Research on productivity, burnout, and mental health all suggest that the average workday is far too long, and that other commitments that we often think of as normal, such as a full course load at college or a commitment to weekly activism, are not sustainable for most people.

I also came to see how the thing that we call "laziness" is often actually a powerful self-preservation instinct. When we feel unmotivated, directionless, or "lazy," it's because our bodies and minds are screaming for some peace and quiet. When we learn to listen to those persistent feelings of tiredness and to honor them, we can finally begin to heal. I spoke with therapists and corporate coaches and learned about the steps a person can take to establish limits in their professional and personal lives. I found that by advocating for our right to be "lazy," we can carve out space in our lives for play, relaxation, and recovery. I also discovered the immense relief that comes when we cease tying our self-image to how many items we check off our to-do lists.

The laziness we've all been taught to fear does not exist. There is no morally corrupt, slothful force inside us, driving us to be unproductive for no reason. It's not evil to have limitations and to need breaks. Feeling tired or unmotivated is not a threat to our self-worth. In fact, the feelings we write off as "laziness" are some of humanity's most important instincts, a core part of how we stay alive and thrive in the long term. This book is a full-throated defense of the behaviors that get maligned as "laziness" and the people who have been written off as "lazy" by society. It contains practical advice for how to draw better boundaries in all the areas of your life where you might run the risk of overcommitting, scripts for how to defend your boundaries and limits to other people, and tons of reassurance that your worst fear—that you are an irredeemably lazy person—is entirely misplaced.

When people run out of energy or motivation, there's a good reason for it. Tired, burned-out people aren't struggling with some shameful, evil inner laziness; rather, they're struggling to survive in an overly demanding, workaholic culture that berates people for having basic needs. We don't have to keep pushing ourselves to the brink, ignoring our body's alarm bells and punishing ourselves with self-recrimination. We don't have to deny ourselves breaks. We don't have to fear laziness. Laziness does not exist.

CHAPTER ONE

The Laziness Lie

I work in downtown Chicago, just off Michigan Avenue. Every morning, I make my way through throngs of tired commuters and slow-moving tourists, passing at least half a dozen people sitting on street corners asking for change. Many times, I've witnessed a suburban-looking parent discouraging their kid from giving money to a nearby homeless person. They say the typical things people say about giving money to homeless folks: they're just going to spend the money on drugs or alcohol; they're faking being homeless; if they want to improve their lives, all they need to do is stop being lazy and get a job.

It enrages me to hear people saying these things, because I know surviving as a homeless person is a huge amount of work. When you're homeless, every day is a struggle to locate a safe, warm, secure bit of shelter. You're constantly lugging all your possessions and resources around; if you put your stuff down for a second, you run the risk of it getting stolen or thrown out. If you've been homeless for more than a few days, you're probably nursing untreated injuries or struggling with mental or physical illness, or both. You never get a full night's sleep. You have to spend the entire day begging for enough change to buy a meal, or to pay the fee required to enter a homeless shelter. If you're on any government benefits, you have to attend regular meetings with caseworkers, doctors, and therapists to prove that you deserve access to health care and food. You're constantly traumatized, sick, and run ragged. You have to endure people berating you, threatening you, and throwing you out of public spaces for no reason. You're fighting to survive every single day, and people have the audacity to call you lazy.

I know all of this because I have friends who've been homeless. My friend Kim spent a summer living in a Walmart parking lot after a landlord kicked them, their partner, and their two children out of the apartment they all shared. The hardest part of being homeless, Kim told me, was the stigma and judgment. If people didn't realize Kim was homeless, then they and their kids would be allowed to spend the better part of a day in a McDonald's, drinking Cokes, charging their phones, and staying out of the oppressive heat. But the second someone realized Kim was homeless, they transformed in people's minds from a tired but capable parent to an untrustworthy, "lazy" drain on society. It didn't matter how Kim and their children dressed, how they acted, how much food they bought—once the label of "lazy" was on them, there was no walking it back. They'd be thrown out of the business without hesitation.

Our culture hates the "lazy." Unfortunately, we have a very expansive definition of what "laziness" is. A drug addict who's trying to get clean but keeps having relapses? Too lazy to overcome their disorder. An unemployed person with depression who barely has the energy to get out of bed, let alone to apply for a job? They're lazy too. My friend Kim, who spent every day searching for resources and shelter, worked a full-time job, and still made time to teach their kids math and reading in the back of the broken RV that their family slept in? Clearly a very lazy person, someone who just needed to work harder to bring themselves out of poverty.

The word "lazy" is almost always used with a tone of moral judgment and condemnation. When we call someone "lazy," we don't simply mean they lack energy; we're implying that there's something terribly wrong or lacking with them, that they deserve all the bad things that come their way as a result. Lazy people don't work hard enough. They made bad decisions when good ones seemed just as feasible. Lazy people don't deserve help, patience, or compassion.

It can be comforting (in a sick way) to dismiss people's suffering like this. If all the homeless people I see on the street are in that position because they're "lazy," I don't have to give them a cent. If every person who's ever been jailed for drug possession was simply too "lazy" to get a real job, I don't have to worry about drug policy reform. And if every student who gets bad grades in my classes is simply too "lazy" to study, then I never have to change my teaching methods or offer any extensions on late assignments.

Life, however, is not that simple. The vast majority of homeless people are victims of trauma and abuse;[1] most homeless teens are on the street either because homophobic or transphobic parents kicked them out, or the foster system failed them.[2] Many chronically unemployed adults have at least one mental illness, and the longer they remain unemployed, the worse their symptoms will generally get and the harder it becomes for employers to consider them as a prospect.[3] When a drug addict fails to recover from substance use, they're typically facing additional challenges such as poverty and trauma, which make drug treatment very complex and difficult.[4]

The people we've been taught to judge for "not trying hard enough" are almost invariably the people fighting valiantly against the greatest number of unseen barriers and challenges. I've noticed this in my professional life as well. Every single time I've checked in with a seemingly "lazy" and underperforming student, I've discovered that they're facing massive personal struggles, including mental-health issues, immense work stress, or the demands of caring for a sick child or elderly relative. I once had a student who experienced the death of a parent, followed by the destruction of their house in a natural disaster, then the hospitalization of their depressed daughter, all in one sixteen-week semester. That student still felt bad for missing assignments, despite everything she was going through. She was certain people would accuse her of "faking" all these tragedies, so she carried documentation with her everywhere she went to prove that these things had happened to her. The fear of seeming "lazy" runs that deep.

Why do we view people as lazy when they have so much on their plates? One reason is that most human suffering is invisible to an outside observer. Unless a student tells me that they're dealing with an anxiety disorder, poverty, or caring for a sick child, I'll never know. If I don't have a conversation with the homeless person near my bus stop, I'll never hear about his traumatic brain injury, and how that affects basic daily tasks like getting dressed in the morning. If I have an underperforming coworker, I have no way of knowing that their low motivation is caused by chronic depression. They might just look apathetic to me, when really they're running on fumes. When you've been alienated by society over and over again, you tend to look totally checked out, even if you're really busting your ass.

The people we dismiss as "lazy" are often individuals who've been pushed to their absolute limits. They're dealing with immense loads of baggage and stress, and they're working very hard. But because the demands placed on them exceed their available resources, it can look to us like they're doing nothing at all. We're also taught to view people's personal challenges as unacceptable excuses.

Zee is reentering the job market after years of combating a heroin addiction. He's been hard at work fighting his addiction in rehabilitation programs, learning life skills in group therapy, and rebuilding his sense of self by doing volunteer work. Yet when potential employers look at Zee's résumé, all they see is a gap in employment that's several years wide, which makes it seem like Zee spent all that time doing nothing. Even some of Zee's family and friends think of those years of recovery as wasted time. We know that drug addiction is a behavioral and mental disorder, and we know that statistically, most people attempt sobriety several times before they succeed. Yet we tend to view people with substance-abuse disorders as if they're morally responsible for having them, and as if every relapse is a choice they gleefully made.[5]

This isn't just true of how we view and judge other people; we also do this to ourselves. Most of us tend to hold ourselves to ridiculously high standards. We feel that we should be doing more, resting less often, and having fewer needs. We think our personal challenges—such as depression, childcare needs, anxiety, trauma, lower back pain, or simply being human—aren't good enough excuses for having limits and being tired. We expect ourselves to achieve at a superhuman level, and when we fail to do so, we chastise ourselves for being lazy.

We have all been lied to about laziness. Our culture has us convinced that success requires nothing more than willpower, that pushing ourselves to the point of collapse is morally superior to taking it easy. We've been taught that any limitation is a sign of laziness, and therefore undeserving of love or comfort. This is the Laziness Lie, and it's all around us, making us judgmental, stressed, and overextended, all while convincing us that we're actually doing too little. In order to move past the Laziness Lie, we must confront it and dissect it so we can see the poisonous influence it has exerted on our lives, our belief systems, and how we relate to other people.

What Is the Laziness Lie?

The Laziness Lie is a belief system that says hard work is morally superior to relaxation, that people who aren't productive have less innate value than productive people. It's an unspoken yet commonly held set of ideas and values. It affects how we work, how we set limits in our relationships, our views on what life is supposed to be about.

The Laziness Lie has three main tenets. They are:

1. Your worth is your productivity.
2. You cannot trust your own feelings and limits.
3. There is always more you could be doing.

How do we get indoctrinated with the Laziness Lie? For the most part, parents don't sit their kids down and feed them these principles. Instead, people absorb them through years of observation and pattern recognition. When a parent tells their child not to give a homeless person money because that homeless person is too "lazy" to deserve it, the seed of the Laziness Lie is planted in the kid's brain. When a TV show depicts a disabled person somehow "overcoming" their disability through sheer willpower rather than by receiving the accommodations they deserve, the Laziness Lie grows a bit stronger. And whenever a manager questions or berates an employee for taking a much-needed sick day, the Laziness Lie extends its tendrils even further into a person's psyche.

We live in a world where hard work is rewarded and having needs and limitations is seen as a source of shame. It's no wonder so many of us are constantly overexerting ourselves, saying yes out of fear of how we'll be perceived for saying no. Even if you think you don't fully agree with the three tenets of the Laziness Lie, you've probably absorbed its messages and let those messages affect how you set goals and how you view other people. As I break down each of these statements, consider how deeply they're ingrained in your psyche, and how they might influence your behavior on a day-to-day basis.

Your Worth Is Your Productivity

When we talk to children and teenagers about the future, we ask them what they want to *do*—in other words, what kind of value they want to contribute to society and to an employer. We don't ask nearly as often what they're passionate about, or what makes them feel happy or at peace. As adults, we define people by their jobs—he's an actor, she's a mortician—categorizing them based on the labor they provide to others. When a formerly productive person becomes less so due to injury, illness, tragedy, or even aging, we often talk about it in hushed, shameful tones, assuming the person has lost a core part of their identity. When we don't have work to do, it can feel like we don't have a reason to live.

> **When we don't have work to do, it can feel like we don't have a reason to live.**

It makes complete sense, of course, that many of us think and talk in these ways. In our world, a comfortable, safe life is far from guaranteed. People who don't (or can't) work tend to suffer; un-

16

employed and impoverished people die at much younger ages than their employed or middle-class peers.[6] Since we live in a world that's structured around work, not working can leave a person socially isolated, exacerbating whatever mental and physical health problems they might be dealing with.[7] The stakes of not being productive are dire. As a result, many of us live in a constant state of stress about our financial and professional futures—which means feeling a ton of anxiety about how much we're working.

Michael is a bartender. He lives in fear that he's not working enough. He grew up on the South Side of Chicago in a working-class Italian family that dealt with a lot of dysfunction and mental illness. He carved out a life for himself despite all that, and learned a skill that's always in demand. Now he can't say no to a job. When you're a talented bartender in Chicago, you get asked to cover a lot of people's shifts. Michael snaps up every job offered to him, hopping from bar to bar all across the city, even if it means getting only a couple of hours of sleep in the wee hours of the morning. It took me weeks to even schedule an interview with him because his schedule was so overfilled.

"My entire life has been burnout," Michael tells me. "When I owned my own bar, I worked ninety hours a week, every week. I was sleeping on the floor of the men's bathroom at night. I was booking the events, writing the food menu, writing the cocktail menu, getting orders from our suppliers, and doing the actual bartending. Then the bar went under, and I had to start taking whatever other jobs came my way."

Michael has always lived this way. As a teenager, he was a ballet dancer. The unforgiving, workaholic world of ballet taught him to fill every waking hour with training and practice, and to ignore any signs that his body was breaking down. He carried that same level of commitment into the adult world, where he's worked without relent for decades. Even when he travels, he puts out feelers for bartending shifts he can pick up while he's in town. He's never known a break. He keeps a meticulous spreadsheet of his hours and earnings, and the figures are mind-boggling.

"I worked three hundred eighty hours this March," he tells me. For reference, a standard forty-hour workweek adds up to about 160 hours per month.

The consequences of Michael's compulsive work habits mirrored mine and Max's in many eerie ways. A few years ago, when the bar Michael owned was failing, stress caused him to start vomiting blood. He also developed a nasty chill that would overtake him every evening, as would happen with me. Yet he kept pushing through his illness, hoping that by working harder, he could save his business.

Those of us who are particularly lucky get to retire after years of living this way. But because we've been taught to make work the center of our identities, we don't know how to handle the change of pace. Retired people often become depressed and see their lives as devoid of purpose.[8] Like unemployed people, retired folks often report feeling directionless and lonesome. Their isolation and lack of daily structure can make them sick, putting them at an elevated risk of heart disease.[9] Many of us spend our entire adult lives dreading this period of life, or we put it off by continuing to work past the point that's healthy for us.[10]

When the coronavirus hit Chicago and all the bars shut down, Michael was immediately overtaken by panic and dread. He had worked nearly every day of his adult life, and with the bars closed, he had no idea what to do with himself or how he would go about making money. So, he set out to open a speakeasy in an empty storefront in the city. He knew a lot of other service-industry folks, and some of them knew which vacated buildings he could sneak into to set up an illegal bar. Many of Michael's non-service-industry friends were shocked that he would put his life and his friends' lives at risk in this way, exposing himself and everyone he knew to the virus by opening up shop. Eventually, someone persuaded him to reconsider.

While I was also dismayed by Michael's speakeasy plan, I understood why it made sense to him. Life had forced him to be self-sufficient, and his only escape from adversity was to work hard without consideration for how much it might hurt him. Work had already made Michael puke blood in the past; from his perspective, risking acute respiratory syndrome didn't seem all that different.

Two weeks into social distancing, Michael texted me: "I can't wait to have a damn job again. This is the most time off I've had since I was fourteen, and I'm going crazy."

Lots of us are like Michael, even if our choices don't always look as extreme. We're unable to cut back on work, always reflexively taking on new responsibilities out of a compulsive fear that if we don't, our lives will fall apart. We've had to trade our health for our financial or professional well-being, choosing between getting adequate time for rest, exercise, and socializing and logging enough hours to get by. Tragically, many of us do this not out of paranoia but because we know just how economically vulnerable we really are. An international disaster like COVID-19 only convinced Michael he was smart to have overworked as much as he did in the past. If he hadn't, he would have had an even smaller financial nest egg to survive on.

Chronic overcommitters are experts at ignoring their bodily needs. Our economic system and culture have taught us that having needs makes us weak, and that limits are negotiable. We learn to neglect ourselves and see health as a resource we can trade for money or accomplishments. This brings us to the second tenet of the Laziness Lie: that we cannot trust our own feelings of exhaustion or sickness, and that none of our limitations are acceptable.

You Cannot Trust Your Own Feelings and Limits

Eric Boyd is a successful fiction writer, but he struggles constantly with the fear that he's going to screw up and lose everything. His fear comes from a very reasonable place: before he became an author, he was in prison. He knows, more intimately than most of us, that the comfort and security his work has brought him could dry up at any moment. As someone with a prison record, he can't dive into the workforce with the same ease that many of us can. So even though his schedule is filled with speaking engagements, teaching opportunities, and paid writing gigs, Eric keeps signing up to participate in paid clinical trials and other side hustles. He never says no to a writing or performance opportunity, even if it means traveling in the middle of the night from one city to another. He still fears that if he doesn't keep pushing himself to the limit, he will descend into laziness and never recover.

I've talked to dozens and dozens of overworked people, and this fear is one almost all of them share. The people who log the most hours, who run themselves the most ragged, who say yes far more often than is actually sustainable for them are the ones who most suspect that they're "lazy." They seem plagued by the fear that deep down they're selfish, needy, and unmotivated. It may sound like a paradox, but it's a core part of the Laziness Lie—perhaps the one with the most dangerous consequences.

The Laziness Lie tells us that we're all at risk of becoming slothful and unaccomplished, and that every sign of weakness is suspect. It has many of us convinced that deep down we're not the driven, accomplished people we pretend to be. That the only way to overcome our selfish, sluggish instincts is to never listen to our bodies, never give ourselves a break, and never use illness as a reason to slow down.

This aspect of the Laziness Lie teaches us to fear and loathe our own basic needs. Feeling tired? That isn't a sign that you need sleep; you're just being lazy. Having trouble focusing on something complicated? It's not because you're distracted and overwhelmed, it's the opposite! You actually need to be taking more on in order to keep yourself sharp! Do you find yourself hating a job you once loved? You're just being a baby. You need to push yourself harder to overcome how shamefully unmotivated you're feeling.

When we buy into this belief system, it becomes very difficult to identify our needs and advocate for ourselves. Back in 2014, when I was debilitatingly sick, I found myself doubting my illness at times. I'd wonder if I was somehow making the fevers up in my mind and secretly manipulating my friends and loved ones into feeling sorry for me. Even my doctor doubted I was as sick as I said I was. He made me record my temperature every evening, in a little journal that I brought to his office. We both discovered I'd been running a fever of 103 degrees nearly every evening. Even then, I still felt guilty about being such a bother. I couldn't understand why willpower wasn't enough to make me well.

> The Laziness Lie has many of us convinced that deep down we're not the driven, accomplished people we pretend to be.

Our bodies and minds have many early alert signals that warn us about oncoming colds, hunger, dehydration, or mental fatigue. If you wake up with a sore throat or a sour taste in your mouth, you can plan ahead, rest up, and nip a virus in the bud. If you find yourself distracted by persistent thoughts of food, it might remind you to grab a snack instead of waiting for full-blown hunger pangs to come.[11] And if reading a single page in a book is too mentally taxing, you can take that as a sign that your brain needs to do something more relaxing for a while.

According to the Laziness Lie, however, these are not useful warning signs—they're deceptions. You don't need a snack, a cup of tea, or a languid Sunday in bed. Those are just your worst impulses, trying to tempt you into behaving badly. The Laziness Lie encourages you to ignore your body's warnings, push through discomfort, and ask for as few accommodations as possible. And at the end of all that struggle and self-denial, there's no reward. You never actually earn the right to take it easy, because the Laziness Lie also teaches you that you can never, ever do enough.

There Is Always More You Could Be Doing

The Laziness Lie encourages us to aspire to an impossible level of productivity. It sets us up to expect full, eight-hour workdays of unbroken focus, followed by evenings filled with exercise, Instagram-worthy home-cooked meals, and admirable side projects. According to the Laziness Lie, a worthwhile person fills their days in ideal, industrious ways. They don't skip doctor's appointments, fail to get their oil checked, or miss days at the gym. If someone lacks the energy to make it to the polls on Election Day because they just finished working a grueling third-shift job, the Laziness Lie says they're to blame for everything going politically awry in this country. When a part-time student doesn't have the mental energy to study after caring for her children all day, the Laziness Lie says she isn't smart enough or virtuous enough to get a college degree.

There's no limit to what the Laziness Lie will do to persuade us that we need to be doing. Our aspirations can climb and climb, but they'll never hit the ceiling, because the ceiling doesn't exist. If you're a diligent employee, the

Laziness Lie will berate you for not volunteering more often, or for not doing enough for your family and friends. If you devote your life to serving other people and meeting their needs, the Laziness Lie will point out that you're not working out enough, or that your home is a mess. If you win a massive award or hit some other life-changing milestone, the Laziness Lie will smile politely and say, "That's very nice. But what do you plan to do next?"

We're all taught to take immense pride in our achievements, but we're also discouraged from resting on our laurels when we do accomplish something great. No level of success grants a person the social permission to stop and catch their breath. We're forever left wondering *What's next? What else?* The Laziness Lie teaches that the harder you work, the better a person you are, but it never actually defines what an acceptable level of "hard" might look like. By forever moving the goalpost and never actually allowing a person to be vulnerable and have needs, it's setting us up for failure right from the start.

This past year, my mom suffered a hip injury that would not heal. Instead of resting and attending physical therapy, she kept aggravating the injury by standing all day long at her job as a dental hygienist. She kept dragging herself to work for weeks (which became months) even though it was clear her body couldn't sustain it.

It got harder for my mom to walk or stand, and she was starting to dread going into the office. Still, she kept putting off retirement. She'd been a dental hygienist for over forty years, she kept reiterating to me; it was who she was, the only job she'd ever done as an adult. So the inevitable kept getting delayed, until my mom's pain got so intense that she had no choice but to call in sick for every shift she had on the schedule. Instead of being the planned, scheduled affair she wanted it to be, my mom's retirement became an emergency decision, announced to her co-workers via text message.

The Laziness Lie kept my mom from admitting to herself that it was time to stop working. It keeps many of us from taking the time we need to recoup, or from spending our younger, typically healthier years doing things we genuinely love. So many of my friends and loved ones are hurting them-selves in similar ways, leaving their health, relationships, and years of their lives as offerings at the altar of hard work. This is what the Laziness Lie has done to us. It has made us terrified of living at a slower, gentler pace.

This understanding of the world has left many of us constitutionally incapable of caring for ourselves, let alone extending full compassion to others. What's worse, the Laziness Lie is so deeply ingrained in our cul-ture and our values that many of us never think to question it. To fully appreciate its far-reaching impact and how it became so integral to our culture, we have to look back centuries, into the origins of capitalism.

Where Does the Laziness Lie Come From?

The Laziness Lie is deeply embedded in the very foundation of the United States. The value of hard work and the evils of sloth are baked into our national myths and our shared value system. Thanks to the legacies of imperialism and slavery, as well as the ongoing influence that the United States exerts on its trade partners, the Laziness Lie has managed to spread its tendrils into almost every country and culture on the planet.

The word "lazy" first appeared in English around 1540; even back then, it was used in a judgmental way to mean someone who disliked work or effort.[12] Many etymologists believe it came from either the Middle Low German *lasich*, which meant "feeble" or "weak,"[13] or from the Old English *lesu*, which meant "false" or "evil."[14] These two origins illustrate the odd doublespeak at work whenever we call someone lazy. When we say someone is lazy, we're saying they're incapable of completing a task due to (physical or mental) weakness, but we're also claiming that their lack of ability somehow makes them morally corrupt. It's not that they're tired or even dispirited in some way we might sympathize with; the word implies that they're failures on a fundamental, human level. The idea that lazy people are evil fakers who deserve to suffer has been embedded in the word since the very start.

23

One of the major factors that caused the Laziness Lie to spread throughout the United States was the arrival of the Puritans. The Puritans had long believed that if a person was a hard worker, it was a sign that God had chosen them for salvation. Hard work was believed to improve who you were as a person. Conversely, if a person couldn't focus on the task at hand or couldn't self-motivate, that was a sign that they had already been damned.[15] This meant, of course, that there was no need to feel sympathy for people who struggled or failed to meet their responsibilities. By lacking the drive to succeed, they were displaying to the world that God hadn't chosen them for Heaven. When the Puritans came to colonial America, their ideas caught on and spread to other, less pious colonists.[16] For many reasons, a belief system that judged and punished the "lazy" was about to become very popular—and politically useful.

Colonial America relied on the labor of enslaved people and indentured servants.[17] It was very important to the colonies' wealthy and enslaving class that they find a way to motivate enslaved people to work hard, despite the fact that enslaved people had nothing to gain from it.[18] One powerful way to do so was through religious teachings and indoctrination. A productivity-obsessed form of Christianity evolved from the older, more Puritanical idea that work improved moral character, and it was pushed on enslaved people. This form of Christianity taught that suffering was morally righteous and that slaves would be rewarded in Heaven for being docile, agreeable, and, most important, diligent.[19]

On the flip side, if an enslaved person was slothful or "lazy," there was something fundamentally corrupt and wrong with them.[20] Enslavers made it a point to keep enslaved people as busy and exhausted as possible out of fear that idle time would give them the means to revolt or riot.[21] Even more disturbing, enslaved people who tried to run away from bondage were seen as mentally ill and suffering from "runaway slave disorder."[22] By not accepting their proper role in society,

> For many reasons, a belief system that judged and punished the "lazy" was about to become very popular— and politically useful.

24

they were demonstrating that they were broken and disturbed. This worldview became the foundation for American capitalism.[23]

The Laziness Lie had been born. It would quickly spread to other marginalized people, including indentured servants, poor white laborers, and Native Americans who had been forced into government boarding schools.[24] These exploited groups were also taught that working hard without complaint was virtuous, and that desiring free time was morally suspect. As the Industrial Revolution changed the landscape of the country, with more and more Americans working long hours in manufacturing plants, the Laziness Lie was pushed even more. The wealthy and highly educated began to claim that poor whites also couldn't be trusted with "idle" time. In fact, too many breaks could make a person antisocial.[25] Propaganda from that time often claimed that if the working poor weren't kept busy, they would resort to crime and drug use, and society would run amok.[26] Laziness had officially become not only a personal failing but a social ill to be defeated—and it has remained that way ever since.

———

We can see the dogma of the Laziness Lie in popular media from that period as well. In the late 1800s, the writer Horatio Alger published numerous stories in which struggling, impoverished characters were able to rise into the upper classes through hard work. The popularity of these books led to the idea that poor people simply needed to "pull themselves up by their bootstraps" if they wanted to live a comfortable life.[27] In the 1950s and beyond, Evangelical preachers promoted a similar idea with the Prosperity Doctrine, which claimed that if a person devoted their life to serving Jesus, they would be rewarded with bountiful job opportunities, wealth, and success.[28]

In the decades that followed, the Laziness Lie found its way into countless films, plays, and TV shows. From the national myths of Paul Bunyan and Johnny Appleseed to the strong, independent cowboys on the silver screen to the memoirs of entrepreneurs like Conrad Hilton, one of the most prevalent legends in American culture became the tale of the single-minded, hardworking man who had created his own success and changed society through sheer force of will.[29] In these stories, the hero is always a strong white man who doesn't need the support of anyone else; he's usually a bit of a social island, with no close connections to other people and a disregard for society's rules in general. In every way, he's the picture of independence, and it's through his strong personality and dog-gedness that he succeeds. These myths, though inspiring and appealing to many, carried with them a dark implication: if a person didn't succeed, it was because they weren't doing enough.

For people who believe in the Laziness Lie, things like economic re-form, legal protections for workers, and welfare programs seem unneces-sary. Those who want to succeed just need to pull themselves up by their bootstraps, after all. Research from the past three decades consistently shows that a majority of Americans do, in fact, think this way. For many of us, our first instinct is generally to blame a person for their own misfor-tune, especially if we can pin that misfortune on laziness.[30] Research also shows that when we believe the world is fair and people get what they deserve, we're less likely to support social welfare programs and have less sympathy for poor people and their needs.[31]

Much like the parents I've seen discouraging their children from giv-ing money to homeless people, many Americans believe that generosity, compassion, and mutual aid is "wasted" on the lazy. Furthermore, if we be-lieve the world was created solely by independent people, we may come to think that there's no need for us to be interdependent and compassionate. We may even come to see relying on other people as a threat to progress.

Decades of exposure to the Laziness Lie has had a massive effect on our public consciousness. It's made many of us critical of other people and quick to blame the victims of economic inequality for their own deprivation. It's made us hate our own limitations, to see our tiredness or desire for a break as signs of failure. And it has created an intense internal pressure to keep working harder and harder, with no limits and no boundaries. The rise of social media and digital work tools has only made these pressures harder to escape.

The Laziness Lie Is Everywhere

Much like the Horatio Alger novels of the past, today's popular media still teaches us to worship hard work and look down on the lazy. From the films we watch to the YouTube videos that keep us company on our lunch breaks, we're inundated with stories that praise diligence and individualism. Some of today's most popular celebrities promote the idea of themselves as "self-made" entrepreneurs rather than extremely privileged and fortunate tycoons. Our fictional heroes overcome evil and accomplish their dreams because they possess unique levels of drive and dedication, not because they support and are supported by other people. Conversely, characters who face limitations and personal challenges such as physical disabilities or mental illness are almost always portrayed as villains or comical side characters deserving of pity but not respect.[32]

John Wick has become an iconic action film character because he defeats throngs of enemies almost entirely on his own, and he's never able to settle into the retirement he keeps promising himself. Many stories about assassins, spies, and supersoldiers follow a similar trajectory, portraying the lives of steely, serious men who just can't seem to give up their jobs, no matter how horrific they are and how much they brutalize them. From *Blade Runner* to *The Usual Suspects* to *Inception*, some of America's most classic and iconic action films feature characters who, like Wick, keep putting off retirement for the sake of pursuing one last job.[33] That last job never actually ends up being the last one, of course. There's always a sequel, featuring new opportunities with even higher stakes.

In *Avengers: Endgame*, Thor is made a laughingstock because he responds to an intergalactic disaster by becoming withdrawn, alcoholic, and lazy. The film also puts the actor in a fat suit, using his fatness to both indicate and mock how much worse his life has become. In the narrative of the film, it doesn't matter that Thor has lost dozens of friends and watched an unimaginable disaster ripple throughout the universe. That's not enough of an excuse for him to descend into a nonproductive, suffering state. A perfectly normal reaction to trauma and grief is rendered mockable and pathetic, and countless fat viewers end up insulted and dehumanized in the process, as do viewers with depression or addiction issues.

This obsession with the strong individualist character has permeated our culture for decades. Films like *The Matrix*, *Star Wars*, and the Harry Potter series all emphasize the importance of their lead characters' being "chosen ones" who must sacrifice everything in order to defeat evil. These characters may have support networks and sidekicks who help them through the story, but when the final moment of triumph comes, they've almost always had to suffer and struggle alone to earn it. They're told they possess a unique ability no one else has, and they have no choice but to use that ability to save the world. This teaches viewers that our skills and talents don't really belong to us; they exist to be used. If we don't gladly give our time, our talents, and even our lives to others, we aren't heroic or good.

Many of the most popular children's TV shows of the moment, such as *Dragon Ball Super* and *My Hero Academia*, also focus on relentlessly hardworking people who exert themselves to the point of injury or pain. I used to watch an earlier version of *Dragon Ball* as a kid, and I identified with the characters who pushed themselves nearly to death for the sake of winning battles. Young children were regularly depicted as sustaining bloody, painful injuries on that show, yet they always continued to fight. At the time, I admired their dedication and wanted to be tough just like them. As an adult, I'm pretty horrified by the violence and outright child abuse that's being celebrated on shows like those as "hard work." Even more morally complex, modern children's shows like *Steven Universe* and *Avatar: The Last Airbender* still teach children that it's up to a singularly motivated individual to save the world. If that person has to sacrifice everything in order to do their job, so be it. In reality, of course, fighting for change is a much more gradual, collaborative process.

> **These stories teach us that if we don't gladly give our time, our talents, and even our lives to others, we aren't heroic or good.**

Instagram influencers and popular YouTubers are also major peddlers of the Laziness Lie. YouTube videos by major "influencers" like Jeffree Star and Shane Dawson are filled with talk about how hard the creators are working and how much they've sacrificed to earn their success. Their obscene levels of wealth are always attributed to their effort, not good luck. Kim Kardashian and Kylie Jenner have spent years (and multiple TV shows) portraying themselves as entrepreneurs, attributing their massive wealth and fame to the fact that they never stop hustling and looking for new opportunities. When the Instagram influencer, model, and comedian Rickey Thompson became famous enough to sell merchandise (around the time he hit four million followers), the first item he revealed was a T-shirt with his catchphrase "Booked and Busy" printed on the front.[34] These massively popular figures cannot stop hammering home the importance of remaining "busy." It's the constant narrative theme in their lives and work.

Video game and comedy YouTubers often dabble in the same themes, talking about how devoted they are to their fans and how much time they're putting into each project. Some streamers regularly fall asleep on camera, because their devotion to constantly generating content runs that deep.[35] Some performers stay on camera for more than twenty-four hours at a time. In one infamous case, a streamer died on camera due to sleep deprivation and physical exhaustion. He had been streaming for twenty-two straight hours at the time of his death.[36]

In some ways, it can be positive for children and other viewers to hear from self-made successes on a regular basis. Social media has democratized who gets to be famous and successful—to an extent. Sometimes Black, queer twentysomethings like Rickey Thompson genuinely do ascend to fame and wealth because they produce excellent videos and work very hard. Yet for every Rickey Thompson there's a Jeffree Star, a massively successful YouTuber and makeup magnate who lives in an opulent mansion while his employees toil away in his warehouses, making the products that earned him his wealth.

When massively successful stars attribute their good fortune entirely to how diligently they've worked, they set people up to have unrealistic expectations about the odds of success, and how wealth is actually meted out in this country. This is especially troublesome when the work habits being promoted are excessive and dangerous. Our media has a selection bias built into it: we rarely get to hear from the people who worked equally hard but failed or lost everything because of it.

The musical comedian Bo Burnham (whose career started on You-Tube) describes this phenomenon very well: "Don't take advice from guys like me who've gotten very lucky. Taylor Swift telling you to follow your dreams is like a lottery winner saying 'Liquidize your assets! Buy Power-ball tickets! It works!'"[37]

Our media rarely shows people setting limits, asking for help, or devoting their lives to the things that make them feel happy and safe. Of course, it's much harder to tell a story about a happy person with a fulfilling, healthy life than it is to show violence, toil, and struggle. Strong, independent heroes are captivating to so many of us because we long to have the power and dedication they possess. As much as I'm troubled by the themes in many of these stories, I still get a rush from watching John Wick murder throngs of enemies with only a library book and sheer force of will. Still, there's a real social cost to the fact that we're taught time and time again that we should never give up or ask for help, when there are many times that a person needs and deserves a break.

———

It's not just popular media that teaches us to work relentlessly without stopping. The Laziness Lie is also promoted in our schools. Our modern-day educational system was formulated during the Industrial Revolution, and was designed to train students for employment in warehouses and manufacturing plants.[38] Today, the structure of the school day remains remarkably similar to the structure of the average workday. There are rigid schedules and arbitrary deadlines that don't take into account what else is going on in a student's life. Absences or changes in the routine can get a child in trouble. Children who struggle to focus or sit still for eight hours are treated as problems to be minimized. Students who aren't naturally gifted in a subject are given less attention and support; so are kids who don't fit the stereotype of what a "talented" student looks like because of their gender, race, or socioeconomic status.[39]

Some people thrive in the standard academic environment. Those of us who have an easy time sitting still and following directions can flourish, receiving praise and encouragement every step of the way. However, a large number of young people are instead given the message that they're not good enough, don't work hard enough, and are destined for failure.

At Loyola University Chicago, the students I teach are working adults. Many of them enrolled in college as eighteen- or nineteen-year-olds, but then something got in the way of their graduating "on time." They got pregnant, fell ill, or had to quit school to take care of a dying parent. Sometimes they just couldn't focus on school or didn't see the point in it. Unfortunately, many of my students absorbed the idea that they're to blame for the challenges they faced. Many think they were just too "lazy" to finish school the first time around.

A few years ago, I was approached after class by an adult student named Maura. She had a couple of facial piercings and dyed hair—just like me. She had just gotten a new tattoo and wanted to show it to me. We talked for a bit about piercing and tattoos, and concerts we'd been to; she and I had a ton in common. Then she asked me how old I was. It turned out we were the same age. As soon as Maura realized this, she immediately started berating herself for having "not done much" with her life compared to me. She did it in a joking way, but I could tell it was coming from a place of genuine insecurity.

I do a similar thing when I discover a successful person who's younger than me. Because I've been taught to constantly measure my accomplishments and see how they stack up against somebody else's, I feel threatened when a person seems to be "ahead" of me, yet I don't tend to evaluate other people's lives in that way.

I started asking Maura about what she'd been doing throughout her twenties. I learned that she'd managed a large retail store for several years while taking classes part-time and raising a child. She also had several roommates, all of whom were younger than her, and often found herself falling into the mom role for them. She had to drive them to work when their cars broke down and look after them when they got sick. On top of all that, Maura's ex-husband was in the military, and for years Maura had traveled with him, unable to find a job on the bases where they lived.

Maura had clearly lived a rich, responsibility-filled life. Her twenties had been much more interesting and challenging than my own, yet she believed she'd done "nothing" with all that time. She was a more mature, well-rounded person than I was. I tried to tell her as much, but I'm not sure she believed me. After all, she'd been told by many professors at that point that she wasn't applying herself or trying hard enough. At the same time she was taking my class, Maura was failing another course because her professor wouldn't let her retake an exam she'd missed because of an emergency at her job.

Like so many of my adult students, Maura seemed sleep-deprived and checked-out from time to time. But from speaking with her, I realized it was because she had so much on her plate. It's easy for a teacher to mistake exhaustion for apathy or lack of motivation, yet I almost always find that when I sit down with students who seem unmotivated, they're impressively productive people who fill their days with full-time jobs, self-improvement, and service to others. Despite all of this, many of my most dedicated students believe they're lazy. Often it's because some teacher in their past berated them for circumstances beyond their control.

The Laziness Lie has also followed us into our homes and private moments. Digital technology and social media fill our spare time with e-mails from coworkers, stressful notifications about appointments we've forgotten, and guilt-ridden messages about what our bodies, homes, and lives ought to look like. Digital work tools have made it possible for many of us to work from home, but rather than making our lives easier, this has created the pressure to be constantly available to our employers. We get our news from phone apps and social media sites rather than printed papers, making

Everywhere we turn, we're told we're not enough.

it harder than ever to get away from upsetting images and distressing information. Even the online spaces that are supposed to bring us pleasure and entertainment, such as Instagram and TikTok, guilt us with advertisements for weight-loss products, intricate home-improvement projects, and complicated beauty regimens. Everywhere we turn, we're told we're not enough. And when we finally disconnect from this constant stream of shame and pressure, we often feel guilty for "disappearing" on our colleagues, family, and friends.

Why You Feel Lazy

When I tell someone I don't believe laziness exists, a funny thing usually happens. The person will almost always try to argue with me about how lazy and terrible they are. They'll admit to me that yes, of course other people who are judged for being "lazy" are actually very hardworking. And yes, a lot of the time seemingly nonproductive people are dealing with tons of legitimate barriers and challenges—but, they insist to me, they're nothing like those people. They're just lazy because there's something deeply wrong with them. They're somehow lazier and more awful than anyone in the world. I've talked to dozens of really accomplished, driven people who remain absolutely convinced that they're uniquely, shamefully lazy.

The first time I had this type of conversation, I was hanging out with an artist friend, Michael Roy, who does street art and murals under the moniker Birdcap. Michael travels the world, covering interior and exterior walls with complex, brightly colored designs that combine ancient mythological figures with nostalgic images from his youth. He's become a successful artist because of his talent and dedication, but when we were hanging out back in 2015, he told me he was horrifically lazy.

I had asked Michael how he had the energy to constantly travel the world

> I've talked to dozens of really accomplished, driven people who remain absolutely convinced that they're uniquely, shamefully lazy.

doing murals, applying for artistic grants, and producing digital art for freelancing clients, all at the same time. He shrugged at me and said that he *had* to push himself like this, because if he didn't, he'd descend into laziness and never make another piece of art ever again. In his mind, being productive seemed somewhat binary: either he was grinding away constantly, painting murals by day and drawing on his tablet at night, or he was a total sloth with no creative drive and no professional prospects.

At that point in his life, Michael didn't have a house or an apartment. He traveled so often that it didn't make sense for him to. He slept on couches or in hostels and lugged a backpack full of spray paint cans with him wherever he went. He didn't have health insurance. He spent full days outside sweating under the hot sun on a ladder, coating walls with primer and decorating them with elaborate designs, yet he believed he was on the brink of succumbing to laziness.

Michael is not a uniquely lazy person. He's an especially busy person. But like so many of us, he feels an intense pressure to keep pushing himself forward. The "lazy" feeling he hated and feared was probably a sign he was tired and nearly burned out, but he had no way of realizing that because everyone around him was singing the praises of hard work, dedication, and showing no weakness.

The world of visual art is competitive and sometimes cutthroat. The people who do succeed have to be constantly active, not only producing new work but also building their online platforms and brands. Every day, Michael sees his colleagues promoting their successes on social media and in interviews. As he goes about painting, applying for grants, and taking on new clients, he also has to worry about gaining new Instagram followers and doing interviews himself.

A professional world like Michael's creates an arms race of busyness, with each person vying for a limited number of opportunities and social media eyeballs. Each artist has to snatch up as many jobs as they can get, because they have no way of knowing what the future will hold. At the same time, they have to build a public reputation for themselves as relevant and cool. Since every person is broadcasting an image of themselves as successful, dedicated, and popular, it can be hard to keep track of where you fall in the hierarchy. And because of all this, it's dangerously easy to feel like no matter how overwhelmed you are, someone out there is doing ten times as much as you are.

―――――――

A lot of people feel the way Michael does, forever burning the midnight oil while fearing that they're on the verge of ruining it all by taking a break. We live in an economically uncertain time, with many industries being disrupted or automated. Freelance jobs and gig work have replaced reliable full-time employment for many people, creating an environment of uncertainty and competition. Digital tools like e-mail and Slack have eroded the boundary between home and the office, making it difficult to ever truly take time off. Meanwhile, social media reminds us constantly of what other people are doing and accomplishing, making us all feel like failures who just can't keep up.

It's a strange paradox, but when we set out to do more than is good for us, we end up feeling like we're not doing anything at all. If there are always more items on your to-do list than you can possibly check off, you will never feel accomplished. If your boss is constantly e-mailing you with questions and requests, you can start to feel guilty for something as simple as turning off your phone to go to sleep at night. When exercise, activism, and even talking with friends is tracked and measured by phone apps, you may start feeling like you're constantly letting people down. We feel lazy, but it's not because we're awful, apathetic people—it's because we're exhausted.

―――――――

Does looking at your calendar fill you with dread? Do you have a deadline that you keep pushing back because confronting it head-on seems impossible? Do you "waste" hours every day scrolling through Twitter or shopping

> **It's a strange paradox, but when we set out to do more than is good for us, we end up feeling like we're not doing anything at all.**

online for things you don't need? If so, you might be feeling very lazy right now—and that might actually be a good thing.

When we feel unfocused, tired, and lazy, it's often because we desperately need some time to rest our bodies and brains. Research has repeatedly shown that a person on the verge of burnout will have trouble staying focused and productive.[40] No amount of pressure and stress can magically help a person overcome that lack of focus and motivation. The solution is to cut way back on expectations for a while. Overextended people have to find space in their lives to sleep, power down their stressed-out minds, and recharge their mental and emotional batteries. You can wait until you reach a breaking point like Max and I did, or you can prevent illness and burnout by being gentle with yourself before it's too late.

The Laziness Lie has tried to convince us that our desires for rest and relaxation make us terrible people. It's made us believe that having no motivation is shameful and must be avoided at all costs. In reality, our feelings of tiredness and idleness can help save us by signaling to us that we're desperately in need of some downtime. When we stop fearing laziness, we can find time to reflect and recharge, to reconnect with the people and hobbies that we love, and to move through the world at a more intentional, peaceful pace. "Wasting time" is a basic human need. Once we accept that, we can stop fearing our inner "laziness" and begin to build healthy, happy, well-balanced lives.

— CHAPTER TWO —

Rethinking Laziness

When I met Julie, she was the executive director of a nonprofit here in Chicago. Her organization provided creative writing classes to Chicago Public School students, particularly those in underfunded, understaffed schools in the city's south- and west-side neighborhoods. Kids love having classroom visits from Julie's organization; the teachers are actors, writers, and performers, and a large percentage of them are Black and Latinx like the children they're teaching. The nonprofit's main goal is to help kids flourish creatively as writers. Each year, hundreds of children go through the program and learn to write short stories, dialogues, and persuasive essays on whatever topics they like.

In her years as executive director, Julie wrote tons of grant applications, found ways to save the organization money without cutting staff or essentials, and built a sizable financial nest egg for the company to fall back on for years to come. She put together professional development events that her staff actually enjoyed. She supported employees when they struggled through personal issues and medical emergencies. When Chicago Public Schools faced budget cuts and school closings, Julie was at the protests and teacher strikes, fighting to protect educational access for the kids who needed it most. She did all of this time-consuming, badass work while raising an infant daughter and coping with an anxiety disorder.

At that time in her life, Julie was a total productivity powerhouse. She worked hard, she fought for causes she believed in, she parented her kid, and she managed her employees with compassion and flexibility. In other words, she was winning the game the Laziness Lie has taught us we have to play. She was "having it all."

Then one evening, the night after her daughter turned a year old, Julie came home and her husband, Rich, said he didn't love her anymore.

Julie's life was about to completely fall apart. The next couple of years would be defined by marital therapy, doctors' and psychiatrists' appointments, a move to a new state, lots of yoga, and the quitting of several jobs. Everything about how Julie set her priorities was about to drastically change. Her long journey toward embracing a slower, "lazier" life was about to begin.

———

Rich became increasingly erratic and self-destructive in the months after he told Julie he no longer loved her. He started an emotional affair with a woman who worked at Julie's nonprofit. He was visibly depressed and started talking about suicide. Instead of contemplating leaving the marriage, Julie chose to support Rich and help figure out what had caused his behavior to change so dramatically. She had a gut feeling that his actions were not a deliberate, malicious choice.

"I was going crazy," Julie says, "because I was like, *This is not my husband. This is not the person I've known for so long.* And we've been together since I was twenty, so we know each other pretty well."

After several psychiatrists' appointments, they discovered Julie was right. It turned out that Rich had bipolar disorder. His symptoms were exacerbated by the stress of balancing parenting with a full-time job that required him to travel often. For years, Rich had been privately trying to manage his symptoms without even realizing it, but as the stress in his life continued to mount, his ability to cope got worse and worse. Suddenly, Julie had to scramble to not only repair her marriage but also keep her husband functioning and alive.

38

One evening, Rich was having a particularly severe mental breakdown, so Julie took him to the hospital. She also called a mental-health crisis line for help. To her surprise, the crisis line operator wanted to talk to Julie about how *she* was doing, and what steps she was taking to care for herself during such an immensely stressful and traumatic time. Julie realized that she didn't have good answers to those questions. She hadn't had time to think about her well-being at all.

"At that point," Julie says, "I was like, *We can't keep doing this*. We can't both be doing full-time jobs. And I'm under all this stress and I have to take care of the kid and my husband and this company and everybody in the company. This just isn't sustainable."

Julie realized she and her husband had to shift their priorities. They were too busy, too stressed, and too overextended to care for their daughter and maintain their own functionality and mental health at the same time. So, Julie created a plan. She realized that since Rich's job could be done from anywhere in the Midwest, not just Chicago, it made sense for them to move somewhere cheaper to live. In a more affordable town, Julie could stay at home and be the primary parent for their daughter, freeing up time for Rich to rest and look after his mental health. And because they'd be living in a suburb rather than a loud, busy, crowded city, Julie would have more space in her life for self-care too.

Rich agreed to give the plan a shot. Julie resigned from her position at the nonprofit. They sold their house and used the money to provide a financial cushion for the move. They found a comfortable, affordable home in Wisconsin, and relocated. "My story just reeks of privilege," Julie says. "We were really lucky with real estate. We knew that we were going to be able to sell our house for a lot."

Julie describes herself as a stay-at-home mom now, though she does run multiple small businesses out of that home. She's started three different small companies in the four years she's been in Wisconsin, in fact. Her drive to work incredibly hard hasn't left her. Still, she says her life now has room in it for her to breathe.

"I have emotional space for other people, and for myself now," she says. "And I'm much kinder and nicer. In Chicago all I had the emotional capacity for was getting to work, picking up my kid, driving across town in traffic to drop her off where she had to go, worrying about parking . . . I had these blinders on."

Nowadays, Julie sets firm limits on how much work she does, and how much anxiety her family is exposed to. She knows the alternative is disastrous. Recently, she took a part-time job teaching at a dance studio. Some interpersonal drama was erupting between other teachers there, and Julie could tell the tension was taking a toll on her well-being. The dance world can also be full of sexism and fat shaming, and Julie didn't want to expose herself or her daughter to it—so she walked away from the job, even though she had just started working there. Saying no so firmly and so quickly would have been a massive struggle for her a few years ago.

Julie's had a taste of what it's like to set her own schedule and rule her life according to her own priorities, and that has changed everything. Now, she can walk away when things aren't working for her.

"This is totally a cliché," she says, "but I do yoga, and every time I'm in a balance pose, I think about how much work balance is. It's constant attention, and you have to keep shifting to find it."

Julie and Rich have attained a healthy balance in their marriage too. They've been incredibly honest and candid with all their friends and family about the struggles they've experienced, and have learned how to ask for help when they need it. Their communication has also opened up in fantastic ways.

"The other evening I was feeling anxious, and Rich was feeling anxious. We were doing things around the house, and I just said to him, *I think we're about to get into a fight*," Julie tells me. "I could feel this tension building up between us, and I thought, *What if I just acknowledged that out loud?*"

As soon as Julie observed the anger building up, she and Rich were able to defuse it.

"Rich was like, *I don't want to fight,*" Julie says. "And I told him, *I don't want to fight either.* It was scary to name this thing I wanted to run away from, but then we were able to deal with it."

Whenever I talk to Julie and Rich, I can't help but notice how comfortable, candid, and downright silly they are with each other. There's a relaxed honesty between them that I've seen in only a handful of couples in my life. Together, they were able to take a relationship that was in tatters and rebuild it into something far more vulnerable and enduring. That never would have been possible when they were both overworked.

————

I think some people might look at Julie's story and see a woman running away or giving up. Julie mentioned that her own mother has a hard time understanding the changes she's made in her life. One way that Julie marked those changes was by getting the word "surrender" tattooed on her upper arm—and her mom found that totally baffling.

"I got a lot of shit from my mom for that tattoo," Julie says. "She was like, *Surrender; that's such a weak word.*"

But Julie's new tattoo and new life reflect her newfound understanding that she cannot control everything. She can't work a full-time job, parent a child, and navigate an evolving relationship with her husband while also maintaining her own well-being and health. She can't prioritize everyone else's needs above her own. If she wants to thrive, she has to give some things up. She's learned not to feel guilt over every opportunity she walks away from or every obligation she says no to.

That is an incredibly difficult lesson to learn. In a world that equates laziness with evil, saying no is often deemed unacceptable. Our culture looks down on people who quit things. Rather than encouraging their good judgment and self-respect, we perceive them as weak-willed or dishonest. When a person juggles dozens and dozens of responsibilities, we laud them for "having it all," but what happens if they decide they don't want it all, or that the constant juggling isn't worth it? Can we actually respect a person who revokes their consent? Can we see a person

41

as impressive for admitting that they no longer want to carry something they've been shouldering for too long? Many of us never learned how to surrender, even when we desperately need to. We've been browbeaten into saying yes for so long that we don't know what a confident no feels like.

———

We so often see "laziness" as an indulgence we never truly deserve. In a world that's beholden to the Laziness Lie, many of us feel we have to hide our desire for free time. I know that when I cancel plans, I try to find a really plausible, virtuous-seeming excuse. *Sorry, I couldn't make it to game night, I had to stay late at work!* The truth (I just didn't feel like going) seems unacceptable to voice. Admitting I want to sit around and do nothing would make me look lazy. It would tell everyone I was weak.

But what if all of that is totally wrong? It seems to me that being upfront about your limits and needs is a sign of strength, not weakness. Cutting back on obligations doesn't mean you're hurting or disappointing other people either. Openly and proudly saying "No, I don't feel like doing that" can help free others to do the same in their own lives. Many of the "lazy" behaviors we've been told to avoid like the plague are actually very mature, responsible choices.

In chapter one, I discussed where the Laziness Lie came from, and the ways in which the Lie sets us up for failure and exhaustion. In this chapter, I want to take that argument even further and explore how resting, quitting things, cutting corners, and all the other actions we typically write off as "laziness" can actually help us heal and grow. A great deal of research actually supports the notion that our lazy feelings are protective and instructive, and that our lives can improve a great deal when we decide to stop judging our desire for idle, "lazy" time and start trusting those feelings instead.

Laziness Is Not Evil

I got into a fight with a college freshman on Twitter recently. Well, not a fight—just a long, tense discussion. He was outraged by my belief that laziness is not the evil, inexplicable thing we've all been taught to view it as. In an essay I posted online a few years ago, I said that seemingly "lazy" people almost always have a sensible reason for why they lack energy or drive.[1] If you under-

> **We've been browbeaten into saying yes for so long that we don't know what a confident no feels like.**

stand what a person is going through, even their most self-defeating, "lazy" behavior can start to make sense. But this young man (let's call him James) thought I was overlooking several types of "laziness" that were objectively senseless and wrong.

Like many people, James seemed convinced that his own inaction and "laziness" were far worse than most other people's. He mentioned that his laziness came from having depression, but insisted that mental illness wasn't a valid excuse for his "bad" behavior. James told me that sometimes whole days would pass before he'd muster the energy to leave his room. Wasn't that clearly unacceptable behavior, he wanted to know? Wasn't that kind of laziness terrible, no matter its cause?

James also told me that in high school, some of his friends prided themselves on their laziness. He said he and his friends procrastinated on purpose, to "stick it" to their school. One student in particular became infamous for writing entire papers in the hour before class started. Surely someone who does that is inexcusably lazy, right?

Finally, James told me that at college, he'd met some people who were truly apathetic about doing well in life. They seemed to have no good reason for failing to work hard. He wanted to know how my belief system accounted for people who didn't seem to be facing any personal challenges and failed to get things done because they simply didn't care.

James's questions touched on three types of people who tend to get pigeonholed as "lazy" in our society: depressed people, procrastinators, and apathetic people who don't see the point in caring about work or school. Managers and professors look down on folks like these. Friends and family find their inaction confounding. Society as a whole tends to resent them for not "contributing" enough to the world. But in these three groups of people, you can find clear illustrations of exactly why a lack of motivation isn't a personal failing or the awful, morally negligent act the Laziness Lie wants us to believe that it is.

Depressed People

The first type of inexcusably "lazy" person James wanted to ask me about was people with depression. He mentioned right out of the gate that he had major depressive disorder. During a depressive episode, James said he looked deeply "lazy" to the outside world.

"Lazy might not be a pretty way to describe it," he tweeted to me, "but it's accurate. In a depressive episode all I do is sleep. I don't get anything done."

When James is depressed, he doesn't have the energy to clean his room or do homework. He misses classes. He sleeps all day. Wasn't he failing in all these areas of his life because he was "lazy"? More to the point, wasn't that laziness *bad*?

This view of depression is disturbingly common. Despite all the work mental-health activists have put into fighting the stigmatization of mental illness, negative and ignorant perceptions of the disorder remain prevalent. Many professors still believe, for example, that depression isn't a valid excuse for a student's lacking the energy to turn in assignments on time.[2] When an employee divulges to their manager that they have depression, they're more likely to be punished for taking sick days than other employees are. Their odds of being fired go way up too, even if the quality of their work remains the same.[3] Parents of depressed children and teenagers often respond to their kids' symptoms by criticizing them rather than by providing them with understanding or support.[4]

Because depression doesn't harm the body in a visible, obvious way, many people fail to understand why a depressed person lacks the energy to get things done. In a massive survey administered in 2018, over 30 percent of respondents agreed with a statement that depression is caused by having a "weak personality."[5] Our culture's propensity to judge and blame the "lazy" still runs very deep. It's no wonder that James had absorbed some of those ideas.

So why are depressed people so "lazy"? The first thing to realize is that fighting depression is a full-time job. Depressed people sleep a lot because their brains get tired from fighting negative thoughts and feelings all day.[6] Depressed people also have lower quality of sleep, meaning they get less energy from eight hours of rest than a nondepressed person does. When you're severely depressed—particularly if you're suicidal—sleep can be the only escape from misery you have. In a very real way, the apparent "laziness" of depressed people is a sign that their bodies and minds are protecting them and working to help them heal.

Depression also saps the brain's ability to plan and execute activities. Something that might seem simple to a nondepressed person, such as doing a load of laundry, can become an overwhelming series of painful tasks to someone who's depressed.[7] It's hard to take a large job and break it down into small steps when your brain is struggling to function. A person's memory gets worse when they experience depression, as does their ability to pay attention and filter information.[8] It's not a moral failure for an exhausted person to let some responsibilities drop. In many cases, it's essential that they be "lazy" in a few areas of life if they want to have the energy to stay afloat in others.

Procrastinators

James wasn't really buying my argument at this point. He still felt pretty confident that being lazy wasn't at all understandable or okay. So, he pivoted a bit and told me about how in high school, he and many of his friends prided themselves on their "laziness" and procrastination.

"We were self-proclaimed procrastinators and took it as a badge of honor," he tweeted. "[It was a] counterculture against the strictness of our school. One friend would wait until an hour before class to start a project."

Surely procrastination is an unacceptable form of laziness, right? Procrastinators lack focus and ambition, and their work is done in a half-assed, last-minute way. The evils of procrastination could easily be avoided if only the procrastinator would just work a little harder in advance—or at least that's what people tend

Fighting depression is a full-time job.

to think. In reality, procrastination is a much more complex beast, one that's often caused by caring a whole lot and wanting to do well.

When a person procrastinates, it's typically because they're paralyzed in some way: by anxiety, by confusion about how to get started on a big, complicated project, or both.[9] I think most people have experienced both of these types of paralysis at one time or another. Imagine you see a job posting for a position that sounds amazing. It's truly your dream job; a rare opportunity. You want to get a wonderful, well-written application in on time so you can dazzle the hiring manager and beat out your competition. But try as you might, you find you can't make progress on it. You don't know what your cover letter should say. You know the application asks for references, but you don't know whom you ought to ask. You're afraid to even look at your résumé, because it's so out-of-date that it's embarrassing.

Soon, just thinking about the job application causes you to feel nauseated and nervous, so you go play a video game instead, to distract yourself from your anxious thoughts. Then you feel guilty for not working on the job application, which makes you anxious all over again, so you take a nap or go clean your kitchen. Before you know it, a week has passed and you haven't even looked at the job application. Maybe you hastily throw one together, hold your nose, and send it off at the last minute, or maybe you give up entirely because you feel like you already blew your chance. Either way, you're left feeling like a lazy screwup.

Procrastinators often get caught in a cycle of perfectionism, anxiety, distraction, and failure. Because they care a great deal about doing well, they hold themselves to an impossibly high standard. They want to do "perfect" work, but their early attempts are far from perfect, so they get discouraged and anxious. As time passes and the deadline approaches, they become even more nervous and concerned about failure. That fear makes it even harder to focus and make progress. To cope with their feelings of anxiety, they

> **Procrastination is a complex beast, one that's often caused by caring a whole lot and wanting to do well.**

46

distract themselves in any way they can. And then, when the deadline finally arrives, the procrastinator must choose between submitting quickly thrown-together work that isn't very good or giving up entirely.

James seemed to think that he and his friends procrastinated for no good reason. In his mind, they were being bad students just for the hell of it. However, if they're anything like most procrastinators, they had a whole host of sympathetic reasons to explain their behavior. Though they're frequently labeled as lazy, procrastinators don't lack motivation. In fact, they tend to care a lot about doing well. Research has repeatedly found that people procrastinate more when a task is one that really matters to them.[10] Unfortunately, they lack the confidence and clarity to start plugging away at it in a productive way.[11]

The good news is that it's possible for a chronic procrastinator to break out of that cycle. With help and encouragement, a procrastinator can be taught to divide large responsibilities into small microtasks, each with their own very short-term deadlines. Something as big and vague as "write a ten-page paper" can be paralyzing, but "write two paragraphs per day" can be manageable. This, combined with treatment for their anxiety, can help procrastinators become far more productive, reliable, and confident in their abilities.[12]

Apathetic People

What about people who are truly unmotivated? People who put off tasks because they simply don't care? James mentioned that his friends put off homework in order to rebel against their overly strict school. This doesn't necessarily sound like a group of kids being lazy because of anxiety or depression or confusion about how to do well. For some of them, at least, it sounds like they truly didn't care. Isn't there something uniquely terrible about being that apathetic? Wasn't the Laziness Lie right to teach us that such people deserve our judgment?

Believe it or not, I don't think so. When someone seems completely apathetic, I don't see them as a failure. Instead, I tend to think that they've been failed in some way. Let's take the ever-popular example

> When someone seems completely apathetic, I don't see them as a failure. Instead, I tend to think that they've been failed in some way.

of the kid who doesn't try hard in algebra class because he doesn't think he'll use algebra in "real life." I used to feel the same way about math myself. I got a C in statistics when I was in college because the class was hard (and boring) and I didn't take it seriously. It was too abstract and vague to seem relevant to my life. Nobody went to the trouble of explaining to me why the subject was important or how it would be relevant to my psychology major. Even within the class itself, this was never made clear.

I continued to feel apathetic about statistics until I was trained as a researcher in graduate school. I quickly realized that I needed statistics to determine whether my experiments had worked. My career wasn't going to go anywhere if I didn't know how to analyze all the data I'd collected, so I put the work in. Bit by bit, I started excelling at stats. Nowadays, I teach statistics classes with enthusiasm (I actually love the subject!) and help organizations analyze their data in my work as a statistical consultant. But I got to this place only because I finally saw why this dull, difficult subject mattered in my own life. Now, whenever I teach statistics, I work hard to help my students see *why* the subject deserves their attention and time. I demonstrate to them why it ought to be one of their priorities. When I've done my job well, they get it, and put in the effort.

So, when I see that somebody doesn't care about a particular goal—whether it's becoming financially independent, finishing a degree, or even voting—I find myself wondering, *Why does this activity seem pointless to them?*

According to James, he and his peers didn't take classwork seriously because their school was overly strict. That makes complete sense to me. When you feel stuck in a controlling environment where nobody treats you with trust, you're naturally going to want to rebel against it. Of course it's hard for a teenager to self-motivate when they've had adults telling them what to do and how to do it all their lives! If James's school had given him and his peers more freedom and agency, they might have risen to the challenge instead of checking out.

Sometimes people become apathetic because of depression or trauma.[13] Other times, people turn to apathy after repeatedly being disenfranchised. Psychologists call this "learned helplessness," and we see it in victims of abuse, people who have been incarcerated, and families that have experienced generations of poverty and racism.[14] When you lose power over your own life, you don't have much reason to stay energized and motivated.[15] So, you protect yourself emotionally by checking out and giving up. In workplaces with ineffective or incompetent managers, for example, employees become apathetic, because they know their hard work will go unnoticed and unappreciated.[16] We also see this in the low voter turnout rate in the United States: a majority of nonvoters are people of color and people living in poverty, who report that they do not feel their interests are being represented by the political options available to them.[17] Pulling back one's effort level in such situations is perfectly rational. It may not be pretty, but it's not a personal failing either.

In so many cases, what we call "laziness" is actually a person coping with a ton of challenges and attempting to set priorities based on their needs. When a person is pushed to their limit, supposedly "lazy" feelings and behaviors tend to pop up. Apathy, low motivation, an inability to focus, a desire to "waste time" doing "nothing"—these are all valuable warning signs. They can teach us a great deal about our limits and needs. However, in order to benefit from this highly evolved, dynamic warning system, we have to learn to stop writing it off as inexcusable "laziness."

Laziness Is a Warning

Scientific research on topics such as productivity and burnout have taught us that there are limits to how much work a person can do. Those limits are more extreme than you might realize: For example, the forty-hour workweek (which is considered quite reasonable and humane here in the US) is still probably too long and demanding for most people.[18] We are not machines. Our bodies and minds aren't set up to perform repetitive or mentally taxing work for eight or more hours per day. Still, many of us push through those limitations, forcing ourselves to work harder, and for longer, than is truly healthy for us.

The Laziness Lie has set us up to expect more productivity out of ourselves than is really feasible or sustainable. As a result, many of us live continuously on the edge of breaking down. For some, that breaking point is dramatic. Julie had to experience mental and physical collapse in order to learn the importance of good work-life boundaries. So did Max. I had to battle illness for months before I finally learned to let myself relax. But it doesn't have to be that way. Our bodies and brains have subtle, gradual signals that tell us to pump the brakes and prioritize our health over our productivity. Unfortunately, the Laziness Lie has convinced us that those signals must be ignored as much as possible.

———

Leo has an uncanny ability to set himself up for frustration and burnout. He's an expert at taking on more responsibilities than seems remotely tenable, and then having to face the drastic consequences of spreading himself too thin. He's just now coming to understand his own limits and learning to listen to his internal "laziness" signals instead of brushing them away—but that process has been long, painful, and full of bumps.

Today, Leo is thirty, but he's been an overachiever and a workaholic since I met him in college. As a student, Leo was ambitious, intelligent, and politically engaged, always organizing fundraisers for politicians and volunteering for local- and state-level campaigns. He was involved in an endless list of extracurriculars, from the campus atheist club to the campus chapter of College Democrats of America. He cared about every conceivable political issue and took it upon himself to fight for his values in every way he could. He traveled the Midwest to aid in get-out-the-vote efforts, registering voters and educating them on the issues. Back at school, he enrolled in the maximum number of classes our college allowed him to take. A few weeks into every semester, he would inevitably fall apart, dropping multiple classes, missing a variety of deadlines, and failing to attend some of the on-campus events he'd so carefully worked to put together.

Leo was often burned out and terribly depressed, but he never wanted to talk about it.

"I'd spend days in my bedroom, too ashamed and tired to leave," he says. "My roommates would think I was out of town until I'd come downstairs in the middle of the day to grab water or something."

Once he was in this burned-out state, Leo couldn't follow through on the many commitments he had previously made. Deadlines would fly by, events would go by unattended, and dirty dishes would pile up on his desk. Yet by the time another semester came around, Leo would yet again find himself signing up for a full course load and taking on mountains of other responsibilities.

"I always thought, *This time will be different*," he says. "I just figured I'd screwed up the last time because I wasn't organized and wasn't trying hard enough to do everything."

Throughout his entire college career, Leo was convinced that his problem was a lack of motivation or effort, not that he was taking on too many responsibilities, so he kept getting buried and burned out. He couldn't seem to see a self-defeating pattern in his actions—or, if he did, the Laziness Lie was preventing him from breaking out of it.

———

As an adult, Leo remained very politically engaged while continuing to overextend himself. During the 2012 presidential election, he redoubled his efforts, traveling, organizing volunteers, and lending his time to the Obama campaign in every way he could. He started taking graduate school classes while working full-time. He also devoted as much of his free time as possible to having conversations with people who disagreed with him. He was willing to invest hours in changing the minds of politically disengaged Ohioans on issues such as LGBTQ+ rights and health care reform.

Leo is a lover of strategy games and an avid reader of history and philosophy books. He lives in his head, and thinks about long-term consequences rather than short-term impulses or needs. I think that's why it was hard for him to notice his own needs and limitations at times. He has to hit a wall before he even starts to see that he's tired. As a result, it took him years to realize his feelings of laziness weren't a threat but rather a signal that he was pushing himself over the edge.

Feelings of laziness are often a sign that someone hasn't been managing the demands of their day-to-day life in an optimal way. Our bodies have amazing methods of forcing us to get what we need. When we're hungry, our minds become preoccupied with food, our stomachs begin to rumble and fill with digestive acid, and we get progressively more cranky and lethargic until we're forced to stop what we're doing and eat.[19] When we don't get enough sleep, our bodies make us feel more and more tired, enticing us to take a nap. If we still refuse to sleep, our brains may force us to by taking millisecond-long "microsleeps" throughout the day.[20] And when we don't give ourselves enough time to relax, the powerful urge to zone out and lose focus bleeds into our everyday lives.

A graduate student of mine, Marvin, decided recently that he wanted to study the ways in which "laziness" leaks into people's lives against their will. He chose to focus on people's distracting themselves from stress and exhaustion by browsing Facebook or shopping online. It's a form of procrastination that most of us have intimate personal knowledge of (I don't know about you, but I do it almost every day), and in the social-science literature it's called "cyberloafing."

The average person cyberloafs many times per day, but it's particularly likely to happen when someone has just finished an intellectually strenuous task or when they're about to mentally "shift gears" from one activity to another.[21] Research suggests that people tend to cyberloaf as a way to relax and reinvigorate their brains, which is essentially the same reason employees do things like chat over the watercooler or futz around in the supply closet looking for a pen they don't really need.[22]

> When we don't give ourselves enough time to relax, the powerful urge to zone out and lose focus bleeds into our everyday lives.

Many employers and productivity experts absolutely loathe cyber-loafing, because they see it as a horribly lazy act, a "theft" of company time. One study conducted in 2014 estimated that cyberloafing "costs" employers $54 billion annually in lost productivity.[23] But estimates like these make a big assumption, one we shouldn't take for granted: that time spent cyberloafing is time an employee could have spent being fully productive, if only they weren't so lazy. Marvin wondered whether this was actually the case.

As he began combing the scientific literature, Marvin found several studies that found cyberloafing to have benefits. A 2017 study by media researchers Shafaat Hussain and Truptimayee Parida, for example, examined cyberloafing among administrative assistants in Ethiopia. The authors found that brief periods of cyberloafing actually helped admins fight the boredom that so often comes from hours and hours of transcribing documents, organizing files, making copies, and running office errands. Rather than sapping their productivity, taking a moment to cyberloaf helped these employees hit the mental refresh button so they could return to their work with renewed energy.[24] Several other studies suggest employees become more productive and focused after a good cyberloafing session.[25]

Additionally, Marvin discovered studies showing that cyberloafing helps work teams to function better, and that employees who cyberloaf come up with more unique solutions to work problems.[26] It turns out that slacking can actually help you be creative and reflective. Marvin also found compelling evidence that some amount of cyberloafing is unavoidable. Just as all employees need time to use the bathroom or take a lunch break, it appears that they also need time to rest their brains.

When an employee spends hours concentrating on something, their willpower tends to erode and their impulse to cyberloaf becomes stronger and stronger.[27] Eventually, their willpower breaks, and they find something—anything—to distract themselves with. Employers usually try to limit this behavior by monitoring employees' computer usage, using software to block websites like Facebook or Amazon, or simply chastising workers when they catch them in the act. However, many studies have shown that cyberloafing will continue to happen anyway.[28] Most people require a bit of loafing time in order to remain happy and focused at work. To see it as a "waste" of company time is like seeing bathroom breaks as an unnecessary indulgence.

When employees are unable to slack off using the Internet, they find other ways to mentally escape. They "waste" time making cups of tea, sharpening pencils, or popping into coworkers' offices to say hello. Most workplace productivity studies consider behaviors like these to be a "waste" of company time as well, yet no one has found a way to get rid of them. That's because "wasting time" is important, healthy, and normal. Management may hate it, but spending time in these ways isn't actually a form of "theft." It's a way of coming up for air. When employees are blocked from engaging in their preferred forms of loafing, their brains still find ways to take breaks, even if the only method available is staring off into space.

So often, the urge to engage in behaviors that seem "lazy" is a sign that a person has worked hard enough and should just sit and be calm for a little while. Most of the jobs that humans perform require time for reflection, planning, or creativity. We aren't computers or robots. Just as we need to eat and sleep, we need time for goofing off and doing nothing. When we ignore that impulse to recharge for fear of seeming "lazy," we risk facing dire consequences.

———

Leo eventually reached his breaking point. When he was in his mid-twenties, he dropped out of graduate school, in part because he couldn't get the required mountains of reading done. To cope with his massive disappointment, he threw himself into his job and into politics, and got involved in even more campaigns than ever before. But it was getting harder and harder for him to ignore how stressed he constantly was. He hopped between a couple of different jobs, raising funds for various campaigns and

> We aren't computers or robots. Just as we need to eat and sleep, we need time for goofing off and doing nothing.

causes. No matter where he was hired, he kept getting into the same nasty patterns. By his early thirties, his workaholism and procrastination had put a major strain on his relationships, as well as his mental health.

"I hadn't dated anybody in a couple of years," he tells me. "I hadn't gone on a vacation in forever. I couldn't justify traveling anywhere with friends because I was too busy, or I was brand-new at a job and couldn't leave. Everybody else had a life, but I didn't."

Around this time, Leo started seeing a therapist. She quickly took stock of his frantic mannerisms, the way his eyes darted anxiously around the room, and the distractibility and overexertion that defined his life, and took a guess at what the source of the problem was.

"She asked me on, like, my second visit if I had ever been assessed for ADHD," he says. "And when I did get tested, I was off the charts."

Before that moment, Leo had never considered it a possibility that he had ADHD. There's a very particular stereotype of the disorder people have in their minds: ADHD sufferers are seen as unintelligent or lacking ambition. Yet for Leo and for many other people with ADHD, the exact opposite is the case. It's very common for people with ADHD to overcommit to a variety of things they're passionate about, and then run quickly and dramatically out of steam because they haven't realistically budgeted their time.

I'll never forget the first time I hung out with Leo after he started taking ADHD medication and working on his overcommitment with a therapist. He didn't interrupt me with tons of observations and questions I couldn't follow the logic of. He had an easy sense of humor, and could speak candidly about how hard his college years had been. He wasn't constantly flitting around the living room, anxiously tidying things or letting out his nervous energy in little verbal tangents and ticks. He could sit through a movie without getting up or being distracted. He had also started recreationally smoking weed from time to time, a thing his younger, driven type-A self would have found downright shameful. My intense, hardworking friend had finally found a way to chill out and stop fearing "laziness."

Around this time, Leo started dating his current boyfriend. He finally had the mental space to prioritize his own feelings and desires, and that made getting close to someone else much easier. In the couple of years that they've been dating, they've gone on several long vacations and adventures, visiting national parks and museums, mountaineering, and kayaking. Leo wasn't someone who could enjoy and luxuriate in downtime like this before, but now he seems to relish it. After repeatedly overcommitting, ignoring his needs, and then dramatically burning out, Leo has slowly learned how to find enjoyment in life. When the two of us discuss politics nowadays, he remains engaged and informed, but there's a clear emotional distance between his self-image and how well his favorite politicians are doing. He's capable of disengaging in a way he never could before. I never thought a straitlaced, politics-obsessed person like him would turn into a chilled-out nature-loving weed smoker, but I'm so happy for him that he did.

———

The seemingly "bad" behaviors we tend to judge as laziness are really powerful signals that something in our lives needs to change. On the organizational level, patterns of employee laziness can tell us a workplace is being mismanaged. One workplace productivity expert I spoke to, industrial-organizational psychologist Dr. Annette Towler, told me that when employees are bullied or mismanaged, they often cope with it through subtle signs of "laziness," such as increased absenteeism.

"That's one of the early, subtle signs that a workplace is toxic," she told me. "You see a lot of employees just not coming in to work, with no explanation or cause. Managers look at that and they think, *Oh, everyone is being so lazy*, or so unreliable—but often it's that they're trying to avoid an abusive or toxic environment."

When a person has been stretched to their limit, they may start to seem flaky and checked-out. They might come in to work late or cancel plans with friends at the last minute. They'll have less drive to do chores or cook meals and may take frequent naps or zone out by playing repetitive video games. In general, they'll have worse impulse control and far less energy than they used to. These aren't signs that someone is a screwup or a failure. They're signs of a person pushed to the brink.

Though these "lazy" behaviors have been demonized for centuries, there's actually nothing evil or damaging about them. Slacking off is a normal part of life; people require idle time in order to remain clear-headed and healthy. Feelings of laziness are also a powerful internal alarm signaling to us that we need additional help, more breaks, or reduced demands. By listening to this laziness, we can better understand our needs and construct lives that are truly worth living.

Listening to Laziness

After Max's dead, necrotic gallbladder was discovered and taken out of her body, she finally got to enjoy some much-needed bed rest, and a break from her grueling job at the information technology firm. She had officially become too sick to work. She had a doctor's note and the healing incisions to prove it.

"Those weeks after gallbladder surgery were the best weeks of my life," Max says, without any irony. "I just slept and lay around and watched movies. It was so fucking fun. I wish it would happen to me again. I'll give up another organ if I can get some more rest."

Max told me when her stress at work was at its very worst, she was so mentally drained that she couldn't sit through films anymore. Though she was an avid lover of horror movies, true-crime documentaries, and all things gruesome and dark, the demands of her job had zapped her energy so drastically that she could no longer focus on them.

"For a whole year," she says, "all I watched was *Bob's Burgers*. Which is a great show! I like that show. But it was the only thing simple and comforting enough for my mind to handle. For a *year*. Because I was working eighty- to

> By listening to laziness, we can better understand our needs and construct lives that are truly worth living.

ninety-hour weeks, and anything that was upsetting or had a complicated plot was just too much for me to process."

Once she finally had a few days to sleep and recuperate, Max found that she was able to sit through long movies and documentaries again. On bed rest, she had renewed interest in her hobbies. She started making witchy handcrafts again. Soon she felt far less hopeless and depressed.

Though we normally think of a medical emergency as being a traumatic and taxing experience, Max's gallbladder surgery marked a significant, positive turning point in her life. When she had the chance to relax, she started reevaluating her life. She'd been given a glimpse of what a healthier, sustainable existence could be like, and how wonderful it felt to get enough sleep. That made it impossible to go back to her old patterns.

Laziness had given Max the gift of insight. And it can do the same for many of us, if we let it.

Laziness Helps Us Be Creative

When we're able to rest and be lazy, we can learn new things about ourselves, or have fantastic insights that would never have occurred to us when we were focused on work. Psychologists who study creativity are often very interested in these big "aha" moments and have put a lot of effort into studying what a person can do to promote them. It turns out that laziness is one of the most effective steps to getting there.

Moments of insight and creativity don't come by trying to force them—they require a period of mental inactivity.[29] Good ideas often come to us when we've stopped trying to come up with them, such as when we're in the shower or on a leisurely walk. While it seems like these ideas have come out of nowhere, the truth is that our minds have been quietly and unconsciously developing them during our downtime. Psychologists call this productive downtime the "incubation period." Like an egg that must be kept warm and safe in order to develop into a healthy chick, the creative parts of our minds require safety, rest, and relaxation in order to produce unique ideas or insights.[30]

Moments of insight and creativity don't come by trying to force them— they require a period of mental inactivity.

Whenever I explain this principle to people, I'm reminded of a moment from the show *Mad Men*. The successful, charismatic advertising executive Don Draper is giving advice to Peggy, a young, ambitious copy-writer who's struggling to come up with a tagline for a client's new product. In just a few short sentences, Don perfectly explains the concept of creative incubation. "Just think about it, deeply," he says to her, "and then forget it. An idea will jump up in your face."[31]

I've had good ideas jump up in my face in that way. In 2013, I was a frazzled graduate student, struggling to come up with a research topic for my dissertation. I spent hours staring at academic articles, trying to make myself arrive at a creative idea through sheer force. Predictably, it didn't work. I started to get really frustrated with myself for "failing" so miserably. Dejected and feeling guilty, I took a few days off to celebrate my birthday and visit some friends.

One day during that vacation, I was on a long walk with a friend, and we found ourselves in the parking lot of a Michael's craft store. We were there to buy spray paint and fake flowers for a wreath my friend was putting together. Suddenly, a fully formed research idea popped into my head. I had to stop right where I was and jot down the details in the Notes app on my phone to make sure I didn't lose them. Though I had felt guilty all that week for being "lazy" and not working on my dissertation, it turned out that my unconscious mind was actually doing a lot of powerful work. I just had to step back and give it the room to be creative for me.

Laziness Helps Us Problem-Solve

In Max's case, it took a period of bed rest (and a ton of bloody horror movies) to realize her life needed to dramatically change. And she needed the creative insight a long, restful incubation period provided her in order to figure out how to go about making that change.

Max knew she would have to fight to build and maintain a sustainable life for herself. It wasn't going to be handed to her. When she came back from medical leave, her office was still going to be inefficient and poorly managed. Her boss would still be the same intense, borderline abusive woman who discouraged her employees from taking sick days. In order for Max to protect her newfound health, she would have to push against these power structures and prioritize her own well-being. And she'd have to be strategic about how she did it.

As soon as she got back to work, Max began documenting whenever her boss gave contradictory instructions. She began collecting evidence of how work was done in her department so she could demonstrate that when applications were late, she wasn't to blame. From there, Max scheduled meetings with upper management to discuss problems she'd noticed in how responsibilities were being assigned. This persuaded them to hire additional employees, who took on some of Max's old duties. Her workload gradually lightened. Now, when Max needs a sick day, she takes it, even if her boss has something undermining to say about it.

"When my boss tries to ask me if I'm 'sure' I need a sick day, I really push back on it," Max says. "Like, I'll make sure that I ask for the day off in an e-mail, and if she hedges, I'll ask her if she's requiring me to come in to work even though I'm sick. She knows that it's actually illegal for her to refuse sick days to employees. But I have to find ways to subtly remind her that *I* know that."

This may seem like a drastic or extreme measure, but it makes sense given her boss's track record. For some of us, the process of learning to set work-life boundaries is largely an internal exercise; in far too many cases, however, the pressure to overexert ourselves comes from the outside.

Overworked, poorly managed employees often have to advocate for themselves using every legal protection available. They may need to band together with other employees and push for a change in policy.

That's what Max did. After several months of repeated problems, she compared notes with other employees and was able to demonstrate to the higher-ups that her boss was not running things correctly. This also helped her to negotiate a more forgiving work schedule.

Things are far from perfect at Max's job. She still regularly fantasizes about quitting, and the work is still generally unrewarding and exhausting. But today, Max says she has only one eighty-hour workweek per month, instead of every single week of the year. She makes time for painting, ghost-hunting tours, and volunteer work. She's also in therapy, working to repair some of the damage that years of being overworked did to her personal life. Perhaps most important, she now has the brain space to watch as many bloody, gothic horror films as she wants.

Max's illness gave her the opportunity to remember how good laziness feels. Those weeks that she spent in bed rejuvenated her and turned her focus back on what truly mattered in her life. With a less stress-addled, run-down mind, she was able to come up with a game plan for how to advocate for herself better and to fix several key sources of dysfunction in her work.

When we consciously make time for idleness and embrace our naturally lazy feelings rather than pushing them away, we can learn what matters to us, and which demands need to be dialed way back. With a rejuvenated, relaxed mind, we can see new solutions to old problems and find new reserves of strength we didn't know we had.

Laziness Reminds Us of What Matters

When you have a lot of responsibilities on your plate, your instinct is probably to hunker down and get as much done as possible. However, a lot of research suggests it's better to hit the pause button, find time to be lazy, and see what realizations and reactions come bubbling up. By slowing down and cutting back, we can figure out which demands in our lives we can afford to let go of. When we stop seeing laziness as the enemy, we can begin to feel good about that act of letting go.

> **When we stop seeing laziness as the enemy, we can begin to feel good about that act of letting go.**

August Stockwell runs an organization called Upswing Advocates, which trains mental-health professionals on how to meet the needs of LGBTQ+ clients, as well as clients with disabilities such as autism and ADHD. It's a time-consuming and demanding job, with lots of administrative tasks, meetings, and phone conferences. It can also be an emotionally difficult job, because it involves speaking with therapists and counselors about some of their struggles with their clients. For years, these demands took a toll on August's mental health.

"I figured out at some point that I was living in a state of hypervigilance all the time," August tells me. "I didn't have good professional boundaries. I would say yes to everything, because there were so many awesome things to be doing! And I'd lose touch with myself."

August tells me that for a long time, they based their priorities on whatever was looming largest at work. Their attention went to whatever seemed to be the biggest "fire" in need of putting out. That's when they put their training as a behavioral analyst to work and developed a way to make it more manageable.

August shows me a spreadsheet that they use to keep track of weekly responsibilities and objectives. It has fields for all kinds of weekly goals, not just work-related ones. There are fields for things like spending time with romantic partners, meditating, taking walks, and scheduling phone calls with loved ones. Everything that matters in August's life is in this spreadsheet.

On the right-hand side of the spreadsheet, August marks down whether they've met a particular goal for the week. *Did I attend this meeting? Did I have a phone call with this friend like I intended to?* In addition, there's also a field where August can record how they feel about whether that particular goal was met. Here's an example of what August's spreadsheet looks like:

Goal Category	Goal for This Week	Priority	Completion	Feelings
Reflection	Meditate at Least Two Days	High	Yes	Good
Physical Health	Exercise at Least One Day	Medium	Need to Exercise	Okay
Rest	Take Three Days Off	High	Took Two Days Off	Okay
Work	Hold Webinar, Send Thank-You Cards to Donors	High	Remaining Thank-Yous	Okay
Relationships	Tell My Partners How I'm Doing	High	Yes	Okay
Errands and Life Tasks	Clean Apartment, Deposit Check	Medium	Yes, Also Sent Password Name Change	Good

This spreadsheet system allows August to notice which goals they regularly miss, as well as how they feel about missing those goals. Rather than judging themselves for failing to meet a goal, August observes where their motivation and their "laziness" has taken them and figures out what lessons laziness has to teach. For example, if they repeatedly miss household-chore goals but don't feel particularly bad about it, that may tell them that having a perfectly tidy house isn't such an important goal. Often, this helps them to create new goals that reflect their actual values, rather than beating themselves up for not being able to do everything all the time.

"All of this helps me focus more on myself and my actual experiences rather than just on other people," August says. "It helps me ask myself, *How am I doing? What do I actually want? Am I happy?* If I'm not, does it still feel worth it to focus on these goals?"

In a world ruled by the Laziness Lie, giving up on an obligation can feel painful. Yet the more we learn to observe our own patterns and learn from them without judgment, the more we can build authentic lives that actually allow us to thrive.

Lin-Manuel Miranda, the writer and star of the musical *Hamilton*, famously came up with the concept for the show while reading a history book on vacation with his wife.[32] He didn't go on vacation hoping to come up with a concept for a new musical; he was just trying to find a way to relax after seven nonstop years of performing in his show *In the Heights*. Yet the moment he had time to truly recharge, he arrived at a creative breakthrough that changed his life forever.

After *Hamilton*'s massive, unprecedented success, Miranda had to force himself to find time for a vacation again. Fans of the show were dismayed when he left the performing cast. But in interviews, Miranda emphasized the importance of laziness.

"It's no accident that the best idea I've ever had in my life, perhaps maybe the best one I'll ever have in my life, came to me on vacation," Miranda told an interviewer in 2018. "The moment my brain got a moment's rest, *Hamilton* walked into it."[33]

Though the Laziness Lie would love for us to believe otherwise, idleness can help us to be insightful creators and problem-solvers. But the value of laziness also goes so much deeper than that. When we give our lives space for slowness, relaxation, and doing "nothing," we can begin to heal some of our greatest wounds and to create lives for ourselves that are nourishing rather than exhausting.

How Doing Less Can Heal Us

When my therapist, Jason, first told me to try sitting around and doing absolutely nothing for half an hour so I could truly "feel my feelings," I thought he was absolutely full of shit.

"Nobody does that," I told him. "Literally no human has ever just sat perfectly still and calmly done *nothing* for that long."

At the time Jason gave me this advice, I was struggling to deal with my emotions. The federal government had just withdrawn its antidiscrimination protections for transgender people. People were being held in cages at the U.S.-Mexico border. Many of my friends were living in fear that the Affordable Care Act was going to be overturned, causing them to lose access to lifesaving medical care. The world felt like it was burning down, and even worse, my more conservative relatives didn't seem to see how they were complicit in all of it. My despair and rage felt too large to deal with. And so I just silenced it as best I could.

All day long, I'd push back any feelings of sadness or anxiety so I could focus on work and activism. I went to protests and rallies. I called my political representatives. I supported my scared friends and tried to stay strong. At night, when I was trying to fall asleep, I'd experience a flood of emotions, either sobbing or seething with rage. My partner hated how I'd mope for hours without telling him what was bothering me. I'd refuse to tell him about any problems I was facing, and then blow up over something trivial days later. I'd waste days resenting something a friend or relative had said but never actually tell them they'd hurt me. Emotions were for weak, unproductive people, I thought. I just had to just keep them at bay.

Jason wasn't on board with the "push emotions away and pretend I'm an unfeeling robot" plan. It clearly wasn't working, and it wasn't a sustainable way to deal with stress or past trauma. So, he told me to schedule time at least once a week to sit and do nothing, and to truly feel whatever emotions came up.

For a few weeks, I protested. It sounded like a completely fake, touchy-feely, ridiculous idea. "It sounds insane to me that anyone would ever do this," I told him. "I can't imagine somebody just sitting there and crying for no reason, and then feeling better somehow. If any patient tells you they actual do that, they're lying to get you off their case, I swear."

Through all my complaints and resistance, Jason laughed and rolled his eyes. He insisted that yes, some people really do just sit there and let themselves feel whatever they need to feel, and that it can be immensely helpful. And he emphasized, yet again, that I really ought to give it a try.

———

It turns out that there's a lot of scientific evidence supporting Jason's suggestion. Over the decades, research has demonstrated that finding time to sit still, be nonproductive, and become attuned with one's emotions can be therapeutic and improve a person's physical and mental health.

In 1985, the therapist James Pennebaker began to study how expressing painful emotions in writing could be healing.[34] Researchers already knew that talking about hard feelings with a therapist was helpful, and having close friends to confide in also helped people to cope. But Pennebaker wanted to know whether people could feel better after sharing their emotions with *themselves* by sitting down and writing about them.

Pennebaker tested this by getting together a sample of trauma survivors and chronic illness sufferers and instructing them to sit down for twenty minutes each day and write about how they were feeling. Here are the instructions he gave them:[35]

1. Find a time and place where you won't be disturbed.
2. Write continuously for at least twenty minutes.
3. Don't worry about spelling or grammar.
4. Write only for yourself.
5. Write about something extremely personal and important for you.
6. Deal only with events or situations you can handle now.

Pennebaker told his study participants to write nonstop for twenty minutes about a source of "emotional upheaval" in their lives. Their writing was allowed to be messy, and even nonsensical. The point of the exercise was to get the feelings out on the page, not to produce something beautifully well-written. If participants ran out of things to say,

Pennebaker instructed them to keep writing anyway, even if it meant just repeating what they'd already put down at the beginning. After the twenty minutes was done, the participants were welcome to throw the pages out.

Pennebaker and his colleagues found that after a couple of weeks of doing this writing exercise, people reported lower stress and less depression.[36] They slept better and had more energy.[37] Even their vital signs and immune system functioning got significantly better.[38] In follow-up studies, Pennebaker and others found that writing about feelings in this way helped a person to ruminate less on the things that bothered them and improved their coping skills. As more and more researchers tested the method on a wider and wider array of patients, the numerous benefits of the practice became even more apparent.

Pennebaker had found a simple, accessible treatment that helped people become more in tune with their feelings and needs, and it seemed to benefit people with a variety of physical and mental illnesses.[39] This research became the basis of Pennebaker's landmark book *Writing to Heal: A Guided Journal for Recovering from Trauma & Emotional Upheaval* and what he called the "expressive writing" method. Expressive writing is regularly used today to help everyone from veterans suffering from PTSD to cancer patients dealing with uncertain futures to all manner of people who suffer from stress, anxiety, grief, and depression.[40] I still find it kind of hard to believe, but countless studies have consistently shown the healing power of slowing down, being nonproductive, and listening to one's emotions.

———

Why does expressive writing work so well? Because it forces us to confront painful feelings that we usually downplay. We live in a world that preaches the gospel of pulling yourself up by your bootstraps and that lionizes the strong and invulnerable. Because of this cultural messaging and all the pressure it places on us, we learn to ignore our needs. We may even hate ourselves for having feelings of weakness or for harboring difficult emotions. Expressive writing seems to work because it gives us the opportunity to locate and listen to the vulnerable side of ourselves that we spend all day silencing.

It's also crucial that the writing process not be about creating something that another person will ever view. When we write for other people, we censor ourselves and focus on whether what we're creating is good enough. Expressive writing is specifically designed to be nonproductive. You allow yourself to write something messy, something that isn't fit for anyone else to ever read, and then you throw it out. This can help a person connect with every feeling they have, no matter how unpleasant it is.

My colleague Dr. Bella Etingen is a researcher at the Veterans Affairs Hospital in Hines, Illinois. She has often used expressive writing to help veterans with PTSD. Part of what makes it such an effective therapeutic method for veterans is that it allows them to be vulnerable and to listen to their emotions in a totally private, unembarrassing way.

"Lots of these macho military guys hate talking about their feelings or their trauma with a therapist," Bella told me back when she was first beginning research on the power of expressive writing. "But if you ask them to just sit down and write down how they feel and tell them that they can throw out the writing after the fact, it's a lot less threatening to their masculinity or to seeing themselves as tough."

I can relate to the "macho military guys" Bella told me about. I'm not tough or super masculine, but I do hate the idea of sitting around and talking about my feelings. I find the whole process kind of cringe-inducing and shameful. Patriarchy and the Laziness Lie worked together for decades to make me suspicious of soft, feminine-seeming things such as crying or talking about emotions—even when my own repression started to eat me alive.

A lot of society's most popular "self-care" methods have gotten an unfair reputation in this way. They're seen as frivolous, feminine, and not suitable for anyone who wants to appear "strong." Taking a bubble bath, lighting some candles, getting a massage—these are seen as lazy, wasteful extravagances, not essentials. Or so we're taught. Eventually, though, many of us come to realize that these gentle, healing activities are absolutely wonderful, and we need to fight back against the cultural brainwashing that tells us to avoid them.

After several weeks of protesting Jason's suggestion, I finally gave "feeling my feelings" a try. Once a week, I set aside half an hour to jot down a few notes about the things in my life that were making me unhappy. To help me get into the right mindset, I'd play music that helped me identify what was bothering me and how I felt about it. I'd cry while I did it, or feel myself getting pissed. Every single second of it sucked. I hated it. It was painful, being reminded of every bit of grief I was carrying, every sad or wounded feeling that was stifled and buried deep inside me. During those sessions, I felt utterly pathetic. After I was done, I'd throw the notes out and go take a walk, trying to shake off the shame I still felt about having human vulnerabilities and weaknesses.

After a couple of weeks of "feeling my feelings" like Jason recommended, I noticed I was no longer crying myself to sleep. I started communicating my feelings to my partner and my friends as soon as they came up instead of brooding for weeks. It suddenly felt less threatening to admit that I was sad or angry. Because I wasn't constantly running away from those feelings, I was able to air them with significantly less shame.

I also started noticing patterns in the things I chose to write about each week. I saw that certain obligations, like a weekly genderqueer support group I used to attend, always came up in my writing as a source of stress. Every single week, I dreaded going. Once I noticed this pattern, I found it a lot easier to stop attending the group.

After a few months of making time to feel my feelings, I was finally able to sit down with my partner and have a hard but necessary conversation about money that I'd literally been putting off for years. It radically changed how we

> Because I wasn't constantly running away from those feelings, I was able to air them with significantly less shame.

divide up responsibilities in our house, and how we think and talk about our future together. My relationships with my conservative relatives improved as well. One day, about six months into the process, my mom said something unintentionally hurtful on the phone. Normally I would have been distant with her for the rest of the call, and then spent the next few days fuming about it. But this time, I had the presence of mind to stop the conversation and tell her that I was upset by what she'd said. I immediately felt like some demon of resentment had been exorcised from my body.

I was getting more attuned to my emotions! This silly-sounding "feeling my feelings" thing was actually paying off!

Expressive writing worked so well for me that I started recommending it to friends dealing with hard, emotionally fraught situations, and to students of mine with test anxiety. I also suggest it to friends who, like me, find themselves getting lost in their own fears about the future of our world.[41] Whenever I mention this to my therapist, he gives the smuggest *I-told-you-so* grin in the universe. But what can I say? That vulnerable-seeming bullshit isn't actually bullshit at all.

———

Expressive writing is a great way to connect with our emotions and enjoy the healing benefits of laziness. Another popular and effective method is meditation. Just as research has highlighted the benefits of expressive writing, science indicates that meditation improves blood pressure,[42] immune system functioning,[43] and mental health as well.[44]

August Stockwell regularly works meditation into their spreadsheet of weekly goals, and they've found that the more they meditate, the more they're able to calm their nerves and identify what matters most to them in life. This, in turn, has helped them to set better boundaries.

"By meditating a lot," August says, "I contacted the calm mental state that I want to live in as much as I can. It helps me see when I need to say no to more things."

Before August started meditating, they didn't realize how anxious and overloaded they constantly were. They had gotten so accustomed to being hyperbusy that they had forgotten there was an alternative. Meditation reminded them that they were capable of moving slowly, appreciating silence, and feeling present in the moment.

> **When we set priorities based on our real feelings rather than society's "shoulds," we feel a greater sense of authenticity.**

"I keep reminding myself, meditating doesn't solve any problems," August says, "and also it's the most important place to start."

To put it another way: Meditation is the most important place to start because it's not intended to solve any problems. Like expressive writing and finding various ways to "do nothing," it's explicitly about abandoning goals for a little while, letting go of stress, and restoring energy and well-being in the process.

Embracing laziness can have a revolutionary impact on our quality of life. When we stop measuring our worth by how many items we check off of a to-do list, we can finally begin to seek out the activities that truly matter to us. When we set priorities based on our real feelings rather than society's "shoulds," we feel a greater sense of authenticity. And when we savor our free time and work to move at a slower, lazier, more intuitive pace, we begin to repair the damage that years of overwork has done.

CHAPTER THREE

You Deserve to Work Less

Dr. Annette Towler is an industrial-organizational psychologist. Her research focuses on how changes to the workplace influence how people feel and behave. For years, she conducted studies on a variety of topics related to how employees are managed in this country, and how management decisions impact productivity and well-being. Her work has examined questions such as whether a manager can be trained to be more charismatic (they can),[1] whether the size of a teacher's salary is related to how well their students do in school (it is),[2] and whether people in healthy relationships make better employees than people in unhealthy relationships (they do).[3]

Annette's expertise is vast. Her work has appeared in some of the most prestigious academic journals in her field. And for many years, she was a tenured professor at DePaul University, just down the street from me in Chicago. But one day, she decided to leave it all behind for a more authentic, joy-filled life.

Annette was at the height of her career when she decided to leave her cushy tenured position for less consistent, less secure work as a freelance writer and consultant. For many this would have been a terrifyingly risky move, but for her the path forward was clear. After decades of studying what makes a workplace healthy, and conversely what can make a workplace toxic, Annette could tell her own academic department was leaning more and more into the "toxic" side.

"Once I got tenure, I felt pressure to start bullying people below me," Annette says. "Faculty would bully students in my department, and senior faculty would bully junior faculty. It was just expected of you to be a part of that."

Annette noticed that faculty and students in her department were stressed-out and overextended. There was a great deal of pressure to perform at a high level at all times, without breaks or time for rest and reflection. People tended to monitor and judge the behavior and productivity of others. Burned-out, miserable faculty members off-loaded their stress onto those below them. There was an overall climate of bitterness and cynicism. In short, Annette's office was like far too many offices in America—almost perfectly designed to create traumatized, exhausted people. Since Annette had personally studied the toll that such workplaces can have on their employees, she knew she needed to get out.

"I pretty much gave up on the profession after that," she tells me.

Today, Annette lives a life that her own research would recommend. She finds time for marathon runs and for making art. She's working on a mystery novel, and volunteers regularly to support survivors of domestic violence. And though she has a lot of freelance work to do, she deliberately puts other things first, including making time to be interviewed by me.

"I prioritize the important things and invest my time and interests in what matters to me," Annette says. "And that's what the psychological literature says a person should do. So, you know, I could be working on some deadline I'm worried about that is ultimately arbitrary, or I could be doing what I *want* to be doing, which is talking to you."

Annette has an easygoing, open perspective on life. She has carved out an existence for herself that lets those wonderful qualities shine. But she was able to build that kind of existence only because she had the privilege and the knowledge to avoid what was bad for her: the conventional, restrictive, overly demanding workplace.

Many organizations have been shaped by the history and values of the Laziness Lie, often with disastrous results. The typical workday is structured around the expectation that a person should be able to sit down and churn out results for eight hours or more, despite overwhelming evidence that this is unrealistic. Managers often believe they must micromanage their employees and attempt to squeeze every last moment of productivity out of them, though research suggests this makes people irritable and unmotivated.[4] Overworked employees are often encouraged to police one another's habits and to spread their shared misery throughout a department, creating a contagion of unwellness and bad boundaries. Thanks to the development of digital work tools, the pressure to be available and useful to an employer at any time of day has only grown, and our shared sense of exhaustion and burnout has gotten more and more intense.

Though many of us feel guilty for not being productive enough, the truth is that most of us are doing far more work than is healthy. We're pushing our bodies and minds to the limit, ignoring the natural warning signs of tiredness and laziness, and encouraging others to do the same. When we push ourselves in that way for a prolonged period, we risk suffering from severe fatigue and burnout. If we want to break free of these damaging patterns, we need to embrace our very human needs and our natural "laziness" signals and find ways to work less, not more.

We're Working More Than Ever Before

In chapter one, I discussed how our collective fear and hatred of laziness has its roots in the history of slavery and capitalism. I also described how the Laziness Lie was used to justify pushing industrial-era workers into grueling, sixteen-hour workdays filled with danger and abuse. Unfortunately, this historical legacy remains very relevant today.

Though there was a time

> Though many of us feel guilty for not being productive enough, the truth is that most of us are doing far more work than is healthy.

when the average workweek kept getting shorter and shorter in length (thanks in large part to unions and the labor movement),[5] that pattern has sadly reversed in recent years.[6] The average workday is getting longer now, not shorter. We see the pressure to overwork in nearly every industry and professional field. Smartphones, laptops, and digital work tools such as e-mail and Slack have made it harder than ever for us to leave our work behind when we go home for the day. And thanks to the rise of the "gig economy," the pressure to fill even our spare moments with additional labor and "side hustles" has expanded our workloads even more.

The Workweek Is Getting Longer

The Industrial Revolution brought with it the rise of the industrial, warehouse-based workplace.[7] Factory employees were toiling all day long in dangerous, dark conditions, unable to make time for anything in their lives other than sleep. There were very few legal protections in place for employees, and many were given no compensation if they got injured on the job.[8] Abuse of employees was rampant, with many not even being given a lunch hour or bathroom breaks.

Workers began banding together and staging walkouts, demonstrations, and strikes in order to protest how they were being treated. This went on for years, and was intensely and violently resisted by employers, as well as police and the US military.[9] Eventually, though, the labor movement began winning legal battles and unions were invited to the negotiation table. Slowly but surely, employees earned the right to more benefits, greater legal protections, and workdays that were less punishingly long.[10]

For decades afterward, there was an overall trend in the US toward shorter workdays, greater pay, and more benefits. Through the mid-twentieth century, many working-class people enjoyed newfound levels of comfort and wealth. Millennials like me grew up hearing about this era from our parents and grandparents. I know it, for example, as the time period that allowed my Appalachian grandparents to make the move from the impoverished Cumberland Gap region of Tennessee up to the middle-class Cleveland suburb where I got to grow up. It was a time of high economic prosperity in the US, particularly for white and white-passing people, like most of my relatives.

That era, however, is long gone. In the past two decades, the average workweek has gotten longer and longer[11] instead of getting shorter as it once did.[12] By 2014, the average American's workweek had crept up from forty hours to over forty-seven.[13] In a survey conducted by Gallup in 2018, 44 percent of respondents said they worked more than forty-five hours per week.[14] Of that 44 percent, 12 percent reported working sixty or more hours per week. That's twelve hours of work per day! While at least 134 other countries have placed legal limits on how many hours a person is permitted to work,[15] in the US there is no legal maximum, so the length of the workweek can continue climbing up and up.[16]

In some organizations, working overtime isn't even viewed as an extra push of effort; instead, it's considered a weekly obligation. When my friend Eli took a job with a massive Silicon Valley tech company last year, they were dismayed to learn that every employee in their department was preapproved for ten overtime hours every single week. This alone made Eli hesitant to take the job. Were these extra ten hours really overtime if they were regularly expected?

In the past few decades, employees have also found a variety of ways to cram greater productivity into each hour they work. Thanks to digital tools, automation, increased computer processing speed, and a ton of other factors, it now takes the average worker just eleven hours to complete what would have been forty hours' worth of work back in 1950.[17] Yet despite how much more people are working, and how much more output they're generating, wages have declined over the years instead of going up.[18]

In addition to working more hours, employees today report higher levels of stress than recent generations did, particularly stress associated with job duties and poor management.[19] Pensions and health insurance have also been affected in many industries, either being removed entirely or made far less generous than they were a decade or more ago.[20] Many companies have moved toward relying on part-time employees instead of full-timers so they don't have to offer benefits.[21] In a very real way, many of us are working far more, and more productively, than ever before, and yet we're getting far, far less in return.

We Can't Leave Work at Work

Though Annette has lived in the US and studied American workplaces for many years, she's originally from England. She's noticed that compared to Europeans, Americans have a particularly dysfunctional relationship to work. "When Europeans go to work, they just do their job and then they come home," she says, "and they understand about the importance of relaxation, that balance that you don't always see in the United States."

It's true that Americans tend to have trouble drawing firm boundaries between work and the rest of our lives. Compared to Europeans, who often have upward of twenty paid vacation days per year, American employees are lucky if they get ten to fourteen.[22] The Laziness Lie has also infected numerous American employees with a strong sense of "vacation guilt," which makes it hard for us to feel comfortable actually using those vacation days up.[23] A survey by Glassdoor found that in 2018, Americans used only about half of their paid vacation days and let the remainder go completely to waste.[24]

We have a similarly tortured relationship to sick days. Almost half of all working Americans don't have paid days off for physical or mental wellness,[25] and those who do are hesitant to use them. Like Max, whose boss manipulated her into not calling in sick, many of us fear that taking time off will make us look like lazy, unreliable workers. And we're not paranoid for having that fear—in 2019, American Airlines was sued by New York City's Department of Consumer and Work Protection for having punished and threatened workers who used their sick days.[26]

> **In a very real way, many of us are working far more, and more productively, than ever before, and yet we're getting far, far less in return.**

When companies fail to provide employees with adequate sick-leave policies and managers bully their workers into working while ill, the public health consequences are massive. Many sick employees spread the coronavirus to their coworkers and fellow commuters because they weren't able to take time off from work in the early days of the pandemic.[27] On a more mundane level, sick food-service employees often have no choice but to come in to work and spread their illness to fellow workers and patrons; 81 percent of food-industry workers have no employer-provided sick days.[28]

When people do get the chance to leave their workplaces, they still struggle with the temptation to continue working remotely. E-mail, Slack, Twitter, and other applications make many workplaces accessible at all times, and as a result, work seeps into all hours of the day.[29] Researchers call this "work-home interference," and since smartphones and other tools have become widely accessible, it's gotten much, much worse.[30] Thirty-six percent of survey respondents told Gallup that they frequently check work e-mail outside of regular work hours,[31] and in organizations where people feel the social pressure to be available online all the time, the work-home interference rate is much worse.

One overworked person that I spoke to, Nimisire, is a sexual-health advocate and educator based in Nigeria. She tells me that she has to place a firm digital boundary on her activism, for the sake of her well-being. "I do a lot of online education and advocacy," she says, "and it can be very exhausting. I have to mute certain words on Twitter—words about sexual trauma or objectification, for example—and sometimes I just put my phone away. Educating people is part of my job, but I have to trust that I can set a limit on how I do that and know that I will still be doing work that's important."

Many people don't share Nimisire's level of self-discipline. We get pulled into an endless loop of replying to messages, checking for new notifications,

> E-mail, Slack, Twitter, and other applications make work accessible at any time, and as a result, work seeps into all hours of the day.

and doing unpaid work long after our time in the office is done. With the rise of things like the gig economy, work-life interference has become an even more pressing problem.

We're Caught in the Gig Economy

Alex works full-time as an administrative assistant in the Chicago Loop. All day long he edits documents, takes meeting notes, makes copies, and runs errands. During rare moments of quiet in the office, Alex tries to catch up on creative projects. He's an actor and a performer, so there are always new lines for him to memorize and new auditions to try to book. At the end of an already long, crammed workday, Alex gets home and fires up the website Upwork to look for some side jobs as a copywriter or a transcriptionist.

"I end up doing the transcription work more often than the writing, even though it pays less," Alex says. "It just takes less energy to do it. I can kinda just zone out and write the words down, even if I feel like a zombie."

When taking Upwork's fees and time spent finding new clients into account, Alex's transcription job pays much less than minimum wage. But it's better than nothing, he says, and it allows him to squeeze a few more hours of earning potential out of his day. A lot of us have turned to sites like Upwork, TaskRabbit, Uber, Lyft, Fiverr, or Grubhub in order to make supplementary income. After all, full-time jobs with benefits are rapidly becoming a thing of the past.[32] The harder it gets to make a conventional, nine-to-five living, the more people have to fill their weekends, evenings, and other spare moments with moneymaking side hustles like these.

I know more people like Alex than I could ever possibly name. The gig economy has arrived in full force, and it's swallowed up the free time and brain space of every driven Millennial artist I know. Ricky drives for Uber in the mornings and evenings when he's not busy giving singing lessons and performing in choirs. Dio used the app Wag to find work as a dog walker, supplementing the income he made as an ice cream shop manager. I used to edit people's academic papers for about twenty dollars an hour on Upwork, until I got too busy to fit that side hustle into my life anymore. I still feel the urge to get on there sometimes and convert my free time into a profit source.

So many of us have been pushed over the edge. Our economy is structured around the hatred of laziness, and it has us working longer and longer hours with each passing year. Many of us don't know how to walk away from our jobs, whether for a vacation, a sick day, or simply to relax at home at the end of a shift. Apps like Foxtrot, Upwork, TaskRabbit, and Uber beckon us to work even in our spare time and tempt us to set even more strenuous and unsustainable goals. All this intense overcommitment and overwork is ultimately self-defeating and harmful. In truth, a person can only work so much.

You Can Work Only So Much

Human beings are not robots; we can't keep churning out consistent results for hours and hours. In fact, we can't maintain consistent output for more than a couple of hours per day. People often find this startling to learn, but it's really true—we were not made to work for a full eight hours per day, despite that being considered the reasonable, "humane" workday length in much of the world.

Though there's a great deal of social pressure and cultural programming that says otherwise, being productive and effective at work is not a simple act of will and determination. To do good work, a person has to rest and find moments to enjoy the beauty of life. More hours of work doesn't equal greater productivity. That's because our attention and willpower have limitations, and quality work requires time for rest.

Working Longer Hours Doesn't Mean More Productivity

Henry Ford famously found that when he cut his employees' hours from forty-eight per week to forty, productivity actually increased.[33] This discovery of Ford's dovetailed perfectly with the labor rights movement, which was pushing for shorter workweeks for the sake of workers' well-being. Over the next two decades, the forty-hour workweek became more and more common in a variety of industries, until eventually it was the American norm.

What happens when we work more than forty hours per week? We get very stressed-out, but we don't get a whole lot more done. The more a person works past that forty-hour limit, the less efficient and accurate they seem to be at their job. Past the fifty-hour point, a person's productivity declines very sharply; past the fifty-five-hour point, and a person is so unproductive and tired that they might as well not be at work at all.[34] Additionally, the longer a person's workweek is, the more likely they are to be absent from work in the weeks to come.

"That's always a warning sign of employee stress: absenteeism," Annette says. "If people stop coming into work suddenly, that's often an early sign that something is wrong."

So, there are good reasons for why the standard workweek became forty hours. Anything beyond that seems to sap an employee's strength and yield diminishing returns to their employer. But these standards were developed during the Industrial Revolution, when people were doing repetitive, manual-labor work. Are these numbers even still relevant today, when most repetitive work is done by a machine and most people's jobs are complex and mentally taxing?

Industrial-organizational psychologists like Annette have observed how employees work and organize their days. They've found that the eight-hour workday is, in fact, unrealistic in many ways. Many workers spend upward of eight hours per day in their workplaces, but when we look closer at their activities, we can see that the lion's share of that time isn't devoted to work. Researchers consistently find that in office jobs, people are capable of being productive for only about three hours per day, on average.[35] The remaining hours are spent doing other things, including preparing food and drinks, chitchatting with

> **What happens when we work more than forty hours per week? We get very stressed-out, but we don't get a whole lot more done.**

coworkers, browsing social media, engaging in online shopping, or even just staring into space. When managers attempt to make up for this supposedly "lazy" time by requiring their employees to work longer hours, it actually backfires, and employees do even less.[36]

When employers (and even some researchers) discuss these trends, they tend to frame it in terms of time that has been "lost" or "wasted," or they wrack their brains figuring out how to motivate people to work harder. But before you let the Laziness Lie tempt you into accepting that, think back to Marvin's research into cyberloafing. When we talk about idle time as being a "waste," it implies that people *are* capable of working nonstop for a full eight hours, if only they had more willpower. But after periods of hard work and focus, people need time for rest. The employee laziness that so many managers fret about patently does not exist. Those distracted, idle-seeming employees are already doing all they can. A major reason for that has to do with how the human brain handles attention.

Our Attention Is Limited

I've taught college students for a decade at this point, so I know how hard it is to hold someone's attention. My students are mature, seasoned adults who are returning to college. They're committed, driven people who have a lot of the tenacity that the Laziness Lie has taught all of us to praise. Yet even among these students, maintaining attention is a major struggle.

Education researchers have known for many decades that the average student cannot pay attention for more than an hour or so without a break.[37] Anyone who leads a class on a regular basis will tell you that they have to use a variety of tools, media, and activities to keep a roomful of students focused. Even if a professor does everything they possibly can to keep the class lively, attentiveness still declines slowly over time.[38] When I worked to design my own online classes, I learned that students typically keep their attention fixed on a video for only about *six minutes*.[39] If the video is any longer than that, distraction sets in, whether the student wants it to or not.

In the workplace, the patterns are similar. Workers have trouble staying on task for more than twenty minutes at a time, and the more distractions (such as e-mail, ambient noise, and instant messages) they have to deal with, the shorter their attention span is.[40] This has nothing to do with willpower or "laziness"; instead, it has everything to do with how the human brain fundamentally works.

One of my first psychology-related jobs was in a neuroscience lab at The Ohio State University. My boss at the time, a researcher named Jay Van Bavel, showed me data from participants who had been sitting in an fMRI (functional magnetic resonance imaging) brain scanner for an hour or more. He described to me how their attention levels curved up and down many times per minute, with tons of experiment time "lost" to distraction, daydreaming, and mental fatigue. These participants had been instructed to pay close attention throughout the entire experiment, but even then, their attention naturally flitted about from moment to moment. It turns out that even when we think we're focusing on something quite intently, our attention is jumping around a bit, even on the millisecond level. Jay told me that these peaks and valleys were pretty much inevitable no matter what the researchers did to keep participants engaged. Rather than dismissing those study participants as horribly "lazy," researchers simply knew the data had to be cleaned and filtered.

Jay's study participants weren't daydreaming or checking out of his studies because they were lazy, or even distracted—there's not much to do or look at when you're sitting inside a dark, gray fMRI machine. Attention fluctuates naturally because the human brain is constantly scanning the environment for new information, potential threats, opportunities for social contact, and more.[41] Even when we're intently working on something, part of our attention is tracking our surroundings, ready to interrupt us if any distractions or threats happen to pop up.[42] Our attention is less like a laser beam (which can be pointed at any single specific point we desire) and more like a rotating lighthouse lantern, temporarily bathing individual rocks in light as it continues to spin across its surroundings.

Since our attention is naturally so scattered, focusing on something requires us to exert some serious effort. That effort can't be sustained forever, which is a big part of why most workers need lots of time to be lazy. It's important that we make time for idle chitchat, dawdling at the watercooler, and daydreaming at our workstations—particularly if we want to engage in high-quality work. The more we overextend ourselves, the worse our work gets.

Quality Work Requires Time for Rest

When we work too hard, and for too long, the quality of our work starts to break down. We become more irritable and are easily distracted by things like random background noise.[43] We get sloppier and more prone to errors, whether they're as simple and low-stakes as making more typos[44] or as catastrophic as a doctor making a mistake in the middle of surgery.[45] Tiredness even makes us more apathetic about doing our jobs in the right way.

A study in the *Journal of Applied Psychology* found when health care workers (such as doctors and nurses) are exhausted from working long shifts, they lose the motivation to follow basic hygiene rules and cut back on how often they wash their hands.[46] A survey of 450 call-center employees found that the more tired and overwhelmed an employee became, the more they tended to withdraw emotionally from their jobs, and the less likely they were to show up for work.[47]

Work fatigue also kills creativity. In the previous chapter, I described how creative insight requires a period of incubation, a restful break that allows the creative mind to unconsciously come up with new ideas and solutions.[48] The flip side of the incubation phenomenon is also true: when people don't get access to breaks and "lazy" time, they think in more conventional, uncreative ways, and are more likely to get stuck.

"If the climate is right," Annette says, "people will be proactive and suggest new things that nobody's ever tried before. But when there's more of a micromanagement approach . . .

> When we work too hard, and for too long, the quality of our work starts to break down.

people will just go along and comply, and you don't see the same level of commitment."

When organizations try to force their employees to work harder than is good for them, lackluster, uncreative work tends to result. The subreddit r/MaliciousCompliance is filled with stories of jaded employees who follow their employers' rules in a super-literal fashion, slowing down workplace processes out of spite. For example, underpaid, overworked, mentally checked-out security staff might slow down admission to an event by asking every patron to empty out every single pocket in their clothing—even obviously decorative pockets on small children's clothing. When Seranine was in the military, her commanding officer once tried to discipline her by demanding that she write an essay that was exactly one thousand words long, on any topic of her choosing. Within an hour Seranine returned a paper covered in random-looking symbols but which Microsoft Word recognized as exactly one thousand words. When her commanding officer asked her what the topic of this "essay" was supposed to be, she said simply, "Following directions."

Often, the work of exhausted employees suffers for reasons other than simple resentment. Tired people also think in more biased ways, focusing on negatives[49] and making more unfair judgments.[50] An employee working for the ninth or tenth hour of the day is a ghost of the upbeat, focused, and engaged person they were in the first hour of the day.

———

All this research makes it abundantly clear that the more we work, the less we're able accomplish—and the less unique and meaningful our work becomes. An overly long, excessively demanding workday erodes a person's capacity to think well, to care about what they're doing, and to produce meaningful results. And that's just what happens to the employee's output. When we examine how overwork impacts an employee's well-being and long-term health, the story becomes far more disturbing.

What Happens When We Overwork?

The social psychologist Christina Maslach was a trailblazer in the field of burnout research in the 1970s and '80s. She initially set out to understand burnout among people in what we call the "helping professions": therapists, social workers, and nurses. Maslach knew those types of jobs could become draining over time and had low retention rates, but she wanted to understand why. As she observed and spoke with workers in these fields, however, what she uncovered was more than she could have imagined: these people weren't just exhausted; they were suffering from the mental and even philosophical toll of their work, and sometimes that suffering was downright traumatic.[51]

Burned-out caregivers weren't just agitated or tired, the way all of us can be after a long workday. Rather, they were losing touch with their patients, their coworkers, and even themselves. These people, who likely went into their fields because they cared about others, were now unable to feel genuine empathy for those they were there to serve. They reported feeling numb and hopeless, or even jaded. Some had become bitter, hating their patients.

I had a tiny taste of that type of emotional numbing when I started conducting interviews for this book. I knew I wanted to sit down with a lot of compulsive overworkers to talk to them about their fears of laziness and the toll such fears had taken on their lives. I wasn't prepared for the number of tragic stories I heard. Friends and strangers started pouring out their hearts to me, telling me about their intense experiences working themselves to the bone.

At first, it felt really cathartic to speak to people with experiences similar to mine. Then it got painful. I was being triggered by all the stories of loss, illness, and stress that I was taking in. My experience with burnout back in 2014 was traumatic. I often think of it as my "lost year." It changed the whole course of my life. Being reminded of what that year felt like, over and over again, made me start to feel jittery, anxious, and unsafe. It made me want to withdraw from the world. I started bailing on my friends and canceling plans so I could stay home and recharge.

Then, for a little while, my feelings got even darker. I started to dread the interviews I had scheduled. When a person sat before me and started talking about their struggles with overwork, I'd find myself getting bored. I'd think, *Oh God, please stop droning on and on, I can't listen to any more of this*. I felt like I was being emotionally vampirized by these people, that their stories were sucking the energy out of me and leaving a bitter, cranky husk behind. Empathy requires a great deal of energy, and it's painful and exhausting to relive other people's suffering repeatedly without a means of escape. Burnout was rapidly heading my way, and I had to switch up my interviewing strategy in order to avoid it. I started putting time limits on the length of my interviews, and tried to do only a few per week.

Maslach found that burned-out people felt adrift and hopeless. As they lost empathy for their clients, they also started experiencing a profound loss of identity, with no sense of purpose. They described their jobs as utterly unrewarding. They became detached from all the things they used to love and be passionate about, including treasured hobbies that had nothing to do with work.[52] Some of these caregivers could no longer understand why they'd ever been interested in working as nurses, therapists, or social workers in the first place. Burnout had robbed them of the people they used to be. Sometimes, there was no bringing those people back.

In the mid-1980s, Maslach expanded her focus beyond the helping professions. She started looking at burnout among people in the service industry, as well as office workers and blue-collar laborers. She had begun to suspect that burnout wasn't just the by-product of hard *emotional* work (such as being a therapist or a social worker) but that it could be a consequence of working too hard in general. What she found suggested that she was absolutely right.

When Maslach began speaking with people who worked in cubicles, restaurants, and warehouses, what she found were the same symptoms those in the helping professions had reported to her. These people also complained of sleepless nights, increased sick days, debilitating self-doubt, and a growing sense of emptiness in their jobs.[53] Like the exhausted nurses and therapists, they had also begun to see their work as meaningless. A pervasive sense of dejection and apathy had descended upon their lives, sapping the joy from everything they did.

Maslach also wanted to know what effect, if any, burnout had on these workers' behavior. In particular, she wanted to know whether it affected their abilities to do their jobs. What she found was that burned-out employees, even though they worked long hours, were actually less productive and engaged than other employees who weren't burned out. These overworked employees were also more likely to suffer from anxiety and to use substances to cope, because drugs were more readily available to them than time off. They also found small ways to "stick it" to their employers, whether by stealing office supplies or fudging their time sheets. Like James and his procrastinating friends or the jaded employees on r/MaliciousCompliance, these burned-out workers had turned to petty misbehavior to express their resentment.

Maslach also found that avoiding burnout wasn't just about working less. It had to do with a person's outlook, and whether their organization rewarded their efforts. Perfectionists were particularly susceptible to burnout, for example, as were people who set unrealistically high goals for themselves. Workplaces where the goals were vague and projects were never completed tended to have more burned-out workers.[54] In other words, when work seems like an endless, pointless slog, and workers have no sense of being recognized for all that they do, burnout is far more common.

Maslach found that burned-out people tended to complain that their workplaces were thanklessly demanding. Because their coworkers often felt just as demotivated and jaded as they did, resentment tended to build and then spread from one employee to another, creating something called the "burnout contagion effect."[55] Once this kind of group burnout set in at a workplace, it was difficult to put a stop to it.

> **When work seems like an endless, pointless slog, burnout is far more common.**

As a result of these observations, Maslach and her colleague Susan Jackson developed a measure of burnout: the Maslach Burnout Inventory (MBI). It's a popular and well-regarded measure of burnout that researchers and therapists still use to this day.[56] The MBI describes burnout as consisting of three things: *emotional exhaustion, depersonalization* (loss of identity), and *a lost sense of personal accomplishment*. Here are a few example items from the MBI; in them, you can hear the desperation and exhaustion that characterizes the condition:

> I feel like I'm at the end of my rope.
> I feel fatigued when I get up in the morning and have to face another day on the job.
> I feel emotionally drained from my work.
> I don't feel that I'm positively influencing other people's lives through my work.
> I have not accomplished many worthwhile things in this job.

I can't help but think that, had I known more about burnout back in 2014, I might have been able to avoid the major health breakdown I experienced. This time around, when I felt burnout nipping at my heels, I was able to be proactive and set boundaries to protect myself from it. I limited the number of interviews I conducted. I restructured the interviews themselves, making sure to ask questions about positive, happy topics as well as ones about doom and gloom. I also started reaching out to people who I knew had changed their lives by embracing laziness and stepping away from overwork. By limiting the amount of upsetting information I was taking in and making time for more encouraging, growth-oriented conversations, I was able to keep the burnout at bay before it was too late.

————

From an employer's perspective, burnout is damaging because it decreases the quality of an employee's work.[57] When we reach our emotional breaking point in our jobs, we skip days or even walk out.[58] It encourages us to cut corners and "check out" whenever we're in the office. Burnout alienates us from our sense of self while simultaneously impacting our choices and our ability to concentrate. But that isn't the most harrowing part of burnout. Not even close.

The worst part of burnout is the impact it has on the sufferer's quality of life. Burning out is like going from seeing the world in color to seeing it only in black and white. When we burn out, we stop being able to feel our emotions as intensely, and may even experience pain and hunger less strongly, making it even harder to remember to be kind to ourselves. In addition, burned-out people also have a reduced ability to recognize emotions in other people, which means that they can't connect as readily with their family and friends.[59] This worsens their social isolation. Even after a burned-out person leaves the situation that caused them to burn out, they may remain emotionally detached and apathetic for months to come. In some cases, burnout erodes relationships so severely that they never recover.

Not only that, but being burned out actually makes us worse at thinking and making decisions across the board. Burned-out people drink more[60] and have worse impulse control in general, which means they're more likely to make bad decisions like gambling or having illicit affairs.[61] They experience far more depression and anxiety, and burnout can exacerbate the symptoms of any other mental illness they already have.[62] Burned-out people don't sleep as well, which means they're likely more irritable and more prone to getting sick.[63] Because they see life as purposeless, burned-out people take more risks, which can lead to terrible consequences (burned bridges, wrecked cars) that they really don't want. Chronic burnout can even cause a person to lose brain volume.[64]

Put this way, burnout is not just a labor issue, it's a public health issue. Overwork strips many of us of our health, our cognitive capacity, and even our passion for life. It makes us less productive and wreaks destruction in our personal and professional lives. In its most extreme cases, it can take years off our life expectancy, or cause us to drop dead at our desks. Yet so many of us are still beguiled and tricked by the Laziness Lie and think burned-out people just need to buck up and try harder.

—————

We all overextend ourselves sometimes, and that choice, when freely made, is not inherently destructive. We might stay out late partying with friends one weekend, for example, or pull an all-nighter working on a creative project that truly excites us. But there's a huge difference between following our passions and pushing ourselves to overwork on a regular basis because the Laziness Lie has convinced us that we have to. And unfortunately, far too many workplaces operate under the assumption that we must all constantly push ourselves past the limit.

Working too hard is bad for us. It doesn't make us more productive. It damages us profoundly, in ways we're still only beginning to understand the scope of. But we don't have to live this way. We can fight to build more healthy, harmonious lives, ones that prioritize laziness just as much as they value hard work.

How to Work Less

Like Annette Towler, Kaitlin Smith is a former academic who's taken major steps to build a more sustainable, burnout-proof life for herself. Kaitlin runs the Wild Mind Collective, an organization that provides stressed and burned-out academics with a digital space to talk about issues such as finding appropriate work-life boundaries, identifying their true passions, and fighting against prejudice and bias within the academy. Her site features interviews with diverse writers and thinkers who seek to build healthy, balanced lives, and her blog offers tools for overworked people who are trying to make their existence more manageable and peaceful.

It's no surprise to me that Kaitlin is doing this vital, timely work. I've known her since we were teenagers, and she's always been deeply reflective and willing to go against the grain. She speaks in a measured, meticulous way that's very soothing. At the same time, her words have always challenged me to see things in a new light.

"Look at how people at work talk about coffee," she said to me at lunch a few years ago. "Everyone talks constantly about how much they need coffee or want more coffee; some workplaces provide their employees with as much free coffee as they want. It's a stimulant that makes us work more, and it causes so many people to have terrible anxiety. And yet most people don't even question why they need to consume so much of it. Instead we romanticize it."

Kaitlin's words stayed with me for years, because I saw myself and so many people I know clearly reflected in them. I've started every single day of my life with a cup of coffee since I was fifteen years old. In fact, I was proud to become a coffee drinker as a teen, because I thought it made me more "adult." Yet it had never occurred to me that relying on coffee was a sign of just how intense my workload and drive to succeed was. If I needed to be on an anxiety-provoking stimulant every single day in order to function, was I really setting my life up in a healthy way? Was I creating expectations for myself that were sustainable? Was I so afraid of laziness that I couldn't let my body just be?

Kaitlin is an expert at avoiding the pressures of the Laziness Lie. She's bravely forged a life that reflects her own ideals, rather than other people's priorities. On the Wild Mind Collective site, she's shared a series of questions that she uses to determine whether her life is on the right track.[65]

1. When am I most in my element?
2. What doesn't bring me alive? What feels dreadful?
3. What do I find inexhaustibly fascinating?
4. When have I been most happy?
5. Who are the people I want to work with?
6. What do I need to be physically well?

Kaitlin's questions point to how vital it is to create a life that we actually find enjoyable and enriching. Using these questions, Kaitlin decided to walk away from environments that were toxic and overly demanding, including an academic department that she once called home, as well as

> **If I needed to be on an anxiety-provoking stimulant every single day in order to function, was I really setting my life up in a healthy way?**

the world of ballet. She stopped devoting her time to dry academic writing and instead put more energy into presentations and blog posts that made research more approachable to a wider audience. And she points out the excessive, unrealistic workloads of so many professional environments, including academia, so that she can help people see through the Laziness Lie and forge new paths for themselves.

———

Since the Laziness Lie has taught all of us to say yes to as much work as possible and to ignore our body's every need, it takes a lot of self-knowledge and confidence to be able to say no to things. The traditional workplace is fundamentally broken in many ways. In order to thrive, we have to detach from mainstream, moralistic expectations of how we should be spending our time. That kind of rebellion is really scary and, in many fields of work, downright risky. Relatively few of us have the luxury and privilege of completely restructuring our work lives.

There are concrete steps we can take, however, if we want to learn how to honor our health more and begin to work less. These tips are rooted in industrial-organizational psychology research, as well as a series of interviews I conducted with therapists and mental-health counselors who help overcommitted, burned-out clients. Put very broadly, the tips fall under three umbrellas:

1. Advocate for Your Autonomy
2. Focus on Quality, Not Hours Spent at Work
3. Break the Work-Life Interference Loop

These pieces of advice are designed to apply to overworked people in a variety of industries, with varying degrees of status and freedom. Someone like Kaitlin or Annette has a lot of power to tailor their day-to-day lives, because they have the status that an advanced education provides. Similarly, I was able to restructure my own work life because I had a PhD and skills I could charge a hefty hourly rate for as a freelancer. If you're working in retail or as a server at a restaurant, that kind of leeway is rarely available. In those situations, you'll need to pool resources (and bargaining power) with your fellow employees and push in a collective fashion for the treatment you need and deserve. These tips are designed to focus on the choices you have control over as an employee, a freelancer, or a hustling victim of the gig economy. They have everything to do with how you schedule your day, how you set goals, and what your mindset about work is.

Advocate for Your Autonomy

One of the greatest predictors of both job satisfaction and employee motivation is how much freedom a person has.[66] Contrary to every micromanager's worst fears, it's not the case that an unwatched, unbothered employee is a nonproductive one.[67] Most people thrive when given a little autonomy to set their own priorities and work at their own pace.[68]

One person I spoke to about this was Markus Nini, a manager and mechanical engineer whose business operates out of Germany. Markus has always based his management strategy on what the latest research has to say on the topic. As a scientist, he has relied on the data to tell him how to lead people in an effective way, just as he relied on the data to inform his engineering work. A few years ago, Markus founded CQ Net, a management training firm that focuses on teaching the principles of "evidence-based management" to other leaders.[69] Markus formed the organization because he noticed that a lot of managers didn't understand how to inspire and motivate people.

"Most employees," Markus says, "have a fire. They have a motivation to really try to achieve something, to do the things they like because they like them. They're self-motivated, intrinsically motivated to do something, which is in stark contrast to what many leaders think about how people work."

At Markus's organization, employees have the ability to set their own goals and to pursue the projects they find the most stimulating. You might think that would make the business chaotic or unproductive—but Markus has consistently found the opposite. The more freedom employees are given, the more satisfied they are, and the better his business performs. When workers are truly invested in the duties they take on, they work harder and deliver consistent, high-quality results. It turns out that trusting employees to get things done is vastly more beneficial than trying to police people's work habits or forcing them to put in long hours. "When leaders push people to be more productive," he says, "it's basically against their human nature. It squashes and pushes down their motivation."

In the psychological literature, this is sometimes called the "overjustification effect."[70] Basically, if you take a job that a person naturally likes doing and then start tying that pleasant activity to rewards or punishment, such as their level of pay or whether they get reprimanded, you'll actually make the task less pleasant for them.[71] Suddenly, they're not doing their job because they like it but because they have to. That creates a tendency toward overwork, stress, and misery.

Annette Towler also brought up the importance of autonomy. She says, "When people feel autonomy, when they feel like they're accomplishing something, that gives them a sense of control over their work, and it leads to higher job satisfaction. And generally, what's good for an employee's well-being is good for the quality of their output and productivity."

On a more personal level, this research means that we don't have to push and pressure ourselves to overcome our "lazy" side. Our motivation will come naturally, so long as we avoid pushing ourselves past a healthy work-life balance. We can listen to our internal "laziness" signals, work slowly and carefully, and take time off as often as we need. That will help us far more, in the long run, than micromanaging our schedules and pushing ourselves to exert effort even when we're running low on energy.

So how do you advocate for autonomy in your workplace? There are several steps you can take, depending on the nature of your work and how receptive the higher-ups at your organization are to change. Many of these steps are also relevant to how you manage yourself. Here are some tips:

1. Share the Science on Autonomy and Motivation

Even though decades and decades of research show that micromanaging isn't effective and that autonomous employees are happier and get more done, most people are completely unaware of that fact. So share the research far and wide, to help legitimize the push for workplace autonomy.

If your boss might be receptive to changing their ways, point them to some of the sources in this book, or to Markus's writing for managers on CQ Net or other science-backed articles on workplace productivity. Point to evidence of it in your own workplace—remind leadership of times when employees were happy and effective because they weren't being pushed too hard. If you don't have the power to influence a boss, educate your coworkers and friends about these facts, and consider organizing a union. The more informed people are, the more they can move toward an "evidence-based" workplace.

2. Ask for Flex Time and Remote Work Options

The outbreak of COVID-19 left many people working from home for the first time in their careers. The shift online was a drastic and sudden change for a lot of organizations, but it demonstrated in a stark way that flexible schedules and telework can be just as effective as coming into the office. At this point in history, every organization needs to be open to unconventional work systems and schedules.

The data shows that flexible scheduling works. When people aren't required to adhere to a specific schedule, they have more freedom to set their own priorities and can build a day that allows time for relaxation, family obligations, and work.[72] When workers can adopt their own schedules, they're more productive and satisfied. Once again, share this data with other people—and emphasize to those in leadership positions that this is the wave of the future and a humane, practical response to the demands of the modern world.

3. Take On Responsibilities That Excite You

This tip may seem out of place—*How can taking on new responsibilities help me work less?*—but hear me out. Many employees discount their ability to create unique, distinctive roles for themselves in their organizations. We often wind up saying yes to whatever responsibilities come our way, too afraid to question whether we're a good fit for those duties. For those of us who do freelance or gig-economy work, the pressure to take on every single job opportunity, regardless of whether we like it, is immense.

To break out of this self-defeating, grueling pattern, we have to focus on defining what we want our professional lives to be. Research consistently shows that when an employee *crafts* their job into what they want it to be, they're more engaged and will flourish on the new career path they've created for themselves.[73] If you can, present your strengths to your employer and prioritize the work you feel the best about. Convince your manager that your time is best spent performing the duties you do well. This isn't possible in every organization, but when you can slowly reshape your position into one that suits you, your odds of satisfaction and of getting promoted go way up.

It takes some serious self-advocacy skills to ask for new levels of responsibility and to reshape your job into something you'll genuinely find motivating, but if you can do it, it's well worth it. Along the way, you may also have to contemplate leaving a job that's painful, unpleasant, or unable to grow alongside you. Not everyone has the ability to leave a job that's punishing and exhausting, of course. But in my interviews for this book, I've found time and time again that many people are afraid to even consider leaving a job that's hurting them, because they fear that doing so is "giving up" or being "lazy." They may also have internalized their employers' beliefs that they're incapable or incompetent, and thus ill-suited for any other work. If you find yourself thinking in this way, make sure to examine it and challenge it to see if it holds water. Abusive managers thrive on making workers believe they have fewer options than they actually do. If you find that your workplace isn't receptive to change, and you lack better options, consider talking to your fellow employees and organizing to get things changed. As a group, you have far more power to reshape the workplace and make it more humane.

Focus on Quality, Not Hours Spent at Work

The Laziness Lie says that virtuous, worthwhile people spend long hours at their jobs, toiling away no matter how drained they feel. In organizations ruled by the Laziness Lie, people are obsessed with keeping up appearances, clocking in early, lingering long after their shifts are over, and watching the habits of other people like hawks. This is both emotionally unhealthy and totally useless from a productivity perspective.

Instead of tying your value as a person to the number of hours you spend at work, focus on the results. This can fundamentally shift both how you think and feel about yourself and how you advocate for yourself to an employer. Consider your work in terms of these questions:

1. What's something I accomplished this month that I'm really proud of?
2. How have my skills grown in the past year?
3. Have I found more effective ways of doing old tasks?
4. Have I improved processes at my workplace or made things run more smoothly?
5. How have I supported other people in doing their jobs more effectively?

You can see that these questions take a holistic look at your work and how you've grown into a role or organization. They also allow you to give yourself credit for things that we don't always count as "productive"— things like teaching a skill to an employee in a different department or learning how to do an old task in a new way. Each of these items touches on ways that an employee develops, becoming more efficient, skillful, and

Instead of tying your value as a person to the number of hours you spend at work, focus on the results.

wise. And none of them have to do with whether you came into the shop earlier than everyone else.

By looking at your work in this way, you can begin investing your energy in things that are enriching and meaningful, rather than in a flurry of stressful, rote tasks that get you nowhere. You can also demonstrate your value to your employer in ways that are measurable and lasting. When you put emphasis on growing your skills and delivering results, you can break out of nasty patterns of overworking and having nothing of substance to show for it. Doing this, however, can require becoming a bit "lazy" and cutting back on job duties that aren't serving you anymore.

Markus put this principle into practice recently with an employee who was struggling to get things done. The employee was clearly stressed and not putting out high-quality work. All the telltale signs of burnout were there, such as increased absenteeism and flat, blunted emotions. But instead of punishing the employee or reprimanding him, Markus sat down with him and tried to come up with a solution.

"I interviewed this employee and his supervisor," Markus says, "and in this case, I found that when he got too great a workload, the employee started to get overwhelmed and frustrated and would begin to burn out. So we made a new plan with him, and gave him a workload that he could handle."

With a reduced workload, the employee began to stabilize. He started showing up for work more consistently and doing a higher-quality job. He actually began taking on greater responsibilities after that—particularly in an area that was interesting and engaging to him. He eventually became a major leader and innovator within that department; he'd found a niche where he could truly excel. But this was only possible because Markus was a compassionate, evidence-based manager and let the employee shape his job around his distinct skills and passions.

I also had to flip my work priorities recently. I used to start my day by reading and responding to e-mails. I tried to maintain a totally empty in-box. Only after I was done getting back to everyone would I "let myself" get to less time-sensitive tasks like writing or planning new lectures for my students. I was often frustrated by how little time I had left to do the things that mattered to me the most.

When I told my therapist Jason about this, he furrowed his brow and gave me a look that I knew meant I was screwing up. "Isn't writing your book more important to you, in terms of your long-term goals and where you want to be in your life?" he asked. "Would you rather have this book be the best thing it can be, or would you rather be caught up on every single random e-mail every day?"

Sending dozens of e-mails every morning made me feel productive, but it was a big drain on my time, and reduced the energy I had available to do thoughtful, quality work on my book. So, I completely reversed my schedule. I put writing time at the top of my day, when I typically have the most energy. I still reply to my colleagues and students eventually, but instead of trying to chip away at every single thing on my digital to-do list, I focus more on doing what matters most—writing—and doing it well. Sometimes, doing a job well means letting other responsibilities drop, at least for a little while.

Break the Work-Life Interference Loop

E-mail used to eat up my weekends and evenings just as badly as it did my mornings. Like so many overworked people, I felt the compulsive need to stay caught up, and treated every work-related message or text from a student as an emergency that had to be immediately addressed. I'd be in bed answering e-mails until midnight, and then wonder why I was too anxious to get to sleep. In order for me to build a life that actually included room for restorative idleness, I had to drastically cut down my digital work time.

Louise Dimiceli-Mitran is a counselor who specializes in helping stressed-out, overextended people. In her private practice, Rhythms Within, she works with clients on setting more appropriate work-life boundaries—and often that involves cutting back on work-related smartphone time.

"I've had a couple of people ask their bosses about cutting back on late-night e-mails," she says. "Often they need help working up the nerve to even ask. But they'll say, *Hey, I'm really having trouble dealing with stress. I'm not going to be available to answer e-mails after eight p.m. anymore.* And sometimes it's gone really well. Sometimes their managers have even said, *You know, that's a good idea. I won't send you anything after that time either.*"

Often, organizations get into a pattern of running on stress-fueled fumes, and sending late-night e-mails becomes an unquestioned norm. As Louise mentions, many bosses themselves suffer with inappropriate work-life boundaries. Sometimes all it takes is a single person questioning the standard way of doing business for toxic expectations to be reduced.

Markus Nini takes a similar approach in his workplace—though for him, setting appropriate work-life boundaries really comes down to an employee's preferences. "It depends on the personality of the person," he says. "I think the key is to recognize how people cope with stress. I had one manager who wanted to turn off all push notifications on his phone; for him it was too much stress at night. But some people like to be online and like to be reachable, and if that's what they want, then I say why not?"

Once again, it comes back to granting people autonomy—and trusting them to get important things done at the pace that feels naturally sustainable and right. Of course, it's not always possible to get this kind of leeway in an organization. Sometimes, asking for the right to turn off your phone will get you reprimanded. In those cases, Louise often observes that her clients need to walk away and find another place to work. "So much of this comes down to self-knowledge," she says, "and knowing what your boundaries and limits are, and leaving a job if it's not interesting to you or healthy."

Because the Laziness Lie has so deeply permeated the workplace, sometimes the only way to break out of the hamster wheel of work-life interference is to leave the wheel entirely. That's scary and risky; Louise knows that firsthand.

"I myself was in a job once that really stressed me out," she says, "and I had people close to me saying, you know, *You've got to leave this job.* I stayed on for another two years, and then I got axed. And it was only after I got axed from that job that I went, *You know what? I'm going to open up my own private therapeutic practice.* And I've never been happier."

————

The Laziness Lie thrives on making us believe we have no options. By making us feel insecure and like we're never doing enough, it convinces us that we don't deserve to find another job or to leave an organization that mistreats its employees. By convincing us that we're lazy and not earning our keep, it pushes us into a constant state of feeling apologetic and paranoid. It's nearly impossible to negotiate for better treatment when we're trapped in a scarcity mindset. Often we need a big wake-up call to realize that we do actually have the skills and drive needed to succeed somewhere that's less punishing.

Annette, Kaitlin, and Louise each had to develop a strong sense of self-knowledge and allow themselves to walk away from professional tracks that didn't line up with how they wanted to live. In Annette's case, her expertise as an industrial-organizational psychologist helped her find the way out; for Kaitlin, getting out of academia required meditating deeply on which work activities brought her

> The Laziness Lie thrives on making us believe we have no options.

joy and which left her feeling miserable; and in Louise's case, it wasn't a matter of free choice but of having the "good luck" of getting fired from a job that had been burning her out for years. Even though she was a trained counselor and worked with burned-out people herself, she needed that external push to break free.

Of course, Louise is far from the only person who gets caught up in overwork like that. The Laziness Lie has taught us that work is the altar at which we must worship. It's scary to step away from constantly churning out productivity—particularly when we believe that our worth is determined by how much we do and what we accomplish.

CHAPTER FOUR

Your Achievements Are Not Your Worth

In 1973, investment banker and writer Andrew Tobias published his memoir *The Best Little Boy in the World*. In it, Tobias describes his life as a closeted gay professional in the 1960s and '70s, struggling to build a successful life while hiding who he was.[1] Tobias had known since he was a preteen that he was gay. Like many queer people of that era, he was deeply ashamed of it. In the book, he describes how he tried to "make up" for his gayness by being the perfect, most lovable, most accomplished young man he could be. He excelled in athletics, winning trophies and ribbons. He studied all weekend long, devoting energy that could have gone toward dating to earning excellent grades. He was a dutiful, clean-cut, polite son who honored his parents.

Once he became an adult with a job, Tobias put his "best little boy in the world" energy toward pulling all-nighters at the office and turning work in days ahead of time, even when doing so was completely unnecessary. He describes one incident in which his manager asked him on Wednesday night to write a memo by Tuesday of the next week: "Hah!" Tobias writes. "I would stay at the office most of the night writing the memo, typing it, xeroxing it, binding it, and there it would be on his desk when he got in Thursday morning. That was as close as I could come to a sexual experience."

Tobias was (rightly) terrified society would reject him for being gay, so he coped with that fear by striving to be accomplished and hardworking. No matter our orientation or status in society, we've all been pressured to win respect by racking up accolades in this way. The Laziness Lie tries to tell us that we must earn our right to be loved, or to even have a place in society, by putting our noses to the grindstone and doing a ton of hard work. The Lie also implies that our intuition cannot be trusted; our cravings for rest must be ignored, our urges for pleasure, tenderness, and love must be written off as signs of weakness. Tobias believed the Lie, so he tried to hide his true self behind a wall of awards.

I'm living in a world that's very different from the one Tobias grew up in. Still, I see myself (and many of my friends) reflected in his desperation to please and overachieve. A lot of queer people still feel an immense pressure to be the "best little person in the world." We accumulate achievements and accomplishments in the hopes that they will help us earn back the respect and love we lost by choosing to live openly as ourselves. We feel insecure about living on the fringes of society and recognize that what acceptance we do receive could be taken away at any moment—and so we work as hard as we possibly can to protect ourselves. We take second jobs, pull long hours, get reports in early, and take on responsibilities that exhaust us, wanting to believe that our trophies, savings accounts, and satisfied managers will protect us from ignorance.

Of course, it's not just queer people who try to self-protect through overachievement. Anyone who feels vulnerable in society can succumb to the pressure to live this way. Women and people of color are often told that they must go above and beyond the expectations set for white men if they want to have a prayer of success. People who grew up in poverty or who struggle with mental illness often feel similarly obligated to overachieve. Anyone who has been told repeatedly that they're not enough may be tempted by the Laziness Lie to strive endlessly for accomplishments and rewards. Our culture teaches us that if we achieve greatness, we may finally deserve to feel safe and at ease.

———

A more contemporary (and straight) example of this phenomenon is the character Leslie Knope on NBC's *Parks and Recreation*. Many Millennials adore Leslie's character, and it's easy to see why. She's chipper and upbeat, with an unending yen for political conquest. She overcomes government bureaucracy, partisan infighting, and her coworkers' bigotry and sexism through sheer determination and optimism. At the start of the series, Knope has a lowly position as the deputy director of her small city's Parks and Recreation Department, but as the series progresses she ascends through the state government, eventually becoming governor of Indiana. She is relentless in her pursuit of success, winning countless political battles along the way.

Fans love *Parks and Rec* because it portrays a hardworking, progressive woman winning at life, despite facing immense opposition, yet I've always found the show's inspiring messages to be kind of hollow. Leslie is a likeable, spunky character, but she's also really pushy and single-minded. She cares a great deal about the environment, justice, and what's right, but to her close friends, she can be rude and steamrolling. She often pushes people to help her accomplish her goals, ignoring their needs and priorities along the way. She doesn't take no for an answer and often forces her husband and best friend to invest time in her schemes even when they don't want to do it. She works herself to illness, and even breaks out of the hospital when she's sick with the flu so that she can continue going to her job.

While the show (and its fans) celebrate Leslie for being a feminist icon, part of me sees her as a spokesperson for the Laziness Lie. She accomplishes great things, yes, but she does so by disrespecting her body's needs and ignoring the boundaries of her friends. Sadly, the show consistently rewards her for this success-obsessed behavior. There's never a moment when

Our culture teaches us that if we achieve greatness, we may finally deserve to feel safe and at ease.

she has to learn to take things easy, or when she develops an interest in activities outside of work.

The show even goes out of its way to mock Leslie's husband, Ben, for getting into stop-motion animation when he's briefly unemployed. Ben's stop-motion films are amateurish; they're never going to win him any awards or help him secure a new job. So, in the eyes of the show and its characters, his interest in it is kind of pathetic. The mild depression he develops as a consequence of being unemployed is ridiculed too. The show consistently implies that a life of hard work and achievement is superior in every way to a life that goes at a slower pace. Unfortunately, a lot of us still believe that's true in real life as well.

———————

On one level, being obsessed with achievement is entirely logical, particularly if you're on society's margins in some way. Being an overachiever can provide you with a buffer when things get rough. When I was growing up, my dad always had a side hustle in addition to his main, full-time job. As I mentioned in this book's introduction, he had a physical disability and felt immense shame about it, so he hid it from his employer. He thought that if other people knew about his condition, they would reject him and see him as unfit to work—so he struggled to "make up" for his disability by being the hardest-working, busiest employee he could be. In addition to working third shift in a warehouse, he mowed lawns during the day to make extra cash. He was following in the footsteps of his dad, who had worked in a salt mine by day and fixed neighbors' cars in the evenings for extra money.

The Laziness Lie romanticizes stories like these of hardworking men toiling away despite all the difficulties they've faced. But I saw firsthand what my dad's life was like, and my grandfather's: often desperate, lonesome, and filled with pain. Hard work didn't buy either of them safety the way they dreamed it would. Both men were in horrible health all their lives, and both died in their fifties.

———————

Rachel is a teacher and a transgender woman. Before she came out and started transitioning at work, she spent years earning teaching awards, racking up accolades, and taking on tons of after-hours responsibilities at her school. She knew she would need to fall back on her reputation as a hard worker when she finally started living as a woman. The second she came out, she was going to face a lot of bigotry disguised as scrutiny.

"As soon as I started coming to work as myself, in feminine clothing," she says, "people started accusing me of being unprofessional and impossible to work with. And they were so cold to me. It was a night-and-day difference."

As complaints began to roll in from intolerant parents and colleagues, Rachel had to point to her awards and sparkling performance reviews in order to protect herself. Her track record proved she wasn't the difficult, inappropriate person some were now claiming her to be. The adoration of her current and former students also helped buffer her against some of the criticism she started receiving. If Rachel hadn't been the "best little girl in the world" at her job, she would have wound up getting canned just for being herself.

I've heard many people of color express a similar outlook on overwork. Many Black parents teach their children that they must work twice as hard as white people, with the expectation that doing so will get them only half as far.[2] If you're marginalized, you can't just be good, you have to be the best. But that striving for excellence comes with a hefty emotional toll. Constantly having to put on a performance of being diligent, motivated, and well behaved can leave people feeling like their lives are inauthentic and don't reflect who they truly are.

———

Achievements are fleeting things. They can never bring us true satisfaction. As soon as you've crossed the finish line and collected the trophy, the joy of running the race is over. There is no victory great enough to overcome the dictates of the Laziness Lie. In fact, the Lie tells us that we must never be satisfied; we must keep running after new opportunities

> **Achievements are fleeting things. They can never bring us true satisfaction. As soon as you've crossed the finish line and collected the trophy, the joy of running the race is over.**

again and again, no matter how many victories lie behind us. In this way, being achievement-obsessed actually makes life less rewarding and enjoyable, because we never get to truly savor or appreciate what we've done or where we've been.

Achievement-hunting can also make us competitive to a fault, seeing other people only as barriers to our next big success. Like Leslie Knope, we can become so intent on "winning" that we forget to take care of our friends or ourselves. We can even see the successes of our loved ones as threats, signs that they're more hardworking and lovable than we are. Our fear of being lazy can swallow up every source of pride and delight in our lives if we let it, until there's nothing left.

The more we adopt an accomplishment-based mindset, the more we come to catalogue, measure, and judge every single thing we do. Unfortunately, the digital age has done a lot to facilitate this obsession. Today, we can easily monitor how much exercise we get, how many likes our Instagram posts receive, how many books we've read this year, and how our "performance" compares to that of our friends. Every enjoyable use of our free time, whether it be cooking, crafting, or travel, can be documented, shared, and assessed relative to other people.

The Laziness Lie has infected so much more than our careers. It has taught us to chase accomplishment in every imaginable realm, even those meant to be relaxing and nonproductive. In the process, it has sapped the joy and leisure out of even the most pleasant and nourishing of activities.

Your Life, Gamified

Taylor started learning how to code this year. They heard there were a lot of good jobs available for people who know programming languages such as Python and Java, and they wanted a way to break out of their unrewarding office job. Life in the tech world sounded cushy and comfortable, and they wanted a bit of that for themselves.

"My friend Heather is totally scatterbrained," Taylor says, "but she knows how to code, so she has a well-paying job and fancy, free lunches at the office every day. Her workplace has a yoga room. God, I should never have majored in English."

So, Taylor started spending their evenings on a site called Code Academy, which offers self-paced lessons in a variety of programming languages. The Code Academy site is colorful and cheery. It's filled with short classes on a variety of programming-related topics; each class features a mix of brief videos, interactive training modules, and online tests. Because the Code Academy site is slick and bright and stimulating, Taylor found it easy to return to every night after work.

"I used to spend my evenings getting into arguments with people online," Taylor says, half joking. "Now I just fire up the Code Academy site and plug away at a few lessons."

It makes sense that Taylor learned to replace one kind of compulsive activity (arguing online with strangers) with another (completing short quizzes online). That's because the Code Academy site is designed to be as interesting, rewarding, and addictive as it can be. The site has a way of getting its hooks into you and making sure you keep coming back again and again. It breaks complex topics into a series of bite-size units. After you finish a unit, you get a little badge. The more courses you complete, and the more often you use the site, the more you're rewarded.

I sometimes use a similar site, Datacamp, in classes of mine that involve programming and statistics. My students find the site motivating, because it makes learning seem like a game. The more miniclasses you take, the more experience points you earn, and there are daily activities you can complete that reward you for continued practice. A student's progress is linked to their social media accounts, so their friends, coworkers, and classmates can see how many achievement badges and points they've racked up and, consequently, what a diligent, virtuous little worker bee they are.

The foreign-language learning app Duolingo operates in an incredibly similar way. There are small vocabulary and grammar exercises that you can complete each day. They take a variety of forms, in order to keep you stimulated and engaged. In one exercise, you might be asked to drag and drop words together to create a sentence; in another, you're asked to speak into your phone's mic and provide the correct response to a question, with the proper pronunciation. Each exercise feels and looks like a game. You get points for logging in every day. If you fail to open the app for a few days in a row, Duolingo's mascot, a cute little green owl, will send you notifications, scolding you for not working hard enough.

These sites and apps provide immediate gratification. They encourage habitual, regular use, just like video games do. And they scratch an itch that the Laziness Lie has left so many of us with: the longing to feel accomplished and worthy. By turning work into a game, they encourage us to cram more and more productive hours into our days, and to feel as if every hour that we don't spend racking up little trophies and new marketable skills is a "waste."

In Taylor's case, learning how to code quickly began swallowing up a ton of free time. It left less space in their life for other passions, like painting and writing.

"Writing just feels stressful right now," they tell me. "It feels subordinate to the coding stuff."

Taylor sometimes performs their writing at local bookstores and coffee shops, but in recent months, they haven't had the time or energy for it. They haven't been setting aside regular painting time the way they used to either. I've wondered aloud—many times at this point—if Taylor's code-learning schedule is grueling to the point of being unhealthy. Taylor seems kind of unsure about that. They'll bring up that it's only temporary. In a couple of years, they'll have enough skills to quit their day job. Until then, they just keep plugging along, racking up skills on the Code Academy site. They're trying to build a future for themselves. They're doing it the way the Laziness Lie taught them to, by putting their nose to the grindstone and trading free time for virtuous hard work.

———

So many aspects of our lives have become gamified. Cooking blogs and YouTube channels have changed food preparation into performance. Twitter can make sharing jokes with your friends feel like a graded comedy class. Sites like Pinterest and Instagram have even turned craft-making competitive. I really love watching videos of people mixing glitter, paint, and food coloring into clear, glue-based putties and slimes. Something about watching people swirl bright colors and sequins into clear goop is just endlessly soothing to me. Yet the online community devoted to these craft videos (they call themselves "slimers") is filled with backbiting, drama, and wrath. Popular accounts constantly fight with one another over who deserves credit for inventing a new slime formula or who was the first to film their videos in a particular style. What was meant to be a soothing, kind of silly activity has somehow transformed into a contentious, status-obsessed one.

This gamification has transferred to how we monitor our wellness too. Our exercise habits are tracked by our phones and watches and shared with all our friends. At any given time, I can open up the Fitbit app and see who in my life is on the "leaderboard" of physical activity, who has racked up the most steps. Then I can use that information to motivate myself to be more active, or I can use another person's achievements as a reason to belittle myself.

Even if you're a relatively passive user of social media, you've probably felt the pull toward gamification in your life. Facebook and Instagram have tailored their algorithms in order to reward regular, compulsive use of their platforms, and to isolate and silence everyone who isn't a power user with a good sense of how to game the numbers. It's widely observed, for example, that if you don't open Facebook multiple times per day, the site seems to "punish" you by hiding your posts from many people on your friends list.[3] Sometimes these apps won't immediately tell you about likes or comments that you've received until you've been an active-enough user that day to have "earned" the right to be told about them. The only way to get a ton of likes or follows on these platforms is to spend hours on them liking other people's posts, leaving comments, and boosting "engagement."[4] The more you use these sites, the more popular you feel.

Both Facebook and Instagram have started dabbling with hiding how many likes another person's posts have. Individual users, however, can still see their own likes and follower counts, and can still measure their success in terms of how many responses they get.[5] In these ways, even the basic act of staying connected with other people has become a craved, achievement-obsessed process. People are constantly vying for attention, likes, followers, and clout. It saps the joy out of almost everything.

How Achievement-Hunting Ruins Experiences

Dr. Fred Bryant is a researcher in the field of positive psychology, the science of optimism, happiness, and what helps people thrive. He's spent more than forty years studying what a meaningful life looks like, a topic he understands on a very intuitive and personal level. Fred's just as cheery and sunny as you might expect a positive psychologist to be; he never stops grinning, and every word he utters sounds reflective and filled with wonder.

"So much of psychology is focused on treating negative symptoms," Fred says, "like depression or anxiety. We act as though the opposite of being depressed is simply being not depressed. But that's not true! We can do more than just be not depressed; we can study what makes a person truly happy, what makes a person feel like their life is beautiful, that it has meaning. We can maximize the good things, not just downplay the bad."

In Fred's work, finding joy and meaning all comes down to "savoring." Savoring is the process of deeply and presently enjoying a positive experience.[6] It occurs at three time points: first, when anticipating an upcoming an event with excitement and optimism; then, when fully appreciating the positive moment as it's happening; and finally, when looking back on the experience with a sense of reverence or gratitude after it's over.

When a person savors, they relish the things they love and devote their full attention to experiencing them in a mindful, appreciative way. You can savor anything you find pleasant, whether it's a picturesque hike in a nature reserve, a cold, refreshing cocktail, or an especially challenging crossword puzzle. All you have to do is approach it with slow, mindful gratitude, rather than seeing it as an item on a to-do list that you have to check off.

"You can't be distracted and savor something," Fred explains. "I could be eating the most delicious piece of pizza in the world—let's say a really amazing slice of Chicago deep-dish. But if I'm grading my students' homework while I'm eating it, I might completely forget to appreciate how wonderful the pizza is. All of a sudden I might look up and say, 'Hey, where did the pizza go? What, it's gone? Well, I guess I enjoyed it; I ate all of it really fast! But I don't even remember what eating it felt like.'"

Fred tells me that a skilled savorer would not distract themselves from the pizza in his example. They would eat it languidly, planning out each bite, maybe even saving the very best bite for last, so they have something to look forward to all the way to the end.

Research by Fred and his colleagues has shown that savoring has many benefits. When a person engages in savoring, time seems to slow down; the details of the moment become lush and vivid.[7] Happy moments feel happier when they're savored, and that happiness lasts longer after the experience is over.[8] Savorers also know how to look back on positive experiences and live them over

> Savoring is the process of deeply and presently enjoying a positive experience.

again, which allows them to boost their happiness even when life isn't going so well.[9] Perhaps as a result, frequent savorers often have much higher levels of life satisfaction and more positive moods compared to people who don't savor very much.[10]

Frequent savorers experience less depression. They cope with issues such as aging and declining health far better than non-savorers.[11] People suffering from chronic pain, heart disease, and cancer experience better long-term health outcomes if they know how to savor the good things in life, and they find their illnesses less depressing and stressful as well.[12] Since happiness generally increases a person's odds of being healthy, savoring can play a role in extending one's life span and warding off illness.[13]

The best thing about savoring is that anyone can learn how to do it. Fred and his colleagues have consistently found that it's a skill that can be learned.[14] There are mental strategies a person can practice in order to boost their savoring ability—just as there are negative, happiness-crushing strategies that a person can learn to avoid. Unfortunately, in a world beholden to the Laziness Lie, it's those negative thought patterns that are far more common.

———

The opposite of savoring is "dampening." Dampening occurs when we suck the life out of a positive experience by distracting ourselves from it, worrying about the future, or focusing on small imperfections that we ought to just ignore. Think of Debbie Downer, from the famous *Saturday Night Live* sketch, who ruins a birthday party by talking about natural disasters and lecturing everyone about how unhealthy birthday cake is. Debbie is a master at dampening a good mood, because she knows how to draw attention away from mindfully savoring the things that make people happy. And she's far from the only one who's impulsively negative in that way. Research has uncovered four mental habits that tend to dampen a person's happiness and make them more miserable. These four habits are strongly encouraged by the Laziness Lie.[15]

Mental Habits That "Dampen" Happiness	
Suppression	Hiding or repressing positive feelings due to shyness, modesty, or fear.
Distraction	Ignoring the joy of the moment and concerning yourself with other things.
Faultfinding	Disregarding the positive side of an experience and focusing on what's lacking or could be better.
Negative Mental Time Travel	Anticipating negative events that could happen in the future or reminiscing about painful experiences in the past.

Consider for a moment the many ways in which the Laziness Lie teaches us to dampen our happiness. By discouraging us from showing any signs of weakness or vulnerability, the Laziness Lie teaches us to engage in *suppression*, the hiding of signs of happiness in order to appear serious or mature. The Laziness Lie also loves keeping us *distracted*; as overachieving workaholics, we're all expected to multitask all day long, never taking a moment to fully luxuriate in a good meal, a golden sunset, or a leisurely walk around the block. Because the Laziness Lie encourages perfectionism, it makes many of us into expert *faultfinders* as well. We set unrealistically high standards of productivity and quality for ourselves, and then pick ourselves apart for coming up short. Finally, the Laziness Lie trains all of us to be *negative mental time travelers*, forever fearing the future and planning for worst-case scenarios, refusing to appreciate what we have because we're so anxious about what comes next.

This is what our cultural obsession with achievement-hunting has done to us. Even something that ought to be pleasurable, like taking a vacation or winning an award, becomes a new obligation to measure, document, and share with the world via social media. Once the experience is over, the Laziness Lie expects us to forget about it and speed ahead to the next credential, the next Instagrammable moment, the next big way to make "productive" use of our time. This keeps us from ever living in the moment or taking genuine pride in the things we've done.

My partner, Nick, once had a coworker who was a stand-up comedian. The guy was absolutely obsessed with how well his jokes did on social media. Every morning he'd post a new joke to Facebook and Twitter, then compulsively check his notifications for an hour to see how well the joke had done. His only benchmark for whether a joke was any good was if it got a hundred likes within the first hour. If it didn't hit that mark, it was a failure. The guy didn't seem to ask himself if he actually *liked* the jokes he was posting, or to view writing them as the creative craft it was. He couldn't take any pride or enjoyment in what he was doing. All he had was a goal to obsess over, an achievement that he had to hit every day.

Research shows that when we're stressed and caught up in routines, we experience time as moving more quickly.[16] Weeks, months, or even years can all blend together in a haze of anxiety and obligation—and we may be left with very few unique, cherished memories to look back on. You can't savor your life—or even remember it in much detail—if your existence is nothing but a series of obligations you have to joylessly meet.[17] Thankfully, there are steps we can take to break out of our overachieving patterns.

How to Reframe Your Life's Value

Life ought to be about so much more than being productive and impressing other people. Chasing obsessively after goals and forever trying to earn social approval will never bring us satisfaction. In fact, it can drain us of our ability to appreciate the good things in life. Instead, we have to take a step back, reconsider our values, and learn to see our lives as having innate worth, no matter what we do or don't accomplish. Changing our mindset in this way is hard, especially after years of the Laziness Lie's indoctrination. There are, however, some

> You can't savor your life—or even remember it in much detail—if your existence is nothing but a series of obligations you have to joylessly meet.

research-supported strategies we can follow to help us get there. Some of these strategies include learning how to savor, making time for awe, and regularly trying something we're very, very bad at.

Learn to Savor

We've already taken a look at the mental habits that dampen people's happiness levels. Now it's time to look at the flip side—the ways of thinking that can actually help us appreciate and amplify feelings of joy.[18]

Mental Habits That Help Us Savor Happiness	
Behavioral Displays	Showing happiness in our behavior: smiling, singing, jumping for joy, flapping our hands excitedly, etc.
Being Present	Living in the present moment, focusing on the experience as it's happening; pushing distractions away and being mindful.
Capitalizing	Communicating about a positive experience with other people; celebrating an event; sharing good news with other people; getting other people excited.
Positive Mental Time Travel	Reflecting on happy memories or reminding people of a pleasant shared past; planning and anticipating desired future events.

You can see how each of these mental habits is the mirror image of the dampening habits. The first one, *behavioral displays*, suggests that if you want to be happy and appreciate your life, you should show your joy when you're feeling it. As someone who loves to flap my hands frantically when I'm excited and who lives to coo and squeal obnoxiously whenever I see a puppy, this is very good news.

Another way to increase our happiness is to *be fully present* in life's pleasurable moments. This means putting down distractions, not trying to multitask, and really drinking in the details of a good experience. One way I've incorporated this into my own life is by taking a real lunch break every day. I've always been tempted to use my lunchtime "productively," answering e-mails while I cram a burrito into my mouth. But doing that just leaves me stressed and shocked at how quickly time has flown by. So instead, I try to make myself walk away from my computer, find a nice spot outside, and force myself to eat slowly, tasting everything, watching people walk by, and enjoying the cool breeze that comes off Lake Michigan.

Next, research shows we can get more happiness out of life by *capitalizing* on good experiences—in other words, by telling people about good things that have happened and making the time to publicly celebrate. Many of us have been taught that it's immodest to brag about our accomplishments, and that instead we should just keep on grinding along, working hard without expecting much of a reward for it. Instead, research suggests that there is value in highlighting the things we're proud of. If we're lucky, we can even boost the moods of people we share our good news with. Research shows that people like to bask in the glory of their friends' and family's victories and feel more pride in themselves when they have successful, happy friends.[19]

The final healthy mental habit to practice is *positive mental time travel*. This, of course, is the opposite of constantly fretting about the future or dwelling on sad moments in the past. Expert savorers know how to reminisce about good experiences. They also expect to have lots of new, joyful experiences in the future, so their lives seem to be filled with happiness, anticipation, and hope.

When he's not doing psychological research, Fred Bryant loves climbing mountains. He regularly goes climbing with two friends who perfectly illustrate what positive mental time travel looks like.

"One guy I climb mountains with is always reminding us of climbs that we did in the past," Fred says. "He'll call me up and say, 'Did you know that two years ago on this day, we were on top of Mount Rainier?' And he'll help me remember all these amazing things that we did that day. Another guy on my team, he's the planner. He's always looking ahead to the next climb, saying, 'Oh, here's what we have to look forward to, here's what we're gonna do.' And he gets us all excited about what's to come."

> Expert savorers know how to reminisce about good experiences. They also expect to have lots of new, joyful experiences in the future, so their lives seem to be filled with happiness, anticipation, and hope.

If you've been taught all your life to focus on accomplishments and to worry about the future, it will be hard to adopt these mental habits at first. But as Fred keeps reassuring me, very few people are naturally good at them. Most savorers got that way over time, by training themselves to focus on drinking in the positives. "It's similar to musical talent," he tells me. "Sure, some people naturally have a good ear, but everyone who plays an instrument has to practice. Savoring is the same. You have to work at it. And then you can get better at it."

Make Time for Awe

Another way to curb an achievement obsession is to consciously find time to experience awe. Awe occurs when we encounter something completely new or deeply inspiring, such as a sparkling, blue sea, a rich, green forest, or an amazing vocal performance at a concert.[20] Awe reminds us of the universe's largeness and our own smallness, in a way that feels exhilarating and soothing rather than threatening. When we feel awe, all our individual problems and worries can seem to drop away, because the vast beauty around us puts everything in perspective.

Awe is also a fantastic burnout-buster.[21] For people in the burnout-prone helping professions, such as nursing and social work, making time for awe is an invaluable piece of self-care. Most of us think of self-care as involving something like getting a massage, buying a new outfit, or taking a warm bubble bath. Those forms of self-care are the easiest to market and to make a profit from, so it's no wonder they're the most well-known. However, pampering is just one form self-care can take. Awe is

> **When we feel awe, all our individual problems and worries can seem to drop away, because the vast beauty around us puts everything in perspective.**

a much deeper and more restorative form of self-care because it has a spiritual component.[22] Even if you aren't religious at all, you can feel a sense of greater purpose, a connection with nature, or a deep bond with all of humanity by seeking out moments of awe and wonder.[23]

So, how do you go about getting awestruck? Novelty and wonder are the keys. Try habitually putting yourself into new situations or exposing yourself to novel, interesting stimuli. There are a lot of ways to go about this. Here are some ideas:

- Visit a new city, with no agenda but to explore it.
- Take a new route to work or walk down unfamiliar side streets in your neighborhood.
- Study a subject you know absolutely nothing about.
- Look closely at an object and consider how many people were involved in creating it and getting it to where it is now.
- Attend a festival, meetup, or workshop for people who are passionate about an activity you know nothing about.
- Try to appreciate an art form you've never spent much time with before (poetry, short film, sculpture, dance, mash-up music, etc.).
- Ask a friend or coworker to tell you about a subject that excites them. Really listen, and try to learn something from them.

An awe-filled life is much easier to appreciate. Unfamiliar places and experiences take longer for our brains to process, which actually creates the illusion that time is slowing down. This is part of why the drive to a new place always seems to take longer than the drive home.[24] When all our senses are focused on taking in the details of a novel experience, it's easier to forget our daily obligations and our worries about the future and to remember that the world is large and filled with possibility. Experiencing awe also uses mental processes that are very similar to those savoring uses, so it's great practice for those hoping to make savoring a regular habit.

Do Something You're Bad At

If you're a habitual overachiever and trophy hoarder, odds are you absolutely *loathe* doing things you're bad at. This is a particularly common problem for people who were "gifted" students in school, or who were constantly told as children that they were smart. When you've spent your whole life chasing praise for being naturally good at things, it's deeply unpleasant to do anything badly.

Doing something poorly is a great way to break free from the Laziness Lie. When we accept failure, we learn that our lives have meaning regardless of what we can (or can't) do. When we pursue an activity we can't ever possibly succeed at, we force ourselves to learn how to enjoy the process rather than the end product. Getting comfortable "wasting" our time on something unproductive and unsuccessful frees us up to choose our own goals and priorities instead of checking off the boxes society has laid out for us.

In the book *The Queer Art of Failure*, Jack Halberstam suggests that failing at something that society has told us to do can be a revolutionary act.[25] When we fail, we find ourselves pushing back against the pressure to generate value for other people—and that changes everything.

"[Failure] quietly loses," Halberstam writes, "and in losing it imagines other goals for life, for love, for art, and for being."[26] In other words, when we fail, we become free to choose what we want our actual goals and priorities to be, rather than following the expectations of others. The Laziness Lie wants us to keep being productive in areas where we're skilled—so when we choose to stick with an activity we're horrible at, we're able to make a choice motivated by genuine love rather than by the external pressure to succeed.

I've always had skills that other people see as valuable: number-crunching skills, teaching skills, even my ability to write. In the past year,

> **When we fail, we become free to choose what we want our actual goals and priorities to be, rather than following the expectations of others.**

I've made regular time each week to do something I truly suck at (and will always suck at): lifting weights. I'm physically weak and uncoordinated, so I avoided going to the gym for years because I knew I'd be just awful at it. But this year, I found myself compelled to learn how to use weight machines. I'd started learning to take better care of my health, and I thought it might be kind of fun to try getting strong. So, I started working at it slowly, three or four days a week.

It's been oddly refreshing, learning a skill that I will never excel at or impress somebody with. Sitting at the weight machines, noticing that I can lift just a tiny bit more weight today than I was able to a month ago, I feel a small swell of pride. I'm never going to be ripped or especially strong, but I've learned how to stick with something that absolutely terrifies me and to get comfortable with not being the best. Sometimes I'm even a bit awed at how far I've come and what my body is capable of.

Learning to Document Your Life Less

Joan was almost Internet famous. She's always been very well-read and incredibly witty, and for years she used to post a lot of droll, funny observations about current events and pop culture on Twitter and Tumblr. Sometimes, when the social media stars aligned, those posts would blow up, getting her hundreds of thousands of responses. People even made fan art based on ideas Joan had shared online. The positive feedback was addictive. Sometimes, the quest for viral success encouraged Joan to behave in ways that weren't healthy for her.

Many of Joan's most popular posts were about some of the darkest and bleakest experiences in her life. She struggled for years with depression and social isolation, growing up in poverty in rural Canada. In her youth, she had a very hard time connecting with the people in her small town, who were mostly straight and didn't share her interest in things like celebrity culture and Old Hollywood. When she posted dark jokes about how it felt to be depressed and obsessed with topics other people found strange, they went viral a lot of the time. Alienated Internet nerds all around the world found they could relate to Joan. But Joan didn't really get anything out of it.

"In some ways I feel that the online community was exploiting my poor mental health at time for 'content,'" she says. "I could certainly be witty and acerbic about my trauma, but at what cost?"

For Joan, everything changed when she finally had the chance to get paid for her writing. One of her posts went more than just viral: it developed into a concept for a feature film. All of a sudden, Joan was in talks with film producers and a well-known director who wanted to take a concept of hers and transform it into a major project. After years of throwing good ideas out into the Internet ether and receiving only a few thousand likes in return, Joan was finally getting recognized for her effort. That really changed her priorities.

"When I realized just how much my thoughts and ideas were worth, I realized I needed to stop giving them away for free," Joan says. "The immediate dopamine hit of several thousand likes and shares, or even an extremely viral post, is nothing compared to the validation of getting compensated."

Joan's behavior shifted almost immediately. She began taking screenwriting classes and worked to build a creative portfolio that would help her pursue a career in media. She started selling her writing instead of giving it away for free online. And she stopped spending so much time chasing virality and high follower counts.

"Those bon mots and witticisms feel very good to write, are easy to write, and will get one a lot of traction, but a full-length project just feels more satisfying," she says. "I had to take a step back and sacrifice the immediate rush of virality and likes for the sustained feeling of accomplishment that comes from a serious, larger project."

Today, Joan shares very little of her life online. She doesn't post about her trauma, and she doesn't waste good joke ideas on Twitter posts.

Instead, she saves them for screenplays, which take more time to craft but pay off far more. The more she disconnects from the competitive, achievement-obsessed world of social media, the more Joan says she's been able to enjoy her life. Her mental health has improved a great deal. She has far more real-life friends, and she's gotten sober. It's not that quitting the Internet magically caused her to become healthier; rather, when Joan stopped focusing on instant gratification and chasing achievements via the Internet, she started having more time to focus on people who actually cared about her and artistic pursuits that really mattered. Instead of looking to her painful memories as a source of potential productivity and "content," she worked on healing those wounds instead.

In recent years, Joan has started attending regular meetings of the Religious Society of Friends (also known as the Quakers). It's fitting that someone who learned to disconnect from the stimulus overload of the Internet now spends one morning per week sitting in contemplative silence with strangers. In a Friends meeting, there's no "content" being provided by anyone—not even a sermon given by a pastor. There's no pressure to speak, no social competition for attention or approval. The community simply joins together and sits in silence, except for those rare, meaningful moments when someone truly feels moved to speak.

Digital tools have made life much easier, but they've also left us with an endless array of accounts to maintain and notifications to worry about. Social media apps have created intense pressure to mine every life experience for achievement points—turning joy into clout. Nearly every activity in our lives has become something to document, measure, and broadcast our success in, despite the fact that a mountain of evidence suggests such obsessive recording and sharing can impair or erode our mental health.

Most of us won't be able to completely go off the grid. Even if we fantasize about chucking our phones out the window, many of us need digital tools to stay organized and connected. But that doesn't mean we have to be fully invested in gamifying our lives. Like Joan, we can work to set reasonable, practical boundaries on how we interact with the digital realm. By reframing our approach to using these tools, we can reorient our lives and detach from the idea that our productivity defines our worth.

Have Phone-Free Time Periods

When our phones are always easily within our grasp, we feel the urge to check them obsessively. This is by design. Most apps have been carefully developed to be as addictive and alluring as possible, with numerous notifications, "rewards" for frequent use, and hard-to-navigate algorithms that keep users refreshing the site every few minutes in search of new content.[27] On top of that, the fear of missing out on important messages, event invitations, and other opportunities keeps us from putting down our devices and ever truly being idle or lazy.

Because smartphones give us access to an entire world of information, they make us feel powerful when we use them.[28] Some research shows that when you take a person's phone away, they feel unsafe, and may even experience a drop in self-esteem because of it. This fear of powerlessness makes it even harder to disconnect.

Despite how much we all rely on our phones, however, there's a growing movement toward taking a "Digital Sabbath."[29] A Digital Sabbath works exactly the way you'd expect: you set aside at least one day per week during which you ignore all your devices and notifications. Most people who practice the Digital Sabbath set aside a weekend day to fully detach, but it's possible to go offline during the week too. Some organizations have even begun encouraging it, because data shows that constantly checking e-mail and Slack messages distracts employees and stresses them out.[30]

For many people, however, going phone-free for a full day just isn't practical or appealing. If that's the case, you can still set boundaries, such as refusing to answer e-mails or check notifications after a certain hour of the night. As Markus Nini mentioned in chapter three,

> Social media apps have created intense pressure to mine every life experience for achievement points— turning joy into clout.

his organization's employees are free to stop answering e-mails at whatever time of the evening they prefer. You can also put limits on what kinds of Internet use you'll engage in, and at what times of day.

Monikah has a second phone with no SIM card in it, which she uses for browsing the Internet at night. She's an avid hiker and naturalist, and in the evenings she likes to go online and research local flora and fauna and plan her next hike. In the past, this relaxing experience was ruined by constant notifications and messages. A disconnected phone allows her to get the best of the Internet without any of the stress. For other people, switching from a bright screen to a Kindle or other e-ink device can be a great way to remain connected to a wealth of information without getting sensory (or information) overload.

Turn Off the Notifications and Activity Trackers

The vast majority of reminders and notifications we receive from our phones are not urgent. That Facebook message from your cousin doesn't have to be answered immediately. The Duolingo owl won't murder you in your sleep if you forget to practice Spanish vocabulary today. When you're caught up in the heat of the moment and your phone is constantly blowing up with noisy, bright beacons of stress and obligation, those facts are easy to forget. Research shows that frequent phone notifications can make people more distractible and hyperactive.[31] Compulsive smartphone use can also exacerbate anxiety and depressive symptoms if a person is already at risk of those mental illnesses.[32]

The best way to protect yourself is to get rid of the temptation to constantly check notifications by turning those annoying reminders off. You can also identify which applications cause you the most guilt and stress, and then work to end your reliance on them. Some organizational apps improve our lives in real ways. The calendar app on my phone, for example, makes keeping appointments less stressful for me, not more. On the flip

> **Research shows that frequent phone notifications can make people more distractible and hyperactive.**

side, I decided a few months ago to delete the Fitbit app, because I realized that monitoring my sleep, daily steps, and exercise levels just made me feel anxious. By tracking my physical activity and sharing it with the world, I felt obligated to always "achieve" the app's recommend ten thousand steps per day. When life got in the way, I felt guilty. The solution was simple: the Fitbit app had to go.

Focus on Process—Not Product

Life has become so intensely gamified that it's easy to think of every activity as a competition. *Did today's selfie get more likes than yesterday's? Did I review more books on Goodreads this year than last year? Am I using my free time more virtuously than all my friends are?* This mindset breeds insecurity and dissatisfaction. To break out of it, we have to treat self-improvement and growth as pleasurable, gradual processes, not goals that we will ever complete.

For Joan, this meant completely changing how she approaches creativity and writing. In the past, she fixated on how well her posts did on social media. It was easy to compare herself to other Internet personalities and focus on the times when her success didn't measure up to somebody else's. She was caught in a hamster wheel of hunting for achievements. The only way for her to move forward was by stepping off it.

Today, almost all Joan's creative work happens in private. She spends her evenings writing. This work doesn't provide the instant gratification that posting jokes on Twitter does. It's slow and gradual. That also means there's no external pressure to push an idea out into the world before it's ready. The long-term payoff is immense, even if she's no longer getting the short-term dopamine hit of a few retweets.

Psychological research shows that it's far healthier to focus on personal growth rather than competition with other people.[33] It's exhausting to be constantly vying to be the very best, the most productive, the most skillful, the person with the most likes. The Laziness Lie loves keeping us insecure because it makes us easy to exploit. If I want to be the very best, I'm never going to stop to take a breather, because there will always be someone out there who is "beating" me in some way. This is a damaging worldview. It leaves no room for healing, experimentation, or quiet, unimpressive, reflective moments. When we choose to feel compassion toward ourselves and stop expecting ourselves to be the very best, we can find joy in all kinds of slow, "unproductive" activities.

Fred Bryant might be a very accomplished psychological researcher, but his true passion is climbing mountains. As you might imagine, reaching the top of the mountain isn't his favorite part. It's making steady progress toward the summit, enjoying the majesty of nature along with his closest friends.

"You put so much effort into climbing the mountain, all for what amounts to just a few minutes at the top of the summit," Fred says to me, smiling. "But it's not a race to get to the top, it's a process—an experience that you're meant to savor and enjoy. I love the journey toward the top of the mountain. I'm not there just to be at the very top. That's what savoring is all about to me. The phrase is 'stop and smell the roses,' not 'run through the field trying to smell as many roses as you can, as quickly as possible.'"

CHAPTER FIVE

You Don't Have to Be an Expert in Everything

"I'm fighting with a stranger on the Internet again," Noah messaged me one night. "Please tell me to stop."

"It's a waste of time and you should stop," I told him, for perhaps the fiftieth time. "They're never going to listen, and you're just gonna make yourself upset."

Noah is an engineer and a voracious reader, so he's accumulated a lot of knowledge about a variety of topics. He's also an avid follower of the news. On the Internet, being knowledgeable and well-read can be a liability just as often as an advantage. It gives you a lot to be anxious and frustrated about. There's too much ignorance out there, too many fights you could potentially have. Yet Noah tries to fight all of them.

"You're right," Noah messaged back. "This guy is never gonna listen. But he's saying that MMR vaccines have mercury in them! I can't believe there are still people who believe this shit!"

Just like that, Noah was back down the rabbit hole, recounting every ignorant and asinine thing the other guy had said to him over the course of the two hours that they'd been fighting. Noah had also spent that time looking up medical studies that proved he was right and sending them to his opponent. He tried asking thought-provoking questions of the man. Then he tried getting more aggressive and confrontational. None of it, of course, was working at all.

"I should walk away," Noah said. "I've said everything I can say."

"Yup," I messaged back, as I was settling into bed.

An hour later, Noah messaged me again. "I just wrote a 1500-word rant explaining how the whole anti-vaccine movement is rooted in the fear of kids having disabilities. Did I just completely waste my time?"

Noah probably *had* just wasted his time. But I said something that was also likely to be true: "It's possible someone else will read the whole fight and learn something from it."

"I hope so," he said, seeming kind of dejected. I turned my phone off, rolled over, and went to sleep, knowing that within a few weeks, Noah would message me again about another Internet fight that he was swept up in—or I'd do the same thing to him.

———

Noah, like a lot of people, has compulsive Internet habits. He gets into needless fights with people he'll never be able to persuade. He obsesses over social problems he doesn't have the power to solve, as if worrying were a productive form of activism. He's struggled with an addiction to reading the news, cramming his brain with as much upsetting information as he possibly can.

Noah has a to-read list that is staggeringly long. When I told him about a book that I was really enjoying, Noah whipped out his phone, opened his Notes app, scrolled for what felt like five solid minutes, and then added the book to the end of the list. I marveled at how long his list was, and how it spanned a variety of topics, from anthropology to marine biology to personal finance to feminism. When he visits people's homes, Noah scans the hosts' bookshelves looking for enticing titles to add to his list. No matter the topic of conversation, he always has at least one or two books to recommend on the subject, sometimes titles he's actually gotten around to reading, sometimes not.

Like so many overextended people I've spoken to, Noah comes from a working-class background. He grew up poor in a run-down area of Detroit. College was not guaranteed to him, nor was a future with strong career prospects. His parents often struggled to get by. That seems to have given Noah a higher-than-average motivation to avoid "laziness" in every possible realm of his life. No matter how exhausting his day job as an engineer can be, he's always committing to doing more beyond that. He's studied multiple languages and traveled abroad to practice his conversational Yiddish and Hebrew. He knows a ton about neuroscience for someone who's never taken a class on the subject. He follows the news on countless platforms. He strives, in every way, to be informed, self-educated, and politically aware.

Noah's computer used to regularly crash from the burden of keeping all his browser tabs open. He's an absolute tab-hoarder, the worst one I've ever seen. He always keeps dozens and dozens open at once—news articles, op-eds, scientific reports, essays, Reddit threads, e-mail chains, and more, some of which Noah's been meaning to read for weeks or even months. He works full-time and has a two-hour commute to work each day, so he never has time to make a real dent in the tabs. I suspect that even if he did find the time, he'd spend half of it reading and half of it finding piles and piles of new sites to add to his list. "I've been meaning to read an article about that" is his constant refrain. "Here, let me send it to you."

A few years ago, I had to ban myself from a Facebook group Noah had created, because he was constantly sharing articles with everyone in the group, often multiple times per day. It annoyed me and stressed me out. I think it probably hurt Noah's feelings that I did that, or maybe it gave him the impression that I don't care about the world as deeply as he did. But I just had to do it. I was already drowning in information. I couldn't let another information addict pull me down even deeper. I think that from Noah's perspective, though, he thought he was doing a vital public service.

It's hard to know how much Noah's reading has enriched his life, and how much it's detracted from it. He has a lot of anxiety about the future, and at times reading the news seems only to stoke those flames. He's educated and wise, and the breadth of his knowledge helps him see how interconnected many social problems are. His intelligence and passion are beautiful qualities, but they also leave him feeling responsible for educating people and correcting every bit of ignorance he sees. I know how stressful that compulsion can be, because I regularly get swept up in the exact same thing. The teacher in me is always trying to educate people, even when it's clear a person doesn't want to be reached.

Nobody can be an expert in everything. There are too many issues to care about, too many rapidly developing news stories to follow religiously. We have access to more knowledge than any other humans in history. As a result, most of us are profoundly overwhelmed with what we know. We're consumed with guilt over the things we feel we should be learning more about but can't find the time to.

Knowledge can be empowering, and access to the Internet has enriched countless lives. The Laziness Lie tells us that we should take full advantage of the privileges of the Internet by forever learning more and more. It sees no limit to how much information a person ought to consume, never acknowledges the emotional and psychological cost of cramming facts into our brains. If we aren't using the wealth of available data to make ourselves more productive and useful to society, what's the point of having it?

While access to information is a privilege, it's also a burden. This is especially true when we treat being well-read as an obligation that can't be escaped. Constant exposure to upsetting news can be traumatic. An unending flood of information makes it hard to pause and reflect on anything you've learned. At some point, even the most voracious of readers needs to pull the plug and stop the constant drip of facts, figures, and meaningless Internet fights. We're living in an era of information overload—and the solution is not to learn more but to step back and consume a smaller amount of data in a more meaningful way.

The Information Overload Era

As human beings have continued to scientifically advance and collect more and more information about the nature of our world, it has become harder and harder to educate the public about all of it. Modern life is incredibly complex, and in order to navigate it well, a person has to be well-informed on a variety of topics and disciplines. Over time, the bar for what counts

> Nobody can be an expert in everything. There are too many issues to care about, too many rapidly developing news stories to follow religiously.

as "well-informed" has steadily risen higher and higher, making it increasingly difficult for anyone to remain caught up.

A good illustration of this is how higher education has evolved over time. Before the 1800s, there was no such thing as a college major. Back then, all students were expected to take courses in all topics. A college degree meant you were very well-educated in all the "liberal arts": writing, philosophy, music, math, astronomy, and more. By the mid-1800s, however, there was simply too much information available for that to be a reasonable expectation anymore. So, the idea of "majoring" was developed. Instead of trying to learn about everything, a student could choose a subject, study it deeply, and become a specialist.[1]

Unfortunately, as human knowledge has expanded even more, many subjects have gotten too dense for a person to fully comprehend them in just four years of study. Now if you want to study a subject such as psychology deeply, you need a master's degree or a PhD, not a bachelor's degree. In many fields, employers have started to treat advanced degrees as the new minimum level of education required, because an undergraduate major just doesn't cover enough of the available knowledge base.[2] In academia, we often say "a master's is the new bachelor's."[3]

As a professor, I find this steady creep of "degree inflation" really distressing. In theory, it ought to be good that humanity has access to so much wisdom. Instead, being well educated is treated as a credential that a person must earn in order to have promising career options. Unfortunately, getting that credential is increasingly expensive and time-consuming. A college education used to open a lot of doors for people, especially those from poor or otherwise marginalized backgrounds. Now, becoming sufficiently educated has become a massive source of pressure and an immense financial strain. It doesn't help that most universities view their master's degree programs as their biggest cash cows.[4]

When it comes to information overload, college is just one piece of the puzzle. Data- and knowledge-sharing has permeated every waking hour of our lives, whether we're in school or not. Each of us is absolutely inundated with facts, opinions, and meaningless Internet fights every single time we unlock our phones. Instead of liberating us, this knowledge is leaving many of us distracted and distressed.

———

Rick knows that he should quit using Twitter. He's been saying as much for years.

"It's just a sea of bad, superficial takes," he tells me. "No matter who I follow, my feed ends up being a bunch of left-leaning comedians trying to find the best joke they can make about whatever horrible thing is happening in the world. Nobody wants to have a meaningful conversation about anything. If you try to insert any nuance, they're hostile to it." Still, he finds the social media site hard to quit. "I check Twitter all day," he says, "and it fills me with despair like every single time."

It's so easy to hop onto Twitter while you're waiting in line at the grocery store or bored with whatever TV show you're watching. Every time you refresh it, there's tons of new content, all of it presented in bite-size packages that the mind can easily digest. There's so much to read and engage with—but because tweets are so short and Twitter conversations move at such a fast pace, most of that engagement is shallow and ultimately unsatisfying. It's no wonder Rick has a compulsive relationship to the platform. It's basically an attention slot machine that never pays out.

> **Being well educated is treated as a credential that a person must earn in order to have promising career options. Unfortunately, getting that credential is increasingly expensive and time-consuming.**

The Internet has revolutionized how we share and access information. It has empowered people throughout the world, giving them access to knowledge that used to be hidden away in universities and libraries. It's raised public awareness of social-justice issues and helped people at society's fringes to find community and understanding. I never would have realized I was transgender if it weren't for online communities where trans people shared their experiences. Hell, if it weren't for the Internet and online writing platforms like WordPress and Medium, I wouldn't ever have become an author. I understand how the Internet can change lives for the better.

But because the Internet has made it so easy to share information, it has also created an impossibly large deluge of data, and each of us is absolutely drowning in it. The volume of knowledge available on the Internet is expanding at a staggering rate. According to IBM, 2.5 quintillion bytes of data are added every single day.[5] The rate of data growth increases further every year. Ninety percent of the information currently available on the Internet was added in the past two years.[6] The volume of unique information the average person encounters in a day is approximately five times what the average person encountered in 1986.[7] It's an unbelievable amount to process—and every projection suggests it's only going to get worse.

———

Unfortunately, a lot of the information that gets thrown in our faces each day is useless, redundant, or damaging. The Internet is awash in comment sections and reply chains where people fight endless battles that go nowhere. Beyond that, much of the data that gets posted each day is "junk data"— random musings, bad jokes, advertisements, self-promotions, and complicated reactions to and critiques of other posts that make no sense without proper context. There's no point in exposing ourselves

> **Ninety percent of the information currently available on the Internet was added in the past two years.**

to that much noise—yet encountering it, and trying to filter through it, is pretty much unavoidable.

In addition to all that relatively benign junk, there's also actively dangerous data being shared: violent fascist rhetoric, hate speech, intentional misinformation, and even traumatic images of death and national tragedy. Though most social media sites have entire teams dedicated to filtering and deleting objectionable and traumatic material, there's just too much of it being posted for it to be completely removed. Some awful images and hateful writing inevitably slip through the cracks, forcing us to figure out how to respond.[8]

The redundancy of information on the Internet is also a problem. Many of us feel the need to help address a pressing social problem or emergency by "signal boosting" posts, sharing them widely with our networks. This desire to educate other people is often very useful, but it can also cause misinformation or panic. When I share a warning about how long viral particles remain alive on a surface such as a kitchen counter, am I helping to save a random friend from getting ill, or am I filling my friends' social media feeds with alarming information they've likely already seen? Am I providing enough context on what that fact means, so a person knows what to do with the information? Or am I just freaking people out? Most of the time it's hard to tell which information is worth sharing and which is either faulty or has already been viewed dozens of times.

It takes a ton of effort to sift through all this data, throwing away the misinformation, nonsense, and hate, and making time for useful facts and meaningful reflections. And it's really easy to get caught up in correcting all the distortions and fighting all the bigots you encounter along the way. It's no wonder people like Noah and Rick get sucked into spending way more time online than is good for them.

Many of us feel an immense internal pressure to stay plugged in and up-to-date. News stories develop at an unprecedented pace. A story can break, spark conversation, provoke a response, and then be entirely disproven all within a few hours. If you don't stay online checking for updates, you risk missing out on the actual truth. Every day there are new attacks on the rights of transgender people, women, and immigrants, and that news is usually served with a side of terrifying facts about climate change, institutional racism, pandemic spread, or gun violence. In this context, turning off our phones and ignoring the news can seem socially irresponsible, yet obsessively overloading our senses with disturbing facts and disgusting propaganda isn't doing any good either.

According to a survey by the American Psychological Association, 95 percent of Americans say that they try to stay up-to-date on the news. However, 56 percent of them also say that following the news causes them significant stress.[9] It's clear that the Laziness Lie has permeated our approach to knowledge and information. No matter how desperately we want to remain knowledgeable, and no matter how strongly we feel a responsibility to stay connected, the truth of the matter is plain: we're taking in too much data, and it's doing us serious harm.

How Information Overload Affects Our Health

After the 2016 presidential election, Noah and I started exchanging long, anxious e-mails about politics. The constant onslaught of frightening news was taking a real, observable physical toll on each of us. And it wasn't pretty.

"I'm pants-shittingly nervous," I wrote to him in an e-mail after Betsy DeVos was named secretary of education. "I literally keep having nervous shits."

"I've also been stress-pooping a lot," Noah wrote back after Trump's travel ban was announced. "I keep feeling totally overwhelmed."

In our e-mails to each other, Noah and I speculated that we shouldn't be reading the news as often as we were. Yet given the circumstances, unplugging was pretty damn hard. I couldn't look away. I was doing myself real damage, flooding my nervous system with constant alarm. But it felt necessary and morally just for me to do so. Between teaching classes,

> We're taking in too much data, and it's doing us serious harm.

I'd open up news and activist sites, call my senators, and make tons of frantic social media posts sounding the alarm bell about everything bad that was happening.

Of course, I was far from alone. According to the American Psychological Association, during that period, two-thirds of Americans reported that the future of the nation was the largest source of stress in their lives.[10] That percentage was at an all-time high. More people were stressed by the state of the nation than they were by their own finances or jobs.

Compulsive, anxiety-fueled news reading only got worse in 2020, with the spread of the coronavirus leaving people all around the world locked indoors. As infections rose exponentially and local and national governments scrambled to respond, staying online for updates no longer felt optional—it was essential if you wanted to know what your risks were and whether you were legally permitted to leave the house or not. Staying well-informed was a civic duty, but it was also a deep torment.

One therapist that I spoke to, Sharon Glassburn of Curiosity Counseling, told me that many of her clients struggle with limiting their news intake. For many of them, upsetting political news is a highly personal threat, and one they can't easily escape.

"I see it a lot," she says. "The [political] situation is so urgent, and a lot of things that are happening are traumatic. And as a therapist, I want to validate clients who are caught up in a situation that they can't control."

If you're a person of color, a sexual-assault survivor, an LGBTQ+ person, or an immigrant, you probably haven't been able to escape worrisome news for years at this point. It's hard to disengage, because each frightening development has a palpable impact on your life. You can't control that or ignore it. However, Sharon warns that fixating on things we can't control can leave us feeling like we have zero agency in our lives. That outlook is never healthy.

"I have to strike a balance between affirming that there are situations that a client can't control and problems that are systemic," Sharon says, "and helping them look to the factors that they can control. Because constantly focusing on massive injustice that you can't change is very unempowering."

In fact, a loss of agency is one of the primary dangers of information over-load. For decades, researchers have noted that consuming too much upsetting news can damage a person's mental health, making them feel powerless and vulnerable.[11] In the 1970s and '80s, communications researcher Grace Levine began recording how often public news broadcasts described negative events as uncontrollable and impossible to avoid. She discovered in multiple studies that over 70 percent of news stories emphasized how "helpless" people were to avoid being victims of things like crime, natural disaster, and untimely death.[12] While it's true that many of these events are difficult to personally control or forestall, there's a real psychological and social danger to portraying the world as so menacing and uncontrollable.

In the 1990s and 2000s, twenty-four-hour news channels and Internet news sites spread in popularity. Watching the news shifted from something you did for maybe an hour per day after dinner to something you could do constantly, even as a primary source of entertainment. During that period, fear of crime and disaster sharply increased—and that increase was directly linked to people's news-watching habits.[13] Studies found that, generally, the more news a person watched or read, the more fearful they felt, and the more dangerous they perceived their surroundings to be, regardless of how safe or unsafe their actual communities were.[14] In the most extreme cases, fear of crime had zero relationship to the actual crime rate itself. Even as the murder rate was going down throughout the country, most Americans were convinced it was on a precipitous rise.

Even worse, this fear seemed to alter people's behavior. Frequent news watchers engaged in more "avoidant" behaviors than other people. They stayed inside more often, didn't socialize as much with other people, and spent less time trying new things and going to new places. Generally speaking, this kind of isolation is very bad for a person's continued growth and development. In some studies, frequent news watching has even been found to increase a person's racial bias.[15]

The old adage is that "knowledge is power," but when it comes to scary, threatening news, research suggests the exact opposite. Frightening information can actually rob people of their inner sense of control, making

> The more news a person watched or read, the more fearful they felt, and the more dangerous they perceived their surroundings to be, regardless of how safe or unsafe their actual communities were.

them less likely to take care of themselves and other people. Public health research shows that when the news presents health-related information in a pessimistic way, people are actually less likely to take steps to protect themselves from illness as a result.[16] A news article that's intended to warn people about increasing cancer rates, for example, can actually backfire and result in fewer people choosing to get screened for the disease because they're so terrified of what they might find.[17] This is also true for issues such as climate change. When a news story is all doom and gloom, people feel fatalistic and become less interested in taking small, personal steps to fight ecological collapse.[18]

The Laziness Lie encourages very binary thinking. People are either hardworking no matter their circumstances, or they're hopelessly lazy. A problem can either be fixed through sheer determination and individualism, or it's impossible to solve, and therefore pointless to try. This framing encourages obsessive devotion to the issues we care about; when working tirelessly to fix a problem becomes untenable, the Laziness Lie tells us we might as well give up. Stressing out about a topic is not actually a means of working to address the problem. It may feel productive, because it keeps our minds busy and engaged, but it actually saps us of the energy to put up a genuine fight.

———

Information overload can even damage our cognitive abilities. Research shows that when a person gets bombarded with a ton of information, they lose the ability to focus. Very little of the information gets stored in their memory.[19] If you've ever "watched" a TV show while screwing around on your phone and then realized that you missed an entire scene or plot point because you were distracted, you know exactly what this feels like. Paradoxically, by trying to cram too much knowledge into our minds, we destroy our ability to make sense of, or hold on to, any of it.[20]

Information overload can damage our decision-making abilities for similar reasons.[21] In order for information to be useful to us, we have to find time to reflect on it, process it, and see if it lines up with the facts we already know. But when we're in a state of information overload, this quiet contemplation can't happen, leading us to make all kinds of errors and mistakes.

Online scams such as phishing try to capitalize on how overwhelmed and mentally vulnerable people are when they're on the Internet. The goal of a phishing scam is to get a distracted person to quickly send their log-in info to someone pretending to be their boss or a representative from their bank without a second thought.[22] Often, the messages sent by scammers are designed to make the recipients panic, telling them that they've been hacked or that their bank account was compromised, and therefore they must e-mail their password to the phisher ASAP. Research shows that when people are distracted or overloaded, they're less likely to notice that someone is lying to them and worse at evaluating the quality or trustworthiness of information thrown their way.[23] Ironically, we might be at the greatest risk of falling for "fake news" when we're habitually consuming too much information.

———

According to Pew, 20 percent of Americans report feeling anxious and overloaded by how much information is available online.[24] However, 77 percent say they actually *like* having access to as much information as they do. This makes sense when we remember the research showing that smartphones (and access to the Internet) make people feel powerful. Most of us feel strongly tempted to learn as much as possible, to avail ourselves of all the stimulation and power the Internet has

> By trying to cram too much knowledge into our minds, we destroy our ability to make sense of, or hold on to, any of it.

to offer. But in order for us to engage with information meaningfully, we have to set limits on how much of it we take in.

Setting Information Limits

Exposure to the wrong type of information can actually cause a trauma response. Social workers, therapists, and the loved ones of assault victims often suffer from something called "secondary trauma," a post-traumatic stress response that results from hearing about another person's experiences of abuse, assault, or violence.[25] It turns out that you don't have to experience a violent act firsthand in order to be severely affected by it. The Internet, sadly, is rife with opportunities for secondary trauma. Videos of shootings, interviews with victims of natural disasters, and distressing graphs of the lives lost to disease can show up just about anywhere. While it's important to know that these problems exist, relentlessly encountering images of them can do us a lot of harm.

Nimisire, the sexual health advocate I discussed in chapter three, told me that she mutes words like "rape" and "sexual assault" from her Twitter feed so she doesn't have to engage with posts about those topics. Even though a key part of her work is educating people about sexual consent and rape culture, she knows it's not productive to fight constantly with anyone who posts something ignorant online.

"Sometimes you have to walk away from the messages that are disturbing," she says. "I can't see all of it. And I can't fight with all of it, you know. I know that in my advocacy work, I'm already doing so much."

Nimisire has reached a key point of realization. She knows it's not her job to read every post and fight with every sexist pig on the Internet. It's not even her job to talk to every assault victim posting about their trauma. The world is huge, and everywhere we turn, some horrific injustice is occurring. We can't engage with all of it, and we don't need to feel guilty or "lazy" for refusing to try. We deserve to give ourselves credit for all the hard work we're already doing.

The way the Internet and social media currently work, it's very easy to get pulled into a constant state of agitation and fear. In order to overcome the heavy informational burden that most of us are saddled with, we have to set limits. At first, taking these steps may feel like plugging your ears and ignoring the cruelty of the world; it may look like apathy or laziness. But remember, laziness does not exist. It's sustaining and self-protective to know our limits. It helps us reorient toward our true priorities. When we focus on the things that we really care about and reduce exposure to things that needlessly hurt us, we become more effective, healthy advocates. If you're struggling with information overload and aren't sure how to dial it back, here are some good places to start.

Use Filtering and Muting Tools

Almost every social media app has a mute function. On Twitter, you can hide any post that contains words or phrases of your choosing, as well as muting individual people. On Facebook, you can mute words and phrases or "unfollow" friends who post upsetting or irritating content. On social media, I have certain anti-LGBTQ+ slurs blocked, as well as the names of a few right-wing bigots whose transphobic comments often make the news. I do a lot to fight transphobia and educate the benignly ignorant. I don't have to fight online with people who wish I didn't exist.

For sites that don't have their own built-in muting function, there are apps you can download that perform a similar function. Sadblock filters and hides news articles about triggering or disturbing topics such as sexual assault.[26] More generic apps like CustomBlocker can be programmed to hide any content that a particular person wants to avoid, whether it's fat-shaming ads for weight-loss products or articles about Donald Trump.[27] All of these tools can easily be toggled on and off, so you can get a brief update on a challenging topic and then hide posts for the rest of the day.

Block Whoever You Need to (and Don't Feel Bad about It)

Sometimes the source of the overload isn't a word or a phrase, it's a person. I had to "unfollow" Noah for a while because he was posting too

> When we focus on the things that we really care about and reduce exposure to things that needlessly hurt us, we become more effective, healthy advocates.

many news articles. I've also blocked friends who get into constant online arguments, including people I agree with on most issues. Even if someone is fighting for the "right" causes, it can be disturbing to watch them constantly butting heads and spreading anger around.

One of the therapists that I spoke to, Louise Dimiceli-Mitran, often helps clients set boundaries on their information consumption. She also recommends blocking people who fight online a lot, or who share a ton of distressing material. She's applied this advice to her own life as well.

"I just went through my own social media, deleting and unsubscribing from things," she tells me. "Now, on Facebook, I get articles from other music therapists, and that's it. And that's what I use it for. Sometimes you have to say, *This is my space and I need it to be clean.*"

People often worry that blocking a friend or acquaintance is "rude," the equivalent of giving them the silent treatment in real life. But when we follow someone on social media, we get exposed to their thoughts and posts throughout the day, often during our private moments and downtime. You don't have a responsibility to let your coworker into your house to rant to you about politics at midnight. You don't have a social obligation to fill your mind with tirades, online fights, and images of war, illness, and environmental collapse at all hours.

Skim the Headlines, and Then Move On

Another step Dimiceli-Mitran recommends is reading the news in a surface-level way. Rather than absorbing every fact about every story as it develops, she suggests merely skimming the news each day to get a general sense of what's going on. After you know the broad strokes of what's happening, you should move on and focus on your own life.

"I encourage people to just, you know, read the headline," Louise says, "and unless it's about a topic that you're really involved with, just do that. Just go, *Okay, I know what's going on; now I'm going to go do my work.*"

Of course, we all have issues that are especially close to our hearts. Even though I've blocked transphobic bigots on Twitter, I do want to be well-informed on issues related to trans people's rights and safety. For those situations, Louise suggests making a "deep dive" on a couple of topics at most; the ones a person has the time and energy to actually address.

"I recommend to people that if you have something that really touches you, some issue that really matters to you—maybe it's climate change, maybe it's domestic violence—whatever it is, you focus on the one or two things that really touch you, and then get involved with addressing those things."

This advice reduces the amount of information a person has to take in. It also addresses the problem of bad news making us feel helpless. If we direct our energy and attention to only a handful of issues and also take proactive steps to address those issues in the real world, we can begin to feel less overwhelmed. By focusing on the small fires that we can help put out with our own activism, we can stop feeling that the world is a constantly blazing garbage fire.

Resist Comment-Section Culture

Comment sections are popular. They capture a lot of interest and clicks. A survey by the Engaging News Project found that 53.3 percent of Americans regularly write online comments on news stories and read the comments other people leave.[28] Yet despite the popularity of comment sections, many people report finding them to be aggravating, stressful spaces.

Comment sections exist because they increase traffic to a website and boost loyalty to a site's brand.[29] If a news article has no comment section, the average person will only ever visit that article one time to read it. However, when an article has a comment section below it, the same people may return to that page dozens of times, checking for new comments, replying to people, and maybe even getting swept up in an hours-long Internet fight. Every time someone returns to the article to leave a new comment, they're giving the site a new page view. More page views means higher advertising revenue. As a result, most sites have a vested interest in stirring up controversy with outlandish "clickbait" headlines, getting tons of outraged comments and letting commenters fight with one another for hours on end.

Most people report that they leave comments in order to express how they're feeling, not to learn from other people or to be persuaded.[30] People like Noah and me get pulled into meaningless Internet fights at times, but it almost never results in our learning anything new or reaching anybody who wants to be educated. Comment sections are designed to manipulate our emotions; they encourage compulsive, angry use. So stop looking at them, and start having private, one-on-one conversations with people you disagree with instead. If you really want to make a strong point, write an essay or a post of your own; don't give attention to people who just want to make others incensed. If that proves difficult, there are apps like Shut Up: Comment Blocker, which hide the comments section of most sites.[31]

Don't Read the News before Bed

Research shows that excessive news watching (particularly coverage of traumatic events) is linked to an increase in anxiety symptoms.[32] The same is true of online news consumption; frequent exposure increases fear and distorts a person's perceptions of how dangerous their surroundings are.[33] These findings have led some wellness experts, such as clinical professor of internal medicine Andrew Weil, to recommend taking regular "news fasts."[34] According to Weil, a news fast should last between a few days and a week. During the fast period, a person should try to focus on their present reality and sur-

> **Most sites have a vested interest in stirring up controversy with outlandish "clickbait" headlines, getting tons of outraged comments and letting commenters fight with one another for hours on end.**

roundings. What Louise Dimiceli-Mitran recommends is a bit more tempered, and perhaps a bit easier to pull off: just don't read the news before bed. After all, there's nothing you can do to address a social problem while you're lying anxious in bed.

"I just don't think it's healthy to constantly know all the details of everything bad that's going on in the world," Louise says. "And the details are so ugly lately. I think they've always been, but we didn't always have access to the kinds of information that we have now."

In some ways, the concept of a news fast reminds me of Fred Bryant's research on dampening happiness. Worrying constantly about worst-case scenarios that may or may not come to pass is a surefire way to distract us from enjoying our present lives. It's much healthier for a person to live in the current moment and focus their attention on information that's truly useful to them and the local problems they can address.

Consume Less Information, More Meaningfully

When we first encounter a new fact or idea, our brains review it in a very surface-level way.[35] In my field, social psychology, it's often said that the first step to understanding something is assuming it's true. We tend to be a bit gullible and uncritical when we're first introduced to a new idea. It's only by taking the time to reflect on new knowledge that we can really make deeper sense of it.

When we spend time carefully pondering information, we're able to reevaluate our preexisting opinions, discover the holes in someone's argument, or see a familiar idea in a completely new light. Researchers sometimes call this process "elaboration."[36] It takes a lot of energy and attention to elaborate on new information. When a person is distracted, tired, or suffering from serious information overload, they can't really elaborate on anything new.[37]

Taking a slower, more contemplative approach to learning can help us to be more thoughtful and critical, and can help us reduce anxiety. As an educator, I've noticed that when I try to make my students memorize too much information at once, they end up understanding almost none of it. But when I slowly work through a lesson and give people plenty of time to digest it, discuss it, and even challenge it, they can come to comprehend it in a more lasting, personal way. What matters is the quality and intentionality behind our efforts, not how hard we're pushing and pressuring ourselves. Here are a few steps a person can take if they want to consume less information in a more meaningful way.

Practice Active Reading

Active reading is the exact opposite of the frantic doomscrolling so many of us do online. Instead of trying to take in as much information as quickly as you can, you work to slowly and intentionally break down small passages. This increases your odds of meaningfully processing what you've read. I recommend active reading to many of my students, especially the ones who are taking classes after many years away from school, but it's really an invaluable technique that can benefit anybody. Active reading something involves using the following six skills:[38]

1. *Visualize what the text is describing.* After reading a paragraph, sit back and try to create a mental picture of what you've just read. For complex or scientific topics, consider looking up videos or charts to help you visualize the phenomenon being described—or try drawing a chart yourself.

2. *Clarify confusing passages and unfamiliar terms.* Slow down to reread something if it's unclear. Write down words or terms that you don't know, and then take a moment at the end of each page to look up their definitions.

3. *Question the author's assumptions and point of view.* Consider why the writer chose to use the examples they're using. Look at the writer's sources and see if they seem trustworthy. Ponder what the author's goal is for the piece of writing.

4. *Predict what will come next.* At the end of each section, jot down a few thoughts about what you hope the piece will touch on

next. What lingering questions do you have? See if you can anticipate where the author is going.

5. *Connect the writing to things you already know.* Does this piece of writing line up with what you already believed, or does it not? What are some other subjects or topics that it seems relevant to? Who else might find this writing interesting?

6. *Evaluate the qualities of the writing.* Was the writing persuasive? Did you find it easy to follow? Did it seem to represent the facts fairly? Even if you disagree with the author's conclusions, can you understand where they're coming from?

It's easy to get distracted by the constant stream of information that the Internet provides us, and to develop bad reading habits. Like anybody else, I can feel tempted to race through as many articles as possible, cramming my brain with superficial facts I haven't taken the time to really contemplate. If, like me, you sometimes struggle with information overload, you can fall back on these methods to slow down and process things with greater intention.

Have a (Real-Time) Conversation

The Internet provides endless opportunities to argue with other people and to be misunderstood. Too much online arguing can actually make a person less willing to open up to someone they disagree with, because it gives them an overly pessimistic view of how those conversations will go.[39] Experimental research shows that when two people speak privately about a disagreement, they feel much greater satisfaction than when they speak to someone in a public, online venue such as a comment section. They also feel more emotionally close to their conversation partner and are more likely to share personal information.[40] The warmth and emotional complexity

> What matters is the quality and intentionality behind our efforts, not how hard we're pushing and pressuring ourselves.

151

of a real-time conversation can help two people reach common ground when they disagree, and can foster feelings of friendship and mutual respect.

Sam learned this recently when they met up with their sister following a big fight via text message. Sam and their sister often get into spats via text. "I'll tell my sister that it would be nice to see her at my Christmas party," Sam says, "and she'll think I'm being passive-aggressive or sarcastic. Even if I add a smiley face, she'll think I'm doing it to mock her! Then again, I do the exact same thing to her. Every little message gets under my skin."

Despite all the hurt feelings and resentments that have brought tension to their relationship, once the two of them are face-to-face, Sam feels much more at ease. "Once I'm actually looking at my sister and spending time with her, I can't maintain the terrible version of her that I've created in my mind," Sam says. "In real life she apologizes if she says something in a rude way. She laughs when things are awkward in this way that's totally lovable. I can't stay angry at her the way I could if I were texting from miles away, stewing over old arguments."

Taking an online conflict out into the real world can really help defuse tension and clarify confusion. If you can't meet in person, try switching from a "cold" medium, like text, to a "warm" one, such as a video conference. This method has helped me calm down panicked students and fighting coworkers in the past. Like Sam and their sister, most people have a harder time staying angry when they can see and hear the person they're speaking to.

This piece of advice won't work for all conflicts, of course. If I'm fighting online with a Neo-Nazi or someone who believes women are inherently inferior to men, I'm not going to have a better time speaking to them face-to-face. There are some disagreements in which a reasonable peace cannot (or should not) ever be found. But when a disagreement isn't a life-and-death issue and both parties do want to understand each other, speaking in person (or in real time) can do wonders to de-escalate conflict.

Get Comfortable with Not Knowing

The absolute best way to combat the urge to overconsume information is to get comfortable with not knowing everything. In a world poisoned by the Laziness Lie, the pressure to constantly improve ourselves is immense. Many of us want to fill our every waking moment with work, achievement, and the development of new skills. The more we strive to be productive and to improve ourselves, the logic goes, the more value we bring to society. Yet our minds need time to recharge, and our lives are more vibrant and pleasurable when we have time that isn't focused on being productive. On top of all that, it's arrogant and unrealistic for us to expect ourselves to be well-versed in all topics. A much healthier approach is to be humble about our limitations.

On the Internet, we're constantly asked to share our opinion. Twitter, Facebook, and Instagram all entice us to share what we're up to and what we're thinking about. Nearly every website has a comment section, begging us to sound off and share our views. "Comment culture" has taught us to speak more than we listen, to form an opinion based only on a headline, and to rush into conversations when we lack relevant expertise.[41] But we don't have to sound off on every issue under the sun. We can choose to read slowly and think before we speak. As all the research shows, taking a more intentional, open-minded approach to these matters helps a person to experience less stress. It also makes us better citizens and more responsible consumers of information. Knowledge can empower us, but only when we take the time to wield it responsibly.

Focus on What You Can Control

In January of 2020, Noah and I had a fight via e-mail about which steps individual people should take to mitigate climate change. Noah was dismayed by how little his friends and coworkers were willing to alter their lives in order to help the environment.

"I'm so frustrated by this super-pervasive thing I see all over leftie, progressive spaces," he wrote, "of emphasizing over and over that it's too late for individual choices around the environment to matter. I still don't see how that fact absolves us of any responsibility to look at what we could do differently."

I told Noah that I understood why people felt dejected and powerless in the fight against climate change. It's challenging, time-consuming, and expensive to make eco-friendly choices, and even if I commit to an entire lifetime of "green" behaviors, it all could be overridden by the environmental damage a single billionaire does in a day. In addition to that, the news on climate change often makes it seem like a foregone conclusion. Under those circumstances, didn't it make sense that people had checked out from the fight?

"I get it; this is a problem that can't be solved by individual choices," Noah replied. "But my point is that this is the only issue I can think of where people actively *discourage* each other from taking steps to address it."

Noah and I went back and forth on this for a while. He argued that society needed to do more to educate people and to encourage them to behave in ecologically sound ways. I claimed that it would be nearly impossible to motivate people to make changes because the news presented it as this looming, abstract fear no one person had any control over. Eventually we stopped the e-mail thread, because it was getting a bit heated. I walked away from the conversation certain I was right.

Then COVID-19 hit the United States. I was astonished by how rapidly and selflessly the people around me responded. Long before any of them were legally required to, my friends and neighbors started isolating themselves. Local theaters and bars canceled performances in order to reduce crowding. Restaurants began offering free food delivery to elderly people and the newly unemployed. People placed loving but firm pressure on those who refused to socially distance. This swift, expansive response rose up in a matter of days and took effect long before our state and local government started requiring us to isolate.

Like climate change, COVID-19 began as a mostly abstract fear. Like climate change, the virus was terrifying to think about, and we knew serious damage was inevitable. The news presented us with dozens of apocalyptic-seeming projections of how the COVID-19 disaster might play out, just as they do with climate change. Yet individual people rapidly started making responsible, altruistic choices to address the pandemic, despite having spent years doing comparatively little to address climate change. Why?

I think the difference is that with the coronavirus, people felt empowered to make a meaningful choice. As the virus spread, fear ramped up, but so did knowledge about which proactive steps a person could take to minimize disaster. The news coverage of worst-case scenarios, such as how brutally the virus hit Italy, filled people with terror, but the response of countries like South Korea and Taiwan provided crucial, motivating counterexamples. In countries where people took the pandemic seriously, thousands of lives were spared. We weren't just being fed messages of doom, we were also given hope.

Though each of us was terrified by the onslaught of bad news about COVID-19, we also knew where to look for advice about how to respond. The steps we needed to take were clear and feasible, and we knew that everyone else was also taking them. Stay inside. Wear a mask. Deliver groceries to elderly people around you. Keep at least six feet away. This advice was as widely spread by the news media as the doom-and-gloom projections were. Instead of paralyzing us with anxiety, the news called us to action. Most of us gladly answered that call, and found solace in the fact that there were elements of this massive problem we could actually control.

Two weeks into the pandemic, I e-mailed Noah and told him I took back everything I'd said about how hopeless fighting climate change seemed.

"Individuals are capable of coming together and making a difference," I told him. "They just have to believe that their choices matter, and that they're not alone in making them."

Information can be used to motivate and inspire. Knowledge can be shared in a way that encourages critical thought and careful decision making, rather than prejudice and panic. The Internet has gotten us addicted to a constant drip of low-quality information, but we can refuse to be overwhelmed into passivity. It's not "lazy" to draw limits on the amount and type of information we consume. Doing so is actually an essential public service.

CHAPTER SIX

Your Relationships Should Not Leave You Exhausted

Grace complains about her invasive and undermining mother, Sylvia, pretty much constantly. Sylvia is an expert at making her daughter feel small and insecure. She seems to have been a disapproving presence for Grace's whole life. When Grace was excited to become second violin in her city's community orchestra, Sylvia asked when she was going to become first chair. Sylvia sends Grace tons of unasked-for gifts in the mail, often things that Grace has no interest in. She gets angry if her daughter doesn't immediately reach out to thank her for her generosity. Sylvia expects constant praise and affirmation of her goodness as a mother, something that Grace really struggles to provide.

"My mom calls me up whenever she's upset about something," Grace says, "and basically demands that I tell her she was a good mom. She'll bring up a handful of good things she did, like taking the family to Disneyland, and ask me, *Wasn't that a good time? Wasn't I a good mom to you and your siblings?* And if I don't bend over backward trying to praise her, she'll get chilly with me or say something totally cruel."

Sylvia can be extremely difficult to deal with, but she isn't all bad. She works as an oncology nurse and is beloved by her patients and their families. Whenever Grace has a violin performance, Sylvia clears her calendar to fly to Chicago to come see it. When other people are around, Sylvia can seem like a warm, proud mother, showering her talented daughter with praise. On paper, her mother is a caring, giving person—yet whenever Grace interacts with her, she feels like she's been emotionally vampirized.

It reached a low point last summer, just as Grace was starting a new job. Her mother and her thirteen-year-old sister appeared unannounced on her doorstep the morning of Grace's first day of work, saying they'd come to "surprise" her. They were holding luggage.

"I thought I was going to projectile-vomit on them," Grace says. "My mom's standing there, and she obviously thinks she and my sister are going to stay with me, even though they never asked. And she can see on my face that I'm not giving her the, you know, *thrilled* reaction she hoped this surprise was gonna get. She can see I'm not grateful. And so she's already starting to get pissed."

Grace let her mother and sister into her apartment and tried to put on a happy face, but the damage was already done. Her mind was racing with anxiety. How was she going to make it to work on time? Was her roommate going to be upset that they had surprise guests? Sylvia could see it. She'd planned this surprise expecting gratitude and praise, and she wasn't getting it. So, she became furious.

"My mother spent that whole visit fuming on the couch," Grace said. "I tried to make dinner plans with her, I offered to take my sister to the museum, I visited them on my lunch break even though it was a total pain. It didn't matter. Mom decided I was being ungrateful, so she made the whole visit miserable. I had to spend the next, like, three months apologizing to her."

As she's telling me this story, Grace gets a text from her mom. She shows me the screen and sighs, rolling her eyes. Grace recognizes how one-sided and unhealthy her relationship with her mother is. Despite that, she halts our conversation so she can give her mother a call. I watch Grace pace the sidewalk, reassuring her mom that yes, she will be coming home to visit for Thanksgiving, and yes, she really is looking forward to it. She looks visibly pained.

Many of us struggle with unbalanced relationships. We don't know how to say no to someone who expects ridiculous things of us. We try to fix other people's problems because we can't stand to see them upset. We take responsibility for all the household chores because we're afraid to ask our partners or roommates to pull more weight. We give more than we ought to, yet whenever we imagine asking someone else to pick up the slack, we feel terrified.

The Laziness Lie has eroded our sense of healthy boundaries and consent. When we believe hard work is the only true "good" in life, and that we must earn our right to be loved, it becomes hard for us to know how to draw limits, even with the people we love. Just as we struggle to cut back on unfair work demands, we also struggle to back down from social expectations that make us uncomfortable. Often, we're left feeling that we have no right to boundaries at all.

Most of us spend the entire workweek ignoring our body's need for rest and idleness, because the Laziness Lie says our feelings are a source of weakness that shouldn't be trusted. That tendency to ignore our needs can seep into our personal lives too, making us horrible at standing up to the people who leech our energy. We get so good at ignoring our needs that we can't even recognize when a relationship is damaging. We end up repeatedly being exploited and manipulated, rather than being nourished and supported.

As an adult with a few years of therapy under her belt, Grace has come to realize that her mother's behavior is inappropriate. She also recognizes that whenever she speaks to her mother, she feels horrible for hours afterward. However, an entire lifetime of being Sylvia's daughter has made Grace very accustomed to swallowing her words and striving to please. Confronting Sylvia about her bad behavior still seems kind of unthinkable. "My mom raised me, and she put me through college," Grace says. "I can't just throw her away like garbage. I love her."

It's telling that Grace thinks pushing back against her mother would be akin to treating her like garbage. When a person has grown up prioritizing the needs of other people, they often mistakenly believe that it's selfish to have any needs of their own. In her book *Adult Children of Emotionally Immature Parents: How to Heal from Distant, Rejecting, or*

> **The Laziness Lie has eroded our sense of healthy boundaries and consent.**

Self-Involved Parents, psychologist Lindsay C. Gibson writes that children who did not receive adequate care and attention from their parents learn that the only kinds of relationships they deserve to have are unbalanced ones. She writes:

> Emotional loneliness is so distressing that a child who experiences it will do whatever is necessary to make some kind of connection. . . . These children may learn to put other people's needs first as the price of admission to a relationship.[1]

While Gibson's work focuses on child-parent relationships, she notes that these dynamics also play out in romantic partnerships and friendships. When a person believes that the only way to be loved is to please somebody else, they end up in all kinds of overly demanding relationships, forever giving more than they receive and never feeling truly seen.

This is exactly what happened with Grace. She's the only roommate in her four-bedroom apartment who cleans the communal living areas at all. She regularly gives her friends rides across town, spots them money for food and drinks, and spends many evenings listening to her loved ones complain about their problems. There's nothing wrong with these loving gestures, of course, but in Grace's case they aren't reciprocated. She never learned how to ask for the same kind of support she compulsively doles out. She tells me it feels incredibly lonely. As Gibson writes, "Covering up your deepest needs prevents genuine connection with others."

Human beings are interdependent. We need social connections and community in order to thrive, yet many of us live in such deep fear of disappointing other people that we compromise our own values and abandon our well-being in the process. The Laziness Lie actively encourages this painful self-erasure by teaching us that our value is defined by what we can do for other people.

In order to form authentic, safe bonds with others, we must get comfortable with letting other people down. We have to be able to say no in our relationships, just as we must learn to dial back our punishingly heavy workloads and other commitments. Emotional overexertion can be just as damaging as professional overwork. The answer to both is to embrace our authentic needs and to stop worrying that saying no makes us lazy.

Dealing with a Demanding Family

Like Grace, Bryan constantly feels pressured by his parents to give them vast quantities of time and attention. Whenever he gets a day off from his high-stress job as a research chemist, his parents expect him to fly home to visit them. Over the years, this has put a ton of stress on his marriage. He and his wife, Stephanie, haven't taken a vacation together as a couple in years. Bryan's parents even demanded that his wedding take place in their hometown several states away instead of in St. Louis, where the couple now lives. Recently, Stephanie reached a breaking point.

"She blurted out at me, *You're married to your parents, not me,*" Bryan says. "And she brought up all these times that I'd dropped whatever I was doing to go help my parents out, even if that meant leaving her behind."

Initially, Bryan felt very defensive. Stephanie is a white woman from a midwestern family, and her relatives have entirely different expectations than Bryan's Korean-American family does. The first few times that Stephanie complained about Bryan's family being overly demanding, he chalked it up to cultural differences that she didn't grasp. Over time, though, he has begun to question whether some of her complaints are valid.

"There's probably a middle ground I could try to strike," Bryan says. "I want to be there for my parents and show that I love them and will always be there for them, but at the same time, I've literally never said no to them or taken space. So maybe it's time to cut the cord a little bit."

———

Kathy Labriola is a counselor based in the San Francisco Bay Area. For decades she's treated clients who work themselves into a frenzy trying to meet the needs of other people. "A lot of people are addicted to approval," she says. "I think most women are, but it's not just women who do it. A lot of people seek out situations that feed into that need they have to feel useful to other people."

Since the 1980s, Kathy has worked to help clients develop assertiveness and reshape unbalanced relationships. Most of the advice she gives consists of relatively small, subtle steps a person can take to gradually reduce their level of commitment to another person. These steps aren't dramatic or cathartic; there's no big moment when her patients confront the friends and family who've berated them all their lives. Instead, Kathy's recommended steps are all about replacing old, ineffective patterns with better ones. Sharon Glassburn takes a similar view, and also recommends that her clients change their relationship dynamics in a gradual way. "People sometimes expect these big moments of big conflict," she says, "but usually building boundaries with a loved one comes down to more mundane steps, and they take time."

Overall, the advice that both Sharon and Kathy give to their clients consists of three broad strokes: challenge expectations that the person has for you, practice disappointing the person, and keep repeating your no, over and over again, even if it makes you feel like a broken record.

Clear Up Expectations

Overly demanding people often assume that you'll meet their needs without ever saying so outright. When a client of hers is caught in a relationship with someone like that, Sharon recommends sitting down with the challenging person and making their expectations explicit. "So often we go into a relationship with unspoken ideas of what to expect from the other person," she says. "And sometimes even just naming what they're asking you for can make a big difference."

In Bryan's case, this involved actually telling his parents that their demands were too extreme. "I had to tell them that not all of my coworkers traveled home to see their parents every time they had a long weekend," he says. "That didn't change what my parents wanted from me, but it did help me explain why I couldn't visit them so often anymore. And it made me feel more like I was being a reasonable person."

In friendships, it's rare for people to have explicit conversations about what they want and what they're able to give to the other person, but Sharon says laying those things bare can clear up a lot of conflicts. It can also illustrate when two people are at an impasse. "Sometimes it can really help to sit down together and just talk about *What do you expect from me? What do I need from you?*" she tells me.

If you find that a person's expectations or needs are overly large or simply aren't a good fit, you can begin to cut back on your commitments to them.

Warn the Person That You'll Be Pulling Back

Kathy Labriola recommends giving your loved one a heads-up that things are about to change. This warning doesn't have to be confrontational; in fact, it doesn't even have to be honest. Sometimes it works better if you soften the blow with an excuse.

"I suggest that people tell their family members they're going through something and that they're going to be less available," Kathy says. "That way you're giving them some advanced warning that it's nothing personal, you just won't be able to do as much for them as you have in the past."

For many people, an effective excuse to fall back on is busyness. Sometimes, the only limit people can fully understand is one created by work. So if you're dealing with someone who does not respect your emotional boundaries, you can actually leverage the language of busyness in order to get away with doing less.

This tactic was effective for Bryan. His parents didn't respect his needs or the needs of his wife, but they did respect his high-pressure job. So, he learned to use it to his advantage. "If I don't have the energy to talk to them one day, I just tell them I'm having a late night at work," he says. "Once, I told them I had a work conference, when really Stephanie and I went camping. If I use my job as the reason I'm pulling back, they don't get mad, and they don't take it personally as much."

> You can actually leverage the language of busyness in order to get away with doing less.

Say No to Small Things

It takes time to retrain a person and adjust their expectations. It also takes time to train *ourselves* to stop reflexively saying yes so much. Kathy finds it's often most effective to begin with small refusals, particularly ones that won't blow up into a huge conflict. "Start by saying no to small things," she says, "because those are easier and the consequences are less. Start to notice when [the demanding person] asks for something small, like getting a ride to the airport, and just start to say no to some of those things."

This step combines very well with the previous piece of advice. If you've already warned the demanding person that you have a lot on your plate and can't be as available for them as you once were, you'll have an explanation to fall back on if they become upset. Over time, you can begin to increase what you're capable of saying no to. It makes for great self-advocacy practice.

Grace was desperately in need of self-advocacy practice, if she was ever going to resist her mom's manipulations. Her therapist suggested she try disappointing a loved one at least once per week—so that's exactly what she did. It started out small, but it helped her recognize which of her friends were really there for her.

"Some people disappeared on me the second I stopped giving them free rides and going out of my way to be there for them," she says. "But other people stepped up their game. I told my friend Phil I couldn't pick him up every time he wanted to hang out, and he immediately started taking Lyfts to my house. Just like it was nothing. That told me he really wanted to spend time with me even when I wasn't doing all of the work to make it happen."

With other relationships, though, the change was not as seamless. In those situations, Grace had to learn to stand strong and reassert her needs and limits as often as necessary.

Don't Be Afraid to Be a Broken Record

When you enforce a new boundary with someone, they'll tend to push back against it. In order to hold firm, you may have to say no and provide your standard excuse over and over (and over) again. "I call it the broken-record technique," Kathy says. "You just have to keep telling them the same thing over again. Eventually, they'll get the message. But it takes time. You can't expect a person to adapt immediately when you've been behaving a different way with them for your whole life."

Kathy has been through this process herself, with a younger sister who used to expect Kathy to baby her and take care of her. After decades of always rushing to help her sister out and meet her every need, Kathy realized she had to dial things back. "About twenty years ago I started changing that relationship," she says. "And it took *years*. I'd been giving in to my sister's manipulations for, like, forty years or something, so I couldn't expect her to just be fine with it the first time I said no. Her belief was that I'm supposed to do everything for her. And why wouldn't she believe that? That's how it had been."

Now, two decades later, Kathy's sister doesn't manipulate her or demand excessive support the way she once did. Bryan is at a much earlier stage of the process. He started refusing his parents this year. But he's starting to see gradual growth too. "This year my mom asked me what my and Stephanie's plans were for Christmas," he says, smiling a bit, "instead of wanting to know which day we'd be arriving at their house. Which maybe doesn't sound incredible to you, but that's huge. They asked. They didn't assume."

This doesn't mean Bryan's work is over, of course. His parents still regularly want to have hours-long chats with him on the phone or ask him to share more about his life than he's comfortable with. When those moments come, he falls back on the broken-record technique. "I just have to keep telling them *Sorry, I'm busy, but I love you so much*," he says.

Lightening the Invisible Load

Riley's marriage to Tom was nearly destroyed by a pile of cardboard boxes.

"He never picks up after himself unless I tell him to," she says about her spouse. "And, frankly, having to ask him every single time is demoralizing. It's not my job!"

Riley's been with Tom since college. Over the years the two had fallen into an uncomfortable yet all-too-common pattern. They both worked all day, Riley as a public-school elementary teacher and Tom at a science museum. At the end of the day, Riley would make time to tidy up the house, picking up empty food containers, sweeping the dirt by the front door, and throwing socks in the laundry. Tom would just flop onto the couch and play *Minecraft*.

One evening, Riley came home late and found that Tom had left a pile of boxes on the kitchen counter. A bunch of Amazon orders had come in that day, and he'd torn open their packaging and left them in a heap.

"I decided I was going to test him," Riley says. "I wanted to see how long he would just let the boxes sit there if I didn't say anything about them."

For weeks, Riley didn't say a thing about the boxes—and Tom didn't touch them. When more mail came in, Tom threw it on top of the pile. Dust accumulated on the boxes, but he didn't seem the least bit bothered by it. A month passed. The counter had gotten so dirty that it was unusable. Tom started prepping his meals on the coffee table in the living room instead.

Two and a half months into the experiment, Riley came home and saw Tom chopping vegetables in front of the TV, broccoli florets falling onto the carpet, the boxes still piled up in the kitchen. She snapped.

"I screamed at him; I said horrible things," she tells me, "stuff I'm still having to apologize for. And when I told him that the boxes, the *fucking boxes*, were the reason I was so upset, all he said was, *Well, why didn't you tell me?*"

———

Riley spent years silently suffering through what researchers call the "second shift": the hours of cleaning and tidying that women typically perform when they get home from work.[2] Women often suffer from an unspoken yet powerful pressure to look after the house, keep track of their family's to-do list, and run countless household errands, while the men in their lives do comparatively little.[3] Like Riley, many women spend all day keep-ing a running mental log of household responsibilities that need to get done, while the men who live with them seem to be completely unaware that there even *is* a list that's forever growing and must be dealt with. When women confront male partners about this imbalance, the common reply is the infuriating "Well, you should have asked me for help."[4]

The second shift isn't exclusive to romantic relationships. Grace did all of the cleaning in her apartment because her roommates (three straight men) couldn't be bothered to chip in. And this phenomenon expands way beyond the home. In professional settings, women take the lion's share of the social and domestic work: cleaning out the office refrigerator, buying the cake when a coworker has a birthday, and making sure meetings are up-to-date on the company's communal calendar. In academia, women faculty members are nearly always the people who organize and lead com-mittees, schedule events, and mentor struggling students.[5] When men don't perform their fair share of this work, women tend to pick up the slack. It's very difficult for most women, who've been indoctrinated by the Laziness Lie and decades of living under sexism, to consider that they deserve to let those responsibilities drop and to be as selfish as the men around them.

Mandy is a professor at a university in Indiana. Recently, she told me her dean berated her for spending hours in her office each week, speaking with students who weren't "high achievers." Many of them were at risk of flunking out, and she was providing them a necessary confidence boost, as well as practical tips for succeeding in college.

"The dean told me I was wasting time I could have spent doing my job," she says. "I had to tell him, *This* is *my job*."

Though supporting students is, in theory, the role of a professor, help-ing them was unlikely to earn Mandy any awards or get her any publica-tions. Yet she saw it as a necessary duty, both because she cared about these students and because her male colleagues had failed to provide their fair share of mentoring. As a result, first-generation college stu-dents, students with learning disabilities, and anybody else who was having a tough time always knocked on Mandy's door, not anyone else's.

This imbalance of power and responsibility gets even worse when you take into account other isms, such as racism, and transphobia. Transgender women, for example, often feel an even more intense pressure to perform domestic labor than cisgender women do. Rebekah explains it this way:

> If a cisgender woman decides to fight the power and say, *Hey, I'm not doing all the household chores anymore*, it's a feminist act. But if I refuse to do those "womanly" activities as a trans woman, people go, *Oh, you're so entitled and lazy—you're acting like a man.*

Race is also interwoven into this issue. Black and brown women tend to take on even more invisible labor at their jobs than white women do.[6] They also expend a great deal more energy monitoring how they speak and act, because even the smallest expression of displeasure can get them labeled angry or rude.[7] In academia, men of color do much more committee work and "service" than white men do. Their time is seen as less valuable, and people expect them to do the thankless work women are also expected to do.[8] People of color are also expected to head diversity initiatives, run inclusion committees, and spend time educating their white coworkers about racial bias, typically with no additional compensation.

The Laziness Lie loves to blame victims for their own oppression. It tells us that if a person wants to succeed in the face of bigotry, all they have to do is work harder than everyone else, and attend to their own needs even less. It's a toxic mindset that can erode their mental and physical health, as well as their sense of boundaries. There are, however, steps a person can take to slowly reduce the amount of invisible, undervalued work they reflexively take.

Track How You Spend Your Time

Kathy Labriola recommends that her clients take stock of how much time they throw away doing work that goes unappreciated. "I ask them to keep very careful track of how they spend their time, at least for a couple of weeks," she says, "even if it's just thirty seconds here, a minute there, so they can see how it all adds up."

Kathy finds that her most exhausted, stressed-out clients spend hours every day doing chores, answering nonurgent messages, updating group calendars, and gener-

> The Laziness Lie tells us that if a person wants to succeed in the face of bigotry, all they have to do is work harder than everyone else.

ally taking care of the needs of other people. They often don't realize how much time gets spent doing these things. All they notice is the nagging sense that they never have enough time to do everything they're supposed to be doing. By keeping track of their daily habits for a few weeks, Kathy's clients can step back and see just where all that time is going. Then they can reflect on whether those small, daily choices reflect their real priorities.

Clarify Your Values

Both Kathy Labriola and Sharon Glassburn mentioned asking their overextended clients to sit down and evaluate whether their day-to-day habits actually align with what matters most to them. "Make a list of all the things you do on a regular basis, and see if some of them can be eliminated," Kathy says. "Are they really necessary? Drop activities that aren't nurturing you or bringing something positive into your life."

Sharon Glassburn helps her clients work through these decisions using a worksheet on values clarification:[9] "Values clarification" is a process in which a person examines their choices and actions and asks whether those choices line up with the ideals that matter most to them. Below is the worksheet Sharon uses, with some example values listed:

Values Clarification

Your values are the beliefs that define what is most important to you. They guide each of your choices in life. For example, someone who values family might try to spend extra time at home, while someone who values success in their career may do just the opposite. Understanding your values will help you recognize areas of your life that need more attention, and what to prioritize in the future.

Select your ten most important items from the following list. Rank them from 1 to 10 with "1" being the most important item.

___ Love		___ Honesty	
___ Wealth		___ Humor	
___ Family		___ Loyalty	
___ Morals		___ Reason	
___ Success		___ Independence	
___ Knowledge		___ Achievement	
___ Power		___ Beauty	
___ Friends		___ Spirituality	
___ Free Time		___ Respect	
___ Adventure		___ Peace	
___ Variety		___ Stability	
___ Calmness		___ Wisdom	
___ Freedom		___ Fairness	
___ Fun		___ Creativity	
___ Recognition		___ Relaxation	
___ Nature		___ Safety	
___ Popularity		___ _____	
___ Responsibility		___ _____	

"What I really like about this exercise," Sharon says, "is that it forces a person to step back and decide, even if they care about all of these things, which ones they really want to put first. Because you can't actually have everything—you do have to make choices about how you're going to spend your time."

Rather than scrambling to do it all—maintaining a clean house, doing countless volunteer duties, working long hours, and supporting our friends—we often need to free up our schedules (and our minds) by doing much less. When we say no to the things that aren't the most meaningful to us, we have the capacity to deeply invest in the things that *are* meaningful. That may require offloading some responsibilities onto somebody else.

Let Other People Do the Job Poorly

After the blowup about the cardboard boxes, Riley finally sat down with Tom for an honest conversation about how chores got divided in their household. She learned something kind of surprising about his outlook. "He told me that every time he does something around the house, I complain about the way he did it," she says. "Like, if he doesn't sweep well enough, I'll just go back and do it again. I guess it fed into his sense that, you know, taking care of the house was something I was in charge of, and he was just supposed to follow my lead."

Riley had spent years paying attention to household chores and learning how to do them correctly. For her, it was cringe-inducing to watch Tom stumble through these same tasks poorly. So, she cut in and did them properly, hoping Tom would notice and adapt. Instead, he got the message that he couldn't be trusted with those tasks. Riley had to learn to resist the urge to "save" Tom from his own ineptitude.

With the help of a couples counselor, Riley finally started passing household tasks to her partner. "Now he's in charge of dishes, laundry, and cleaning the bathroom and living room," she tells me. "It's not my job. What I have to work on is not accidentally doing any of it, or telling him how to do it."

Now, if Tom flounders while cleaning, Riley doesn't step in. She'll sit on the patio and read a magazine while he takes twice as long to scrub the bathroom as it would take her. Her inaction might look downright "lazy" to a stranger, but she's proud of having finally learned to let go a bit.

"I had one client who was working a full-time job, raising children, trying to do everything she was supposed to be doing. She told me,

I could either have a life, or have a clean house," Kathy says. "And she decided to have a life."

Coping with Parenting Guilt

It's no coincidence that the client who gave up on having a clean house was a mother to small kids. Parents face perhaps the greatest social pressure to meet others' needs of anyone. There are so many ways to get parenting "wrong," in society's eyes; so many choices that can earn a parent judgment and disdain.[10] This makes an already tiring, demanding responsibility even more anxiety-ridden and grueling. And, once again, the source of this problem is the Laziness Lie.

Competing yet incompatible perspectives on how to do parenting "right" become popular every few years. Every generation of parents finds something new to feel bad about. From about 1920 until the middle of the twentieth century, psychologists such as John B. Watson warned parents not to cuddle or kiss their children and to limit physical contact to a handshake or a pat on the head.[11] Watson claimed that too much affection could make a child weak-willed and soft. In the latter half of the twentieth century, the big parenting fad was attachment parenting, which suggested the exact opposite approach.[12] Suddenly, the fear became that children who *weren't* held and cuddled enough would develop low self-esteem, depression, and tons of other issues. By the 1990s, things flipped again and fear of "helicopter parenting" began to build, and parents started worrying that being too attentive could erode a child's sense of self.[13]

"There is no way to not mess your kids up," says Aiden, a stay-at-home father to three boys.

Aiden is a transgender man, and says he's worried about how to be the best father to his kids since the day he realized he was pregnant. "You can read all these books about what not to do and make yourself sick worrying about it. Even when you're pregnant, you can read all this competing advice—*Don't eat this, don't exercise, no, wait, you* should *exercise*—and you never know if any of it actually matters in the end."

Today's parents are inundated with conflicting advice. "Mommy blogs" and parenting-focused social media accounts dispense endless judgment on issues like breastfeeding, co-sleeping, allowances, and day care. Nearly every choice is highly politicized, from preschool selection to purchasing gender-nonconforming clothes and toys. Many parents report feeling guilty and uncertain about their choices, and fear being socially rejected for failing to raise their kids perfectly.[14] These anxious parents worry that they're not doing enough to set their children up for success; in short, they feel lazy.

Aiden says he used to take all these competing perspectives to heart, and it drove him absolutely batty with worry and self-doubt. His mother-in-law contributed to his anxiety by critiquing everything Aiden did and said as a parent too. "She meant well, but she had all these ideas that were so out of date," he says. "She wanted me to raise my sons in this really stereotypically masculine way—which, as a trans person, I'm just not going to do. But she didn't get it."

Facebook and Instagram gave Aiden's mother-in-law a regular window into his family's life, allowing her to judge him from thousands of miles away. When Aiden posted online about his kids, he'd sometimes get critical comments from total strangers as well.

"I'd share pictures of my kids to private parenting groups," he says, "but even there, other people would tell me what I was doing wrong, how I should have nursed my kids longer, how I needed to sign them up for sports, all this stuff I didn't even ask for anybody's opinion on. Parenting is always kind of solitary, but this made it especially isolating."

Some studies suggest that parenting anxiety is on the rise, due in part to social media use.[15] Yet again, digital tools have made it easier than ever for the Laziness Lie to pursue us, constantly reminding us that there's more we could be doing, and that we're letting people down in an endless variety of ways.

> **Many parents report feeling guilty and uncertain about their choices, and fear being socially rejected for failing to raise their kids perfectly.**

Rather than succumbing to this pressure, Aiden chose to reject it. "By the time you have your second kid, you realize you've screwed up a thousand times, and you're gonna screw up again," he says. "And each time it happens, it terrifies you less. The world doesn't end."

Instead of aiming to be a flawless dad, Aiden decided to embrace just being "good enough." It turns out that research suggests "good enough" is a great goal.

Be Just "Good Enough"

In the 1980s, developmental psychologists started embracing the concept of the "good-enough parent."[16] After generations of passing down rigid rules for how a parent (usually a mother) was supposed to behave, researchers began to realize that parenting perfection didn't really exist. Every parent had flaws, and trying to eradicate those flaws didn't work. Instead, parents coped better if they entirely abandoned the hope of being perfect.

According to developmental psychology, the good-enough parent provides their child with love, shelter, and adequate food; they make mistakes, but nothing that causes their children significant trauma.[17] They don't obsess over society's ideas of what a parent "should" be doing; instead, they find a balance between their own needs and the unique traits and passions of their child.

For Aiden, being a good-enough dad means cutting some corners. "We eat a lot of microwaved chicken tenders in this house, and sometimes I'll put the kids to bed early without a bath," he says, laughing. "My mother-in-law would hate to hear that. But my kids are happy, healthy little goblins, and my husband and I actually have time to have sex once in a while."

Embrace Mistakes

A key feature of the good-enough parent is that they don't beat themselves up when they make a mistake; instead, they try to make amends for it and learn from the experience. Research suggests that it's the comfortable, self-accepting imperfection of the good-enough parent that helps a child learn how to deal with life's inevitable setbacks and disappointments.[18]

Another parent I spoke to, Emily, openly discusses her mistakes with her daughter. One of her biggest mistakes was engaging in corporal punishment. "I used to think spanking was good discipline," she tells me. "That's how I was raised. But then I learned all about the research that it's just bad, it just doesn't work. My daughter's twelve now, and we've talked about it. I told her, *Here's why I used to think that was okay, and here's why I stopped.*"

When parents discuss mistakes with their children, they create an open line of communication that makes the relationship more resilient and capable of growth. Research also suggests that parents who are comfortable with making mistakes are more accepting of their children's flaws and screwups as well.[19]

Live Your Own Life

Famed couples counselor Esther Perel has frequently written that in order for parents to maintain their own mental health and sense of identity, they must make time to pursue hobbies and social activities that have nothing to do with their kids.[20] This can benefit the children in a direct way: when parents choose to detach a bit from their parenting role, they give their children the freedom to entertain themselves and find their own passions.[21]

Aiden put this principle into practice a few years ago, shortly after his middle child was born. Though having two children left him busier than ever before, he made a conscious choice to carve out time for one of his favorite activities: rock climbing.

"I told my husband, *Look, I'm gonna start climbing again, and, like, one weekend a month, I want to go out to the*

> The good-enough parent doesn't beat themselves up when they make a mistake; instead, they try to make amends for it and learn from the experience.

state parks and go up some cliffs," he says. "And my husband was like, *Okay, I'm going to start scheduling Dungeons & Dragons sessions with my friends too."*

Years later, both Aiden and his husband still make regular time for their hobbies. When their plans overlap, they hire a babysitter, and try not to feel guilty about it.

"Sometimes one of the boys will be sick, and one of us will go, *Oh, I should cancel my plans and stay with them,"* Aiden says. "And in those moments one of us will correct the other and go, *Look, it's good for the family to do what's good for ourselves.* And usually that helps."

Setting Limits with Exhausting Friends

Years ago, I had a friend named Ethan. We met online, on a forum for fans of the show *Mad Men.* I loved the dark wit Ethan brought to his weekly reviews of the show's episodes. Our online conversations evolved into a friendship, and a few years later, Ethan moved to Chicago to take a new job.

Once he arrived in Chicago, Ethan's behavior changed. He hated his job, and quickly became depressed. He had no other friends in town and became reliant on me for social contact and emotional support. He started telling me about abuse he had endured as a child, often going into upsetting detail. He complained about his boss and said his life looked hopeless. Eventually he started talking about suicide.

I didn't want Ethan to hurt himself. I felt responsible for his well-being. After all, he'd moved to Chicago knowing nobody else but me! If I didn't listen to him pouring his heart out, nobody would, so I did everything I could to help. I'd talk to him late into the night, reassuring him that his life had meaning and that he should keep going. I researched therapists in his area and created a list of providers I thought would be a good fit for him. I searched for jobs he could apply to and sent them his way. I had a social-worker friend call him up and work through solutions with him.

One night, Ethan was caught in a deep, depressive spiral, and kept texting me the same words, over and over: "I don't have any hope. I don't have any hope. I don't have any hope."

"Ethan, I'm so sorry," I wrote back. "I don't know what to say. Did any of the therapists I recommended look like a good fit?"

"All a therapist would do is tell me to look on the bright side or do yoga or something," he replied grimly. "That's not going to help me."

I kept encouraging him to get additional help. My support was clearly not enough, I told him.

"To be honest," Ethan replied, "I haven't even opened up the list you sent me."

In that moment, I realized I was trying harder to help Ethan than he was trying to help himself. I felt so used and underappreciated that I stopped talking to him right then and there. I was furious at Ethan, but even more disappointed in myself.

———

The Laziness Lie has fundamentally warped our sense of boundaries, making many of us believe that other people's problems are ours to solve. It tells us that if we care for someone, we have to suffer to help them. Unfortunately, we can't actually fix another person's problems. So, we end up frustrated and run-down, realizing we've been pouring energy into helping someone who can't (or won't) meet us halfway. Kathy Labriola works with a lot of clients who struggle with this.

"It's a wonderful impulse, to try to help people," she says. "But it can also become a compulsion some people have to always run in and help, without even asking if they're the person who should be doing it, or if there's anything they can do to help."

The Laziness Lie guilts us into taking on responsibilities that aren't ours to carry. Before we get wrapped up in yet another dramatic, ill-fated attempt to "save" someone, we ought to ask ourselves if another person's problems truly warrant our involvement, and if so, which *kinds* of involvement. From there, we can begin breaking out of the insecure, approval-seeking patterns that make us throw away hours of effort trying to help a person who isn't receptive to that help.

Determine Whether You Should Help, and How Much

When Kathy has a client who struggles with emotional overcommitment, she presents them with a series of questions that are designed to help them reflect on whether being involved is their responsibility. Here are those questions, followed by some alternative methods of addressing the problem that don't involve trying to "fix" the situation.

Questions to Ask before Trying to "Save" Someone:
Can they solve this on their own?
Do they want help?
Do they want *my* help?
Am I the right person to provide help right now?
Can I direct them to seek help from a professional or a close loved one?
What are my motives for helping?
What will helping cost me?

These questions point to how many people reflexively attempt to "help" others in ways that are excessive, unrealistic, or even downright invasive.

"I see clients take up all these caregiving responsibilities for someone who's just a casual acquaintance," Kathy says, "and suddenly they'll become a major support person in this near-stranger's life. And I'm like, *You barely even know this person!*"

If I had stopped to ask myself these questions about Ethan, I would have realized that his depression and trauma history weren't issues I could solve, and involving myself so deeply in his life was wildly inappropriate. Ethan needed to seek out therapy himself, when he was ready. I'd wasted hours making a list of therapists for him when that wasn't what he wanted. What he wanted was for me to be on call to support him twenty-four seven. I could have spared myself and Ethan a lot of frustration if I'd refused to give in to that oversized expectation. It never occurred to me to draw those types of boundaries. At the time, I was too addicted to being "useful" to other people.

Ask Yourself Why You're Trying to Help

A few months later, I listened to an episode of the advice podcast *Dear Prudence* and heard something that knocked me right on my ass. One of the advice-seekers in the episode was caught up in a very one-sided friendship with their next-door neighbor. This person provided their neighbor with free babysitting, groceries, and tons of emotional support. The neighbor had never so much as thanked them for their generosity. The advice-seeker felt resentful, burned out, and taken advantage of. They wanted to know what Prudence, aka Danny M. Lavery, thought they ought to do.

Danny's response began with a few practical tips about how to deflect the needy neighbor's requests. But then he went deeper and challenged the letter writer to ponder why they had felt so compelled to do thankless, unnecessary work for someone who was barely even their friend. *Do you believe that if you take care of enough people,* Danny mused, *eventually someone will notice and finally decide to take care of you?*

Danny's question might as well have been directed at me. The Laziness Lie had browbeaten me into hiding every vulnerability and need and left me obsessed with proving my worth to other people. I couldn't imagine asking for emotional support or care. Whenever I felt lonely or sad, I would try to boost my mood by helping somebody else. I had always secretly hoped that somebody would notice how hard I was working and approach me out of the blue, saying, *Oh, you poor thing, you've already done so much. Let me take care of you.*

Kathy Labriola recommends that people ask themselves why they want to help people in need, and what they expect to get out of helping. "We all

> I had always secretly hoped that somebody would notice how hard I was working and approach me out of the blue, saying, *Oh, you poor thing, you've already done so much. Let me take care of you.*

have a mix of healthy and unhealthy motives for doing things," she says, "and that's okay. But you do want to get a sense of what the ratio is there."

In other words, it's normal to have somewhat selfish motives for helping other people. None of us is perfectly altruistic. But if you find yourself compulsively helping other people in a desperate bid to win their approval, it's time to dial back your commitments. In particular, you should disengage from enmeshed, unfair relationships in which you don't feel appreciated, and in which interactions leave you feeling used up or taken advantage of.

Stop Rewarding Inappropriate Behavior

In his book *How to Deal with Emotionally Explosive People*, the psychologist Albert J. Bernstein discusses how providing tons of mental-health support to demanding friends can create a self-defeating feedback loop. If you're always there to help your friends feel better when they're down, you may accidentally train them to rely on you in order to feel better. Instead of using their own resources and problem-solving abilities to address their problems, they may begin to feel that they *need* you to fix things for them. "The things that make people feel better the quickest," Bernstein writes, "usually make them do worse."[22]

This was exactly what happened with Ethan and me. When Ethan was feeling suicidal and hopeless, he should have called a mental-health crisis hotline, a therapist, or someone he was genuinely close with. But because I was always there, ready to listen for hours to his every complaint, he learned that I was the place to go with all his concerns. Without meaning to, I had trained him to avoid taking proactive steps to improve his life and instead develop a reliance on me.

When faced with a distressed person, many of us feel tempted to do all we can to help. But often, our best attempts at helping can harm everyone involved. There's a huge distinction between providing help and being someone's sole crutch or unofficial therapist. By refusing to take on responsibilities that don't belong to us, we can empower an unhappy person to troubleshoot their own problems. They won't be happy that we've refused to rescue them, but they'll usually be much better off in the long run.

In his book, Bernstein describes several reasonable, productive forms of help that compulsive "helpers" can use to replace the more intense enmeshments they're used to.

Instead of:	Try This:[23]
Offering solutions to a person's problems	Ask them how they will solve it: "What do you plan to do?"
Trying to make a person's bad feelings go away	Let the person express their feelings without trying to change them.
Letting a person vent, cry, or rant for hours without resolution	Listen supportively, but suggest a distraction or a break when the person gets "stuck" fixating on the problem.
Listening while a person spirals into greater and greater anxiety, sadness, or rage	Interrupt them when they start to repeat themselves or escalate. "Let's focus on the present situation right now."
Trying to guess what the person wants	Make them clarify expectations: "What would you like me to do?"
Providing more support than you're comfortable with	Identify other sources of support: "Who else can help with this?"
Taking responsibility for the person's situation	Deflect responsibility: "I'm flattered that you care what I think, but you're the expert on what's best for you."

If I had responded to Ethan's panic by taking the steps on the right instead of those on the left, our friendship might not have taken the toxic, parasitic turn it did. I saw Ethan's suicidality as something I had to make go away. Every time I tried to take charge of the problem by telling him to call specific therapists or apply to specific new jobs, I robbed him of even more agency.

After I stopped providing Ethan with boundless emotional support, he had no choice but to reflect on how he was going to solve his own problems. Months after we stopped talking, a mutual friend told me that he had a new job he liked and roommates who enjoyed spending time with him. By setting myself free of Ethan's unrealistic demands, I inadvertently liberated us both. It wasn't "lazy" or uncaring for me to detach from the relationship. We both needed me to.

When we stop struggling to meet other people's expectations, we can finally begin to see ourselves and our own values clearly. And when we begin to challenge the demands that individual people place on us, we become better able to cast off the massive, far-reaching ones that society imposes on us as well.

> **When we stop struggling to meet other people's expectations, we can finally begin to see ourselves and our own values clearly.**

CHAPTER SEVEN

Shrugging Off Society's "Shoulds"

I've already found a few excuses for talking about *Mad Men* in this book, but please indulge me one last time. The show does a fantastic job of illustrating the pressure to conform that has always haunted the American workplace. Peggy, the ad agency's first female copywriter, has to learn to overcome her colleagues' sexism by talking, writing, and even dressing more like a man.[1] Rather than fighting sexism head-on, she learns to cope by following its "rules" by never being too emotional, too feminine, or too sexy. Similarly, the agency's first Black employee, Dawn, has to project a persona of unassuming cheeriness so people don't find her "angry" or threatening.[2] Even the show's white male lead, Don Draper, has to hide every sign of his upbringing as a poor child of hillbillies. His history doesn't line up with the "professional" image he's cultivated, so it has to be buried under a mask of middle-class, white-male conformity.

As the descendant of Appalachian hillbillies myself, I find Don's story very relatable. When my relatives left rural Tennessee for suburban Cleveland, they started trying to hide their hillbilly background. Whenever my dad or grandmother accidentally did something that was too "hillbilly," someone else in the family would mock it, not-so-gently "correcting" them. Often these embarrassingly "hillbilly" acts were just sensible, thrifty behaviors, like trying to bargain for a cheaper price at a garage sale or taking a piece of decent-looking furniture from someone's garbage.

Matthew Weiner, the creator of *Mad Men*, once said that the show was about "becoming white."[3] Don Draper is already white at the beginning of the show, of course; what Weiner meant was that as Don ascends the corporate ladder, he learns to erase more and more of his former self until he fully embodies the wealthy, white Anglo-Saxon Protestant persona he needs to be in order to get ahead. In my family's case, "becoming white" was a bit more literal. My family on my dad's side is Melungeon, a mixed-race group of people from the Cumberland Gap region of Tennessee.[4] Many of my hillbilly relatives were white or white-passing, but others were dark-skinned and were read as either Black or Native. When my family moved from Tennessee to northeast Ohio, it was easy for the light-skinned members to disappear into a privileged, middle-class life. All they had to do was hide their accents and "hillbilly" traits, and never acknowledge their nonwhite roots. Even as a kid, I learned to rebuff questions about where my family was from or what my ethnicity was, because the complicated truth would bring out people's bigotry. Historical records show that many Melungeon people have followed this exact path, obscuring their nonwhite ancestry, adopting a white identity, and blending into mainstream society through a blend of conformity and self-erasure.

The Laziness Lie encourages people to conform for the sake of succeeding at work. We're rewarded when we choose to "become white" in our presentation, professionalism, and work habits. From a young age, we're taught to admire the women writers who had to take male pen names in order to be published, and to celebrate the Black inventors and scholars who had to work twice as hard as their white peers for a fraction of the money and acclaim. The people who resist the world's bigotry are branded as "lazy" complainers who don't have what it takes to succeed.

The Laziness Lie wants us to believe that the solution to every social problem is casting aside your grievances and getting to work. The more a person can buff out all their rough edges, becoming as smooth and featureless and "normal-seeming" as possible, the more they and everyone around them can ignore systematic problems and focus on being productive. But like every other false promise the Laziness Lie makes us, it's a self-defeating trap.

———

Before starting Wild Mind Collective, Kaitlin worked at a nonprofit that aimed to help low-income Black youth find decent-paying jobs. In theory, she appreciated the organization's mission. In practice, their processes disturbed her.

"The organization focused on finding low-income youth of color who needed jobs, and then kind of transformed them into highly obedient corporate automatons," she says.

Kaitlin says the nonprofit trained Black youth to be endlessly polite and uncomplaining. Staff and volunteers policed the kids' mannerisms and words; anything that made them seem at all "unprofessional" was harshly discouraged. The nonprofit also trained the kids to keep their anger and outrage in check, no matter how much unfairness or racism they witnessed.

"If any of the young people had a problem obeying or had questions about the way things were run," Kaitlin says, "people at the organization would have these phrases they would parrot constantly, telling them basically to hide their emotions and thoughts and keep on working."

I was once a teacher at a charter school that taught its Black students similar lessons. Elementary school children were expected to sit "at attention," with their arms folded and their eyes on the teacher at all times. If a child fidgeted, looked around the room, or expressed their selfhood in any other way, they would be punished.

In our deeply victim-blaming, Laziness-Lie-loving culture, marginalized people are often told that they must solve the problem of their own oppression. Black women are regularly told to straighten their hair because a naturally coiled hair texture is considered distracting and "unprofessional" by white people.[5] Native Americans are often discouraged from wearing traditional jewelry to the office because it's been deemed too big and "flashy."[6] Transgender people like me are often punished for openly being ourselves in the workplace. Even something as simple as using the correct restroom can result in a reprimand or an attack. We're often told that our very existence is a "distraction" to other employees.

In the mainstream, workaholic workplace, nothing is more threatening than "distracting" nonconformity. The very concept of what counts as "professional" behavior is rooted in the desire for social control. The nonbinary writer, voice actor, and activist Jacob Tobia writes about this beautifully, in their essay titled "Why I'm Genderqueer, Professional, and Unafraid":[7]

> For years, professionalism has been my enemy because it requires that my gender identity is constantly and unrepentantly erased. In the workplace, the gender binary can be absolute, unfaltering, and infallible. If you dare to step out of line, you risk being mistreated by co-workers, losing promotions, or even losing your job.

Jacob wears a lot of bright, tailored dresses, chunky jewelry, and smart, work-ready heels. If they were a cisgender woman, no one in any office would have a problem with how they look. But because they're a visibly nonbinary person with facial stubble and body hair, their cute, kicky workplace attire is deemed unacceptable.

In our culture, lots of people are told that honest expression of their selfhood is distracting or unprofessional. Fat people are expected to contort their bodies or starve themselves in order to fit into a world built for the thin. Disabled people are discouraged from asking for accommodations because it might make them seem "weak" or "lazy." The Laziness Lie demands perfection, and it defines perfection in very rigid, arbitrary ways: a body that conforms; a tidy, presentable life; a day filled with "productive," virtuous

Marginalized people are often told that they must solve the problem of their own oppression.

activities that benefit society; a life that has no room in it for rebellion or complaint. If we don't check off each of these boxes, we're made to feel as if we've failed.

Of course, we were always going to fail. These ideals exist to set our priorities for us and to keep us busy, distracted, and feeling apologetic about our needs. But we don't have to measure ourselves against these unfair yardsticks. If we take a step back and really reflect on all of the things society tells us we "should" be doing, we may find that many of them don't line up with who we are at all. We shouldn't have to struggle to make ourselves palatable, understandable, and small. Resisting these "shoulds" makes us strong, not lazy.

I could have tried to be a perfectly gender-conforming, polite, pretty young woman, but years ago I decided I'd rather live as myself. Julie the former nonprofit director could have kept trying to work full-time while raising a family, to project the perfect image of the woman who "has it all," but she chose to prioritize her family's health instead. Kaitlin could have stayed at an organization that went against her morals, but instead she chose to create a new path for herself and uplift other "wild minds" that aren't easily contained and controlled. Each of us has an opportunity to push back against the dictates of the Laziness Lie and ask ourselves how we truly wish to live. But doing this requires staring down some of society's most pernicious "shoulds" and rejecting them, because we've finally recognized that those rules don't serve us.

To set ourselves free, we have to refuse to meet the expectations that harm us. Deciding not to conform to these unreasonable restrictions may get us branded as "lazy," but in truth it's some of the hardest, most virtuous work around.

Your Body Is Already Perfect

When you've been taught all your life that your productivity determines your value, it's really easy to become alienated from your body. Instead of seeing your body as a fundamental part of who you are, you come to see it as a means to an end. Our culture views bodies as tools that exist to be used and objects that exist to win the approval of others.

This is especially true for fat women, who are constantly told by society that their bodies are failing to perform their "job," which is to be as small and conventionally beautiful as possible.

"It's constantly exhausting to be defined by beauty," says my friend Jessie Oliver. "That is something none of us actually really signed up for."

Jessie Oliver is a voice coach, an amazing opera singer, and an activist for fat positivity. On her podcast *Fat Outta Hell*, she and her cohosts discuss everything from the joy of finding adorable plus-size bikinis to the difficulty of locating restaurants with chairs that can comfortably hold large bodies. She's been an active voice for fat liberation for many years, pushing back against the judgment and exclusion fat people face at work, in the doctor's office, and in the performing arts. Because she's been on the receiving end of fatphobia for her entire life, she's intimately aware of how society's hatred of fatness is tied to the Laziness Lie.

"The diet industry is the only industry I can think of that profits equally whether you succeed or fail," she says. "If you don't lose weight, you have to keep trying; if you succeed, they can sell you all these products to help you maintain your weight—because God forbid you ever become fat again."

Hatred of fatness is immensely profitable. In 2019, the weight-loss industry was worth over $72 billion in the United States alone.[8] The industry grew 4 percent from 2018 to 2019, and most analysts predict it will continue to grow for many years to come.[9] The weight-loss biz is a massive beast with many far-reaching tendrils, peddling everything from diet pills to "fat-blasting" workout classes to cosmetic surgeries to waist-training belts. If you believe your body needs to change, there are lots of options into which you can pour your money—and a lot of businesses that are eager to feed your insecurities to keep that money flowing.

Society's hatred of fatness pushes many of us to work incredibly hard in pursuit of an arbitrary standard of "perfection." It keeps us overexerting ourselves in gyms and fitness classes, trying desperately to mold our bodies into trim, "toned" shapes, regardless of whether that's healthy for us. It tells us that all bodies are capable of resembling the bodies of the wealthy, white Europeans on whom the beauty standards were based.[10] It convinces us that our bodies' natural hunger signals are not to be trusted and ought to be suppressed with pills or meal-replacement shakes. It leads us to spend thousands of dollars per year on desperate attempts to "improve" ourselves, even though, statistically, those methods almost never work.

"So much of the research and so much of the science that historically has been done about fatness has been funded by the diet industry," Jessie says, "so all the results are being presented in a way that allows them to say, *We have this thing that will fix you.* We're constantly being told that we need fixing."

Despite this immense pressure on people to "fix" their bodies through weight loss, nearly all attempts at weight loss fail.[11] This is true no matter the method a person attempts: dieting, exercise, surgery, and supplements are all ineffective when it comes to changing people's bodies, especially in the long term.[12] Studies show that between 95 percent and 97 percent of people who attempt to lose weight end up gaining back all of the weight that they lost within five years.[13] And though we're all taught to see fatness as "unhealthy," a great deal of research shows that repeatedly losing and gaining weight is far worse for a person's health than maintaining a consistent high weight.[14]

Despite all of this evidence, many of us keep trying to battle fatness, because we've been taught to see fat as a sign of inexcusable "laziness." "Fat" and "lazy" are two terms that often go together. Both are used to pass moral judgment on a person and to express disgust at who they are and how they live. Just as the Laziness Lie punishes economic victims for their own misfortune—*You could succeed if you would just work harder*—it also punishes the victims of fat hate and body negativity by saying all they need to do is eat less and exercise more.

From my teens until my late twenties, I had a pretty severe eating disorder. I used to deny myself food as much as possible and force myself to

> "Fat" and "lazy" are two terms that often go together. Both are used to pass moral judgment on a person and to express disgust at who they are and how they live.

exercise for more than an hour every single day, no matter how busy I was or how tired I felt. When I got incredibly sick back in 2014, poor nutrition was definitely a contributing factor, alongside overwork. To me, the two are inextricably linked. Both my compulsive overwork and my eating disorder came from my fear of being lazy and my need to constantly prove that I was doing "enough."

To get healthy, I had to unlearn my belief that physical suffering was a sign of virtue. I also had to challenge my fear of gaining weight. For my entire life up to that point, I'd been taught that fat people were inexcusably lazy and were themselves to blame for the exclusion and judgment they faced. To escape my eating disorder, I had to challenge my biases against fat people.

Embrace Fat Positivity

When I was first trying to heal from my eating disorder, one thing that helped immensely was exposing myself to beautiful, celebratory images of fat bodies. I started following the blogs and social media accounts of cool, fashionable, badass fat people, and began to really listen to, and appreciate, the fat people in my life. I devoured the comedy videos of Joy Nash, a fat actor who later went on to star in the show *Dietland*. I pored over the images of fat fashion models like Arcadio Del Valle and Kelly Lynn.[15] I read writing by fat people about their experiences of prejudice and exclusion. I listened to the struggles of my fat friends. Over time, I could feel my fatphobia *and* my discomfort with my own body beginning to erode. As I began to judge others' bodies less, I became more compassionate toward my own body as well.

Studies show that when we expose ourselves to diverse images of fat people, our negative stereotypes of them begin to go away.[16] Research also shows that spending quality time with fat people out in the real world helps to make thin individuals less fatphobic.[17] Exposure to positive images of people of a variety of sizes and shapes helps us become compassionate toward our own bodies as well.[18] By coming to recognize the beauty of fat bodies, I stopped being a pawn the diet industry could manipulate and profit from. More important, I became a less cruel, less judgmental person toward the fat individuals in my life.

Remember That Your Body Is Not an Object—It's You

When psychologists study people suffering from negative body image, at the core of the problem is something called "self-objectification."[19] When we view our bodies as objects or "things" that are separate from our minds, we're engaging in self-objectification. In particularly damaging cases, self-objectification can even involve seeing one's body as a collection of separate parts, all of which have their own perceived flaws, rather than a worthwhile whole.

Research shows that people who routinely think about their bodies as objects report much lower self-esteem than those who don't, and are much more likely to engage in eating-disordered behaviors.[20] One study even showed that women who spend a lot of time thinking about their bodies actually get worse at solving math problems as a result of the distraction and distress that self-objectification causes them.[21] Unfortunately, the more a person is exposed to media images that uphold a thin-body ideal, the more likely they are to think in these damaging, self-objectifying ways.[22]

How do you fight the urge to self-objectify once it's already there? Well, you can focus on what your body can do, rather than what it looks like.[23] Exercise can become a process of celebrating what your body is capable of, or of enjoying the pleasure a good run or a tough weight lifting session can give, rather than a form of punishment.[24] Being gentle with your body is also important. Listening to your body for signs of pain, discomfort, and hunger can help you feel more attuned to your needs and less apt to punish yourself with overexertion. Most of all, you have to work to abandon the fear that being idle or gaining weight is a sign that you're "lazy."

As we talked about back in chapter two, great healing can be found in listening to our bodies and honoring our needs for rest and idleness.

It's revolutionary—and deeply healing—to listen to our bodies' pain or exhaustion and respect it rather than judging it. Unlearning a lifetime of fat hate and body shame is a long, complex process, but you can begin that unlearning as soon as you accept that you don't need to put any effort into changing your shape. It's society's rigid, fatphobic expectations for people's bodies that need to change, not you.

Your Life Can Be Messy

Another damaging "should" the Laziness Lie promotes is the idea that our lives "should" look a certain way. The competitive nature of capitalism leaves many of us feeling that we have to attain a certain kind of lifestyle, one that impresses other people and signals our wealth and success. This is yet another trap, and another needless source of stress.

The phrase "keeping up with the Joneses" comes from the title of a comic strip by Arthur "Pop" Momand, first published in 1913 in the *New York World*. The comic follows the McGinis family as they struggle to keep up with their showier, classier neighbors, the Joneses. The McGinises are new to the upper-middle class and lack their neighbors' manners, tidiness, and sense of style. Ever since the creation of the strip, the phrase "keeping up with the Joneses" has been used to describe the pressure many people feel to maintain a classy, presentable lifestyle to impress the people around them.

Interestingly, the Joneses never actually appeared in the comic, though it ran for more than twenty-five years. You never get to see the perfect, respectable family the McGinises aspire to be like. To me, this makes perfect sense: if readers had been able to see the Joneses, they would have found flaws to pick apart; instead the family remained mysterious, always superior to the McGinises in countless ways, yet never being critiqued themselves.

As odd as it sounds, this same dynamic of anxiety and comparison to a perfect, unknowable "other" is still maintained on social media today. The people we compare ourselves to are hypervisible and permanent fixtures of advertisements, Instagram feeds, and YouTube channels, but we know very little about their actual lives. This allows us to project an image of perfection onto them. Their spotless homes, stylish outfits, and exciting vacations make our lives seem lackluster and leave us feeling as though we're kind of pathetic and sloppy in comparison.

In reality, many of the people who appear to be doing "better" than us on social media are simply curating their lives more. They're amplifying the glamour and downplaying all signs of struggle or pain. Unfortunately, this creates an arms race of flawlessness, with more and more humanity being smoothed away until the only thing deemed acceptable is an unreal level of perfection.

———

Until a few years ago, Essena O'Neill was an Instagram darling. As a teenager, she accumulated over half a million followers by posting glitzy photos of herself on the beach and at various lush vacation spots. She wore beautiful gowns in rich jewel tones; she bared her flat stomach while donning sleek workout gear; she drank weight-loss teas while wearing shortshorts and tank tops and tousling her artfully messy hair.

By the time she turned eighteen, Essena was completely burned out and disillusioned with the "influencer" game. She was sick of projecting a false image of herself and exhausted by the work that crafting such an illusion required. So, she deleted hundreds of Instagram posts in the span of a day and altered the captions on all the posts that remained. Each new caption laid bare the techniques she'd used to create the impression of easygoing perfection that had defined her "brand."[25]

On an old photo of herself lounging on the beach in a bright pink bikini, Essena added the new caption: "NOT REAL LIFE—took over 100 [photos] in similar poses trying to make my stomach look good. Would have yelled at my little sister to keep taking them until I was somewhat proud of this. Yep so totally #goals."[26]

On a photo of herself in a tank top and running shorts, Essena changed the caption to read, "A 15 year old girl that calorie restricts and excessively exercises is not goals."

In her other edited captions, Essena revealed that many of her spontaneous-seeming posts were carefully planned sponsorship deals. She laid out the countless photo-staging and editing techniques that allowed her to appear as thin and radiant as possible.[27] In the years following Essena's caption-editing frenzy, a handful of other social media darlings have come forward about similar deceptions and apologized for the damage they'd done.[28]

Psychological research shows that exposure to these posts takes a toll on how people feel about themselves. A study of Facebook users found that encountering glamorous or aspirational images was associated with a drop in users' self-esteem.[29] Another study found that teens who compared themselves to online personalities experienced more depressive symptoms,[30] while a third study found that adult women who edit and filter their selfies have much more negative self-images than those who don't, and experience greater self-consciousness.[31] Other studies have observed similar effects in teen girls.[32]

Every unrealistic standard that we encounter on social media can breed a new source of anxiety. Whether it's a stunning outfit or a luxuriously decorated living room, every ridiculously perfect image gives us a new thing to feel guilt and "lazy" about. But we will never catch up to any of those Joneses, because they were never real people in the first place. They're just facades, designed to keep us busy, distracted, and feeling insecure— because those insecurities keep us both productive and profitable.

Thankfully, a growing body of research is shedding light on the steps a person can take to fight these pressures. In short, if social media leaves you feeling as if you're not enough, you can counteract it by avoiding comparisons with other people and seeking out the successful people who inspire you rather than make you feel bad.

Avoid Upward Comparisons

In nearly every psychological study on the damaging effects of social media use, "upward social comparison" is a key variable.[33] When we look to someone who seems more accomplished or high-status than us and use their perfection as a stick to beat ourselves up with, we're engaging in upward social comparison. If you find yourself feeling threatened or judged every time you view a particular celebrity or influencer's posts, odds are you're doing it.

Upward comparison is, in essence, a way of using other people's accomplishments to determine what our own goals should be. It kills contentment and self-acceptance. There's always someone doing better than we are in one way or another; if we constantly seek out people to unfavorably compare ourselves to, we'll never feel like we're enough.

Research suggests that people who do a lot of upward social comparing tend to work themselves to the point of burnout.[34] In many ways, the urge to look upward and compare ourselves endlessly to those "above" us is at the heart of the Laziness Lie. Often, though, that idealized person sitting above us doesn't really exist. It can be helpful to remind ourselves of that fact; some studies suggest that there's a psychological benefit to being reminded of how doctored and curated most social media images are, for example.[35] But it's even better to avoid exposing ourselves to those shame-inducing images in the first place.

You don't need to beat yourself up by comparing yourself to those who seem more productive or glamorous. You won't suddenly become "lazy" if you get rid of all that guilt. You can trust yourself to determine your own goals, and to follow through with them at the pace that's right for you.

Seek Inspiration, Not Shame

There are a variety of ways to look upward, and not all of them do damage. There's a great deal of value in having someone to admire as a source of motivation and encouragement; that's not the same thing as using a glamorous celebrity's beauty as a source of shame. The psychologist and researcher Pieternel Dijkstra describes it this way:

Individuals may *contrast* themselves with a comparison target (i.e., focus on the differences between themselves and the target), or they may *identify* with a comparison target (i.e., focus on the similarities between themselves and the comparison target).[36]

> There's always someone doing better than we are in one way or another; if we constantly seek out people to unfavorably compare ourselves to, we'll never feel like we're enough.

Dijkstra and his colleagues have observed that when we identify with someone we see as being "above" us, it can give us feelings of hope and admiration. Rather than making us feel inferior, this upward gaze can leave us inspired.

I'll return to an example from early in the book: the Instagrammer, comedian, and model Rickey Thompson. I have very little in common with Rickey. I'm a white academic, not a Black social media star. I don't have his good looks, high energy, or sense of comedic timing. Yet when I see Rickey's modeling deals and media appearances, I feel a swell of pride and identification. I identify with Rickey's creative drive and snarky attitude, as well as his queerness and his offbeat personality. When he does well, I feel like there's hope for all the intense weirdos out there, myself included.

I'm not holding myself to Rickey's standards of success; rather, I view him as a guiding light. I'm not in the same line of work as he is, and I don't want to emulate his career path myself, but his victories remind me that I can be my own best, weird self and make a place for myself in the world. Fighting the Laziness Lie, after all, isn't about abandoning all goals. It's about connecting with the goals that truly light a fire inside us—and pursuing them in a healthy way. I think that's why I find Rickey so inspiring. He's clearly living his own life on his own terms, and flourishing.

It's Not Your Job to Save the World

Nearly every person I interviewed for this book mentioned feeling deeply anxious about the future of our world. Many said they feel guilty about not doing more to address the world's problems. Even people who've taken concrete steps to embrace rest and do less in their lives, like Julie and Leo, mentioned feeling remorse that they weren't doing enough to

SHRUGGING OFF SOCIETY'S "SHOULDS"

fight climate change, racial injustice, the persecution of immigrants, and dozens of other problems.

My friend Kim, whose experiences with homelessness I described in chapter one, knows this feeling very well. In the years since being homeless, Kim has built a new life for themselves. They've gotten engaged, moved into a house in Wichita with their partner and daughter, and become a prominent activist. On Facebook, they run several online activist groups, with a combined membership of over 150,000 people. The groups inform followers about things like homelessness, economic inequality, climate change, and dozens of other topics close to Kim's heart. They pour hours each week into keeping the groups active. In real life, Kim also does homeless outreach, giving people money and food and directing them to resources.

Unfortunately, there has been another development in Kim's life in the past few years, one that threatens their ability to juggle these many responsibilities. After moving to Wichita, Kim developed Charcot-Marie-Tooth disease, a rare and painful neuromuscular condition. The disease is debilitating, and it saps Kim's energy in massive ways. "My husband does the lion's share of the housework, because I'm fatigued by physical labor so quickly that it would never get done otherwise," Kim says. "Sometimes I run a load of laundry or wash four dishes, but then I have to lie down to rest."

Kim's disability puts major limits on how much work they can get done, both as a parent and an activist. Running errands, going to doctor's appointments, picking their daughter up from school—each takes a significant physical toll, and sometimes Kim doesn't have the strength to do any of it. Kim and their husband are constantly burned out, and when things get especially busy, activism has to fall by the wayside.

"Last September, I compiled a list of about two dozen climate-related reports and articles, dealing mostly with how climate change disproportionately harms people living in the Global South,

> **Fighting the Laziness Lie is all about connecting with the goals that truly light a fire inside us— and pursuing them in a healthy way.**

Indigenous people, and disabled people," Kim says. "I intended to create a big social media post for each of these reports and post them during the Climate Strike in September."

Unfortunately, Kim wasn't able to make these posts in time. Life got in the way.

"I had to get wedding invitations in the mail, and I felt guilty every minute I wasn't working on that," Kim says. "Caleb and I got married over a year ago, and it's taken us this long to even plan an actual wedding. I had to finally get it done. So, the Climate Strike passed by without my ever getting around to those posts. There are optimal times and days to post certain stories if you want to elicit a response, and I feel terrible when I miss those dates."

When I asked Kim what steps they take to manage their burnout or reduce their workload, they don't have much to offer. "I don't know that I do anything to prevent burnout," they say. "It's never not on the horizon. To some extent, having a neuromuscular condition forces me to rest sometimes. Sometimes, instead of feeling guilty about what I'm not getting done, I just sleep all afternoon instead."

Even though Kim clearly has tons of valid reasons to need a break from activism, they still feel guilty for not giving more time and energy to it. Climate change is an urgent, pressing issue—a literal fire that needs to be put out. It's hard to set reasonable work-life boundaries when matters seem that dire. If you care deeply about a variety of social issues, it's easy to feel that you must sacrifice your own well-being in order to save the world.

When I spoke to Kathy Labriola about this, she noted that this feeling of panicky urgency is nothing new. "The thing that seems so striking to me is that at any given moment in the last fifty years, there are lots of people saying, *Oh my God, this is the most important issue ever in history, and we must sacrifice everything for this cause*," she says. "People said that exact thing ten years ago, twenty years ago, thirty years ago, about different issues. And then they got so burned out after a relatively short time that they just dropped out totally from doing anything."

As much as we might want to devote our lives to solving the political problems that keep us up at night, intense, panic-fueled activism is rarely sustainable. No individual has the power to actually save the world through sheer hard work. It's both ridiculous and destructive to set such high expectations for ourselves. Instead, if we want to fight injustice or work to improve the world, we ought to do so in a collaborative way that recognizes our unique strengths and needs.

I spoke with several mental-health professionals who regularly treat clients for activism fatigue, and their overall advice was this: prioritize causes that genuinely inspire you, set realistic goals for your activism, and work to accept that there are certain problems you cannot fix, no matter how hard you try.

Set Goals Based on Compassion, Not Guilt or Fear

If you care about fighting a social problem, it's easy to get swept up in feelings of panic or guilt. When you take a break to rest, to care for yourself, or even to enjoy a vacation, the problem remains, unfixed and looming in the back of your mind. And in many activist spaces— both in-person and online—there's a great deal of pressure to remain focused on pressing, upsetting issues all the time, often to the detriment of our health.

"There are a lot of traumatized people in activist spaces," says Sharon Glassburn. "They've experienced a lot of injustice and abuse, and they don't have the ability to walk away from it completely, and so they become really emotionally dysregulated, and they can re-traumatize the people around them."

I know exactly what Sharon means. I've seen it firsthand in my own activism. A few years ago, I got involved in a campaign to shut down a solitary-confinement prison in southern Illinois called Tamms Correctional Center. I joined up with Leslie, an activist and

> No individual has the power to actually save the world through sheer hard work. It's both ridiculous and destructive to set such high expectations for ourselves.

political organizer who had been fighting to get Tamms closed for more than ten years.

Everywhere she went, Leslie carried a massive suitcase filled with letters from men who were in solitary confinement. She worked a full-time job during the day, then spent four to six hours every night answering letters from these men. Every weekend was filled with meetings with politicians and activist groups fighting to close Tamms. I admired her drive, but I could see that it was corrosive to Leslie's health. Eventually, her intensity took a toll on me too.

One chilly Saturday in March I came down with a cold. I'd made plans to spend that day with Leslie, going door-to-door campaigning for a political candidate she believed would help us get Tamms closed. It was a bitterly cold day, the sidewalks were encased in snow, and I was running a fever. I should have bailed on my plans with Leslie, but I knew that if I did, she'd think I didn't take the cause seriously. So, we worked all day, barely taking time for a single break. By midafternoon my cold had gotten far worse, and I was barely able to walk. Even then, I could tell Leslie expected me to keep working, and was disappointed in me for running out of energy.

Leslie's activist group meetings regularly stretched late into the night, and she was constantly creating long to-do lists that overwhelmed me and her other volunteers. I quit the campaign shortly after that bitterly cold day in March, because I just couldn't take it anymore. Instead of burning myself out, I wish I'd set reasonable limits on my activism and hadn't let Leslie's expectations manipulate me into overwork. Now when I decide to fight for a cause, I ask myself a few quick gut-check questions about it:

1. When I think about this activism, do I feel excited, or do I feel guilty?
2. If I say no to something or miss an event, do I worry that I'll be judged by the activist community?
3. How much time can I safely give to this cause every week? Every month?

4. How will I know when I need to reduce my commitments or take a break?

5. What other steps am I taking to make the world a better place?

When I reflect on these questions, I'm better able to make a reasoned decision about how much work I can afford to put in. Instead of seeing every single social issue as a blazing fire that I must personally snuff out, I can view activism as a regular, healthy habit, like exercise. I can't do everything, but I can help chip away at big problems by doing my own small part.

Grieve the Things You Cannot Change

One of the mental-health professionals I interviewed about this was Xochitl Sandoval, a counselor who works with the Chicago-based therapy group Practical Audacity. A queer, transgender Indigenous person, Xochitl knows very deeply what it's like to be impacted by injustice on a day-to-day basis. One way that ze deals with it is by giving lots of space for mourning and grief. "I think we don't know how to grieve as a society," ze says. "I think a lot of the conversation about activist burnout is actually about grieving, about being really able and willing to just sit in this space of *This is fucking awful. And there might not be anything I can do to solve this.*"

Xochitl shares with me that ze often mourns the harm that has already been done to the planet due to industrialization and climate change. Though society can take steps to reduce carbon emissions and slow the damage that's occurring, there's some harm that can never be undone.

"The Amazon is burning. So many animals have gone extinct because of climate change," ze says. "And there's always, I think, this natural impulse to make sense of it all. Like, *What are the ways in which you can take action? Like, you sign some petitions? Can you commit to not using plastic?* And we can talk about those steps. But let's start with the grief. Let's start with the fact that even if I cut out all plastic from my life, that doesn't take away all the plastic in the ocean."

The American Psychological Association issued a massive report on "climate grief" for the first time in 2017, with chapters detailing how fear about the planet's future is linked to depression and anxiety among adults and children alike.[37] A survey from Yale, conducted in 2018, found that 62 percent of people say they're worried about climate change—up from around 30 percent back in 2015.[38] So, Xochitl and zir clients are far from alone in feeling this despair. Instead of trying to ignore these hard feelings or to solve them with activist work, Xochitl recommends honoring them.

It may sound very demotivating to sit and mourn loss like this, but feelings of grief can't just be brushed away. When we treat social problems as emergencies that we must fix, we delude ourselves into thinking that we can control them, if we only work hard enough. Realistically, though, that just isn't the case. I can fight and fight to make the world more just, but if my goal is "fixing" a decades-old problem or making it go away, I'm destined to fail and burn out. Sometimes, the best way to deal with those feelings of panic and guilt is to really let them wash over us for a moment, and really accept that we're not fully in control—or fully responsible for it. This can be an immensely sad experience, but it can also be liberating. When we mourn the losses that cannot ever be brought back, we come to accept the reality we're living in. This allows us to address problems realistically and sustainably.

Make Your Activism Small

Another way to make activism less stressful and all-consuming is to stop thinking of it as a big, abstract obligation and to focus instead on the small, concrete steps you can take each day. Research from the American Psychological Association suggests that when we look at an abstract, scary problem and focus only on how massive and complex it is, we tend to feel a lot of powerlessness and grief.[39] Conversely, when we turn our attention toward the small, local steps we can take to address the problem, we feel more in control of the situation, less anxious, and more motivated to keep up the fight.

For example, I can spend my free time researching how the changing ecosystem will impact Chicago's local and indigenous plants, or attend a talk at the Botanic Garden on how to help plant and protect more native species.[40] I can fight back against local industrial development that would make climate change worse. I can vote for politicians who take the issue seriously and donate to local, Indigenous-led organizations that are growing native plants and looking after the land in traditional ways.[41] I can't stop climate change, but that doesn't mean I have to give up. I can take solace in the fact that I've helped bring life into the world.

———

It took years for Kim and their partner, Caleb, to plan their wedding. Kim was always too busy with things like managing their illness, raising their daughter, and engaging in their daily activism. Caleb was always too busy with his full-time job and keeping the house relatively clean and organized. It's been really hard for them to find the time and energy to move to the next stage of their lives.

Recently, though, I opened up Instagram and was greeted with a photo of Kim in their wedding dress, smiling and sitting on a hotel bed with their daughter, Sophie, at their side. Normally when I hear from Kim, I hear all about how exhausted they are and how difficult everything in their life has been, so seeing them looking happy and relaxed was a really welcome sight. I teared up, and then eagerly hopped over to Kim's profile so I could look at all of the other beautiful, joyful wedding photos that had been uploaded. I know Kim probably still feels bad about having taken time away from their activism in order to plan this wedding—but as their friend, I'm so happy they did.

Compassion Kills the Laziness Lie

I started this book with the example of a parent telling their child that homeless people are lazy and don't deserve generosity. Beginning there was a deliberate choice. Lots of people have been taught to see homeless folks as the epitome of laziness, and to believe that laziness is the root cause of homeless people's suffering. This tendency to blame people for their own pain is comforting, in a twisted way: it allows us to close up our hearts and ignore the suffering of others. This same tendency also keeps us running endlessly on the hamster wheel of hyperproductivity.

When we view homeless, unemployed, or impoverished people as victims of their own "laziness," our motivation to work backbreakingly hard gets stronger than ever. The fear of ending up homeless morphs into the fear of not working hard enough, which in turn makes life an endless slog of pushing ourselves past the brink and judging anyone who doesn't do the same. Lacking compassion for a struggling group of people actually makes it harder for us to be gentle with ourselves.

Fighting the Laziness Lie can't stop at just encouraging people with full-time jobs to relax a bit and take more breaks. The compulsion toward overwork is a key component of the Laziness Lie, and resisting it is important, but we have to go so much further than that. Our culture's hatred of the "lazy" is all-encompassing. It bleeds into how we view relationships, child-rearing, body size, barriers to voting, and so much more. The Laziness Lie teaches us that people who do more are worth more. When we buy into that method of assigning value to people, we doom ourselves to a life of insecurity and judgment.

The remedy for all of this is boundless compassion. If we really want to dismantle the Laziness Lie and set ourselves free, we have to question every judgment of "laziness" society has taught us to make, including those that are very challenging for us to unlearn. If you're entitled to moments of rest, of imperfection, of laziness and sloth, then so are homeless people, and people with depression, and people who are addicted to drugs. If your life has value no matter how productive you are, so does every other human life.

It's hard to unlearn this stuff. For me, I think it will be a lifelong project. As much as I encourage my friends, peers, and students to exercise empathy and tolerance, I often struggle with it myself. I'm prone to getting infuriated and judgy the second a slow-walking person blocks my path on the sidewalk. I get impatient when a coworker is late in responding to an e-mail or a calendar invite. When a friend of mine complains about needing to make a change in their life and then doesn't actually go ahead and do it, I'm baffled by their inertia. I ought to know better than to have these reactions, yet I still do. I really hate this side of myself.

It's normal to have these disapproving thoughts. The Laziness Lie has indoctrinated us into having them. These knee-jerk reactions are reflections of the society that we were raised in and the biases that were ingrained in us.[1] Thinking this way doesn't make me a bad person; if you're similarly short-fused, you're not a bad person either. What matters most is how we deal with these feelings. We always have the option of reflecting on where our negative thoughts came from, challenging them, and releasing them when they're no longer doing us any good.

There are a lot of things I do to keep the Laziness Lie at bay and to quiet my mind's constant stream of shame and criticism. These steps are rooted in research from social psychology—the field that has shaped me as a thinker and a writer. If you're still struggling to unpack the Laziness

Lie and the influence it's had on your life (and I think most of us are), these steps are a great place to start. I find that they really help me to be more gentle with other people and to have more compassion for myself.

Practice Compassionate Curiosity

We often dismiss people as "lazy" when we can't understand the reasons for their inertia or inaction. If someone's behavior makes no sense to us, passing judgment on it feels very natural. *He won't apply to jobs, he sits on the couch all day, and he hasn't washed a dish in weeks—he must be lazy.* Labeling someone as "lazy" can turn a complex, challenging situation into an open-and-shut case.

Instead of dismissing a person so quickly, it's much more effective to get curious. Every person has reasons for why they act the way they do. Even if someone's inaction strikes us as totally self-defeating or pointless, within the context of that person's life, it makes sense. So, when you find yourself inclined toward judgment, try reflecting on why a person might do the things they do. Here are some questions to ask yourself:

What need are they trying to meet by acting this way?

What challenges or barriers are getting in the way of their making a change?

What hidden struggles (such as physical disability, mental illness, trauma, or oppression) might explain the difficulties they're facing?

Who might have taught them to act this way?

Do they have other options? Are those options really attainable for them?

What kind of help might they need?

Research shows that exercising curiosity is a fantastic way to unlearn our prejudices and biases.[2] And the more we learn about someone's circumstances, the more compassion we have for them and their apparent shortcomings. I've put this principle into practice with my students more times than I can count. If a student is missing assignments, showing up late, and failing to respond to my e-mails, my initial reaction might be to write them off as lazy or unmotivated. I could give up on them right then and there—but it always works out better if I get curious instead. When I check in with a student to see if they're doing okay, I often find that their apparent "laziness" is actually caused by a ton of turmoil and difficulty in their life. When a student trusts me enough to share this information, it gives me an opportunity to offer them help. These moments of connection and collaborative problem solving are some of the most meaningful experiences I get to have as an educator—and if I'd remained judgmental and committed to the Laziness Lie, they never would have happened.

I have a close friend who struggles with addiction, and I find myself applying the same thinking to his situation. He has a really hard time falling asleep at night, and has experienced suicidal thoughts and urges his whole adult life. Sometimes, his best option is to get so drunk that he falls asleep and can't harm himself. It's not a pretty solution, but it makes complete sense to me. I've encouraged him to reduce his drinking and I cheered him on when he started seeing an addiction counselor, but I don't blame him for choosing to drink instead of ending his life. I'm glad he's alive to fight another day, and I respect his decision-making process.

I also find these questions useful for understanding my own behavior. I used to vape nicotine, and for years I felt embarrassed by how wasteful and stupid the habit was. Then I asked myself: *What situations make me vape more? What do I enjoy about doing it?* I realized pretty quickly that I was using vaping as an appetite suppressant, and to give myself a little jolt of extra energy, the same way I might use caffeine. Once I realized this, it was pretty easy to replace vaping with eating snacks and drinking more coffee. Shame would never have gotten my behavior to change; compassion and curiosity were what I needed.

Look to the Broader Context

Sometimes, we don't have the chance to ask a person about their situation and why they behave the way they do. Even in the absence of that information, we can practice compassion by looking at the big-picture factors that limit them or make their life hard. It's much easier to accept a person's actions (or inaction) when we recognize that there are outside factors that influence how they behave. Sometimes the outside factor is something as simple as their having a bad day. Other times, the external factor is something massive and systemic, like classism or racism.

As I've already outlined in this book, fighting against the Laziness Lie is particularly difficult when a person has been pushed to society's margins. People of color and women are often expected to be unfailingly productive and uncomplaining, above and beyond the level white men are. People with mental illnesses and physical disabilities are shamed for having needs and limitations; looking after their health can be viewed by other people as an indulgence. Even people like my Appalachian relatives had to struggle against this—just think of how often movies and TV shows play with the stereotype of the lazy, ignorant hillbilly.

The Laziness Lie encourages us to label people and to pass judgment on them, rather than looking at the broader context they've been placed in. By zooming out and examining their social context, we can get better at seeing them as complex, dynamic people instead of hollow stereotypes. This helps us to stop expecting flawless behavior and productivity from them and to start seeing them as people who are worthwhile no matter how much they do or don't produce.

It's also useful to apply big-picture thinking to our own struggles. If I fail to meet my goals for the day, I could beat myself up for being a lazy failure, or I could ponder what else is happening in my life that might be slowing me down. Maybe I had trouble sleeping the night before, or I'm about to come down with a cold and I just don't realize it yet. Maybe I just learned that my employer-provided health insurance won't cover any gender-transition-related expenses, and so I'm feeling really excluded and undervalued. These things affect me. They'd probably affect you too. I'm not a flawlessly productive robot—nor is anybody else. In fact, it's a *good* thing to be sensitive to the situation I'm in, and to react to setbacks and disappointments. Remember Xochitl Sandoval's observation that we all need time to mourn. Having emotional reactions to one's circumstances is a sign that you're adaptable and alive. It's only because of the pervasiveness of the Laziness Lie that we see natural reactions as weaknesses.

Stop Associating Productivity with Goodness

After you've gotten into the habit of reflecting on why people act the way they act, you can take it even further. Question your root assumptions about which actions are "better" than others, and why. Curiosity about a person's context helps us to be understanding when their actions strike us as ineffective or bad, and that's a great place to start. But it's even more radically compassionate to stop labeling behaviors as "bad" at all.

The Laziness Lie is rooted in capitalism and a particularly harsh breed of Christianity, and it preaches that salvation comes from hard work. That belief system carries over into how we talk about productivity, effort, and achievement. It teaches us to view idle time as a waste and to try to constantly keep ourselves occupied. It leads us to assume that there is more virtue in doing something than there is in doing nothing, no matter what that "something" is.

This mindset can lead down many dangerous paths. If work is always better than unemployment, then it's better to serve an abusive boss in a corrupt, environmentally damaging industry than it is to quit. If keeping busy is a sign of virtue, then it's okay to burn through tons of resources traveling the world and having big, expensive, Instagrammable experiences, rather than having time alone at home. If being active is always superior to being passive, then it's more important that we talk and express our opinions to the world than that we listen to the experts who might have something to teach us.

The Laziness Lie pushes us into unfettered, frantic individualism, leaving no room for reflection, listening, or quiet, inward growth. I'm reminded of a quote often attributed to Irish statesman Edmund Burke that's often shared with children when they first learn about the Holocaust: "The only thing necessary for the triumph of evil is for good men to do nothing." It's a powerful statement about the necessity of standing up against evil, and I think a lot of kids connect with the words when they first hear them. Leaders of all stripes call on this quote to justify some of their boldest actions. Doing something is better than doing nothing, after all. At the very heart of the quote and its popularity is the Laziness Lie lurking within it: it says doing nothing is akin to condoning evil.

There's a problem with this quote, though: Edmund Burke never appears to have said it.[3] In fact, no one knows where the quote came from. It seems to have been made up, then widely adopted by a variety of political leaders, activists, and nonprofit directors throughout the world. Burke's actual words are far less individualistic: "When bad men combine, the good must associate; else they will fall, one by one, an unpitied sacrifice in a contemptible struggle."[4]

This is not a statement about how "good men" must be active and engaged in order to fight evil head-on; rather, it's a call for good people to band together and stand firm against the evil forces attacking them. This quote doesn't praise activity for the sake of activity, it praises community. It suggests that not all battles for good are direct clashes of power, and that violent "contemptible struggles" often will fail. Sometimes, the best thing good people can do is hunker down, care for one another, and survive.

I wonder how many times the fake Burke quote has been used to justify bombing an impoverished country, invading an independent state, or even forcing marginalized people into prisons or corrective camps. If standing by and doing "nothing" is the same as permitting evil, then almost any action you take in an attempt to fight evil can be seen as justified. If doing nothing is evil, then doing something is good, even if that something is foolhardy and destructive. I've sometimes counteracted the (fake) Burke quote by telling people that all that's needed for harm to persist in the world is for evil people to think they're doing good. When productivity is equated with goodness, it becomes hard to tell the difference.

The indoctrination of the Laziness Lie runs deep. Even once we come to realize how unreasonable and dangerous it is, we may find that it still has a hold on us. In order to combat the Laziness Lie fully, we have to identify the signs of it that linger in our minds and work to slowly uproot them.

Here are some indications that you may still be associating productivity with goodness:

> When you get less done during the day than you anticipated, you feel guilty.
>
> You have trouble enjoying your free time.
>
> You believe you have to "earn" the right to a vacation or a break.
>
> You take care of your health only in order to remain productive.
>
> Having nothing to do makes you feel "useless."
>
> You find the idea of growing old or becoming disabled to be incredibly depressing.
>
> When you say no to someone, you feel compelled to say yes to something else to "make up" for it.

Throughout this book, I've outlined the various ways in which over-exertion is damaging to a person's health, their well-being, and even the quality of their work. While all of this is true, saying it over and over again can have an unfortunate implication: It might seem like the purpose of taking care of yourself is just so that you can do better work for longer. If you're still thinking about breaks and rest as a means to an end in this way, then you're still letting your productivity define your worth.

When I first wrote the essay that became this book, I got a lot of e-mails from people who wanted advice on how to boost their productivity. The whole point of the essay was that when people seem "lazy," it's usually because they're facing unseen barriers and challenges. Many readers wanted to know how they could go about finding those barriers and challenges in their own lives and excising them. Time after time, I had to tell those readers that I didn't have advice for how they could overcome their every limit and get more done. I didn't even think they *should* aspire to be more productive. If they wanted to get more done in one area of their life, they'd probably have to cut a few other things out. More important, I wanted them to get comfortable with being less productive than society tells them they ought to be.

Taking breaks, drawing boundaries, and learning to listen to our internal feelings of "laziness" are each worthwhile for their own sake, not because they make us better workers. If you really learn to prioritize your health, it's likely that you'll become less productive overall. That's because you were always doing too much from the outset. Learning to take care of yourself in a holistic way means accepting that you might never be as prolific as you once were, and coming to see that as a good thing. As a result of following the advice in this book, your bedroom might get messier, your in-box might start to develop a backlog, and people might stop praising you so much for your work ethic. You'll know that you've really made progress in unlearning the Laziness Lie when each of these changes feels comfortable and natural rather than threatening.

Of course, no one arrives there in a day. I'm still constantly tempted to evaluate my life in terms of how much I've gotten done. I still find myself judging people who aren't workaholic achievement-hunters. One kind of offbeat thing that helps me detach from this line of thinking is taking time to consider my pet chinchilla, Dump Truck.

Like most pets, Dump Truck has never done a "productive" thing in his entire life. All he does is eat, sleep, and destroy the various wooden toys I put in his cage. When I see Dump Truck slumped over asleep in the middle of the day, I don't feel any disdain over how "lazy" he's being. I don't think he needs to earn the right to food, rest, or playtime. I just love him and find him adorable. His worth to me has absolutely nothing to do with his activity level or anything he "contributes" to my household or my life. His worth comes from his being beautifully, imperfectly alive.

If this little animal's life is innately valuable and beautiful no matter what he does or doesn't do, maybe that means my life is innately valuable too. In fact, if I can love Dump Truck just as much when he's doing nothing as when he's doing a lot, then maybe I can care for and appreciate every human regardless of how they spend their time. It's wonderful to realize that all people are deserving of love and comfort, and that this worthiness has nothing to do with productivity. I don't always remember this, but when I do consciously take the time to focus on it, it fills me with a feeling of peace. It helps me realize that I don't need to struggle or to punish myself with overcommitments and hard work either. I'm okay just as I am.

Be Gentle with Yourself

The Laziness Lie has a far-reaching history, one that's deeply embedded in the legacies of industrialization, imperialism, and slavery. It has permeated almost every piece of media we consume, from the largest blockbuster films to the most intimate-seeming YouTube channels. Since we were children, most of us have been told constantly about the value of hard work and the dangers of not being ambitious and driven. This kind of intense cultural programming cannot easily be undone.

Unlearning the Laziness Lie isn't really about trying to scrub every sign of its influence from our minds. No matter how carefully we reexamine our thought patterns and question our old assumptions, its influence will always be there. Over time, though, we can get better at dismissing the parts of ourselves that have been conditioned to letting go of and judging, and start observing with compassion instead.

It's ironic, but learning to resist the Laziness Lie takes a lot of ongoing, internal work. Continue to practice self-compassion and gentleness, and know that change doesn't come instantly. The path forward is not linear, and there's no trophy to be won by being the best at fighting it. You're still learning. You'll never be perfect, and that's okay. You're fine exactly the way you are. So is everyone else.

Acknowledgments

Thank you to Kim Rosencutter/Mik Everett for your friendship and moral guidance. Knowing you has helped me to grow so much as a person, intellectually and emotionally. Your writing has taught me more about taking a compassionate approach to social issues than any class I've ever taken. This book would have never happened without you.

Huge thanks to my agent, Jenny Herrera. Before you reached out to me, I had kinda resigned myself to just being a hobbyist when it came to my writing. You gave me the confidence, inside knowledge, and critical feedback I needed to aspire to more, and I can't thank you enough for it. Your support has changed my life.

Thank you to Harris Sockel and the editorial team at Medium. Your continued support of my work has helped me grow as a writer, and reach literally millions more readers than I ever would have otherwise. You and your team's edits have taught me a ton about how to make my work more approachable and less long-winded.

Sarah Pelz, I am so grateful to you for championing *Laziness Does Not Exist* at Atria, and for helping the book take its final shape. Your input on the book's structure and early chapters was integral to the final product becoming what it is. Your encouragement and faith in the project helped me feel capable of seeing it to fruition. Thank you for taking a chance on me.

Massive thanks to Amar Deol for taking this book on as an editor. Your feedback was thorough and precise, and also incredibly motivating, and really took the manuscript to the next level. I have some of your feedback screenshotted and saved in my phone, because it always helps me feel better when I start doubting myself as a writer. It's been a total delight working with you.

Christopher Piatt, thank you for seeing my potential and helping to nurture it over the years. Thank you to the other voices in Chicago's Live Lit Community who have helped me hone my own style: Josh Zagoren, Ian Belknap, Tom Harrison, Megan Steilstra, Bilal Dardai, Carly Oishi, and Samantha Irby, and so many more. Any time my writing is remotely engaging, it's because I've spent years imitating each of you.

Thank you to Kevin Johnson and Dio Owens for giving me the pep talk I needed when I was deciding between book cover designs. You both helped give me the language I needed to describe the book's tone, and how to evoke that tone visually. Thank you, Collin Quinn Rice and Jennifer Bowser, for helping me get comfortable with having my picture taken.

Ida Cuttler, thank you so much for giving me all kinds of insights into the bookselling process, including spending hours with me at Women & Children First in Andersonville looking at covers and blurbs. You've been such an actively supportive friend throughout all of this, and it means so much to me.

Thank you to all my Tumblr Writing Community friends, who have traded stories and rants with me over the years and done so much to support my growth: Melanie O'Brien, Jessica Jones, Stephen T. Kennedy, Kayla Ancrum, Roxy MacDonald, Chuck McKeever, Liz Sharp, Sarah McCoy, and so many more.

Thank you to every burned-out (and formerly burned-out) person who spoke with me for this book: Imani, Jessica, Nimisire, Rick, Michael, Kaitlin, Jessie, Jess, Amanda, Kim, and everyone else who appears in this book, I am deeply thankful to you for being so generous with your time and vulnerability.

Thank you to all of the researchers, mental-health advocates, activists, and psychologists who allowed me to interview them for this book: August, Xochitl, Kathy, Sharon, Fred, Louise, Markus, Paul, and Annette, I learned a ton from speaking with each of you.

Thank you to all of my students, particularly the ones who trusted me and shared their limitations and needs with me. I'm sorry that other teachers and professors have left so many of you feeling like there's something wrong with you. There isn't.

Thank you to my mom and sister for constantly trying to teach me how to lighten up and enjoy life once in a while. I swear I have internalized at least some of it. Finally, thank you to my partner, chinchilla co-parent, and best buckaroo, Nick, for your patience, weirdness, creativity, and love.

Notes

Chapter One: The Laziness Lie

1. European Federation of National Organisations Working with the Homeless (FEANTSA), "Recognising the Link between Trauma and Homelessness," January 27, 2017, https://www.feantsa.org/download/feantsa_traumaandhomeless ness03073471219052946810738.pdf.

2. National Coalition for the Homeless, "Homeless Youth," August 2007, http://www .nationalhomeless.org/publications/facts/youth.pdf.

3. Arthur Goldsmith, PhD, and Timothy Diette, PhD, "Exploring the Link between Unemployment and Mental Health Outcomes," American Psychological Association, April 2012, https://www.apa.org/pi/ses/resources/indicator/2012/04/unem ployment.

4. D. Vojvoda and I. Petrakis, "Trauma and Addiction—How to Treat Co-Occurring PTSD and Substance Use Disorders," in *The Assessment and Treatment of Addiction*, Itai Danovitch and Larissa Mooney, eds. (New York: Elsevier, 2018), 189–96.

5. Nicole L. Henderson and William W. Dressler, "Medical Disease or Moral Defect? Stigma Attribution and Cultural Models of Addiction Causality in a University Population," *Culture, Medicine, and Psychiatry* 41, no. 4 (December 2017): 480–98.

6. Victoria Pillay-van Wyk and Debbie Bradshaw, "Mortality and Socioeconomic Status: The Vicious Cycle between Poverty and Ill Health," *The Lancet Global Health* 5, no. 9 (September 2017): e851–e852.

7. Marja Hult and Kirsi Lappalainen, "Factors Associated with Health and Work Ability among Long-Term Unemployed Individuals," *International Journal of Occupational Health and Public Health Nursing* 5, no. 1 (2018), 5–22.

8. K. B. Adams, S. Sanders, and E. A. Auth, "Loneliness and Depression in Independent Living Retirement Communities: Risk and Resilience Factors," *Aging & Mental Health* 8, no. 6 (November 2004): 475–85.

9. Nicole K. Valtorta, Mona Kanaan, Simon Gilbody, Sara Ronzi, and Barbara Hanratty, "Loneliness and Social Isolation as Risk Factors for Coronary Heart Disease and Stroke: Systematic Review and Meta-Analysis of Longitudinal Observational Studies," *BMJ Heart* 102, no. 13 (2016): 1009–16.

10. Betty Onyura, John Bohnen, Don Wasylenki, Anna Jarvis, Barney Giblon, Robert Hyland, Ivan Silver, and Karen Leslie, "Reimagining the Self at Late-Career Transitions: How Identity Threat Influences Academic Physicians' Retirement Considerations," *Academic Medicine* 90, no. 6 (June 2015): 794–801.

11. Jake Linardon and Sarah Mitchell, "Rigid Dietary Control, Flexible Dietary Control, and Intuitive Eating: Evidence for Their Differential Relationship to Disordered Eating and Body Image Concerns," *Eating Behaviors* 26 (August 2017):16–22.

12. "Lazy," Online Etymology Dictionary, https://www.etymonline.com/word/lazy.

13. Ibid.

14. "Lazy," *Webster's New World College Dictionary*, 5th ed. (New York: Houghton Mifflin Harcourt, 2014).

15. Max Weber, *The Protestant Ethic and the Spirit of Capitalism*, trans. Talcott Parsons (New York: Dover, 2003).

16. Sydney E. Ahlstrom, *A Religious History of the American People*, 2nd ed. (New Haven, CT: Yale University Press, 2004), 125.

17. "A History of Slavery in the United States," National Geographic Society, https://www.nationalgeographic.org/interactive/slavery-united-states/.

18. J. Albert Harrill, "The Use of the New Testament in the American Slave Controversy: A Case History in the Hermeneutical Tension between Biblical Criticism and Christian Moral Debate," *Religion and American Culture: A Journal of Interpretation* 10, no. 2 (Summer 2000): 149–86.

19. Noel Rae, *The Great Stain: Witnessing American Slavery* (New York: Overlook Press, 2018), chapter 5.

20. Dr. Samuel A. Cartwright, "Diseases and Peculiarities of the Negro Race," *De Bow's Review*, 1851, http://www.pbs.org/wgbh/aia/part4/4h3106t.html.

21. Heather E. Lacey, "Nat Turner and the Bloodiest Slave Rebellion in American History," *Inquiries* 2, no. 1 (2010), http://www.inquiriesjournal.com/articles/147/nat-turner-and-the-bloodiest-slave-rebellion-in-american-history.

22. "Drapetomania," Ferris State University, Jim Crow Museum of Racist Memorabilia, November 2005, https://www.ferris.edu/HTMLS/news/jimcrow/question/2005/november.htm.

23. Matthew Desmond, "In Order to Understand the Brutality of American Capitalism, You Have to Start on the Plantation," *New York Times Magazine*, August 14, 2019, https://www.nytimes.com/interactive/2019/08/14/magazine/slavery-capitalism.html.

24. "History and Culture: Boarding Schools," Northern Plains Reservation Aid, http://www.nativepartnership.org/site/PageServer?pagename=airc_hist_boarding schools.

25. Weber, *The Protestant Ethic and the Spirit of Capitalism*, chapter 5.

26. A. P. Foulkes, *Literature and Propaganda* (Abingdon, UK: Routledge, 2013), 46.

27. John A. Geck, "Novels of Horatio Alger: Archetypes and Themes," Cinderella Bibliography, University of Rochester, https://d.lib.rochester.edu/cinderella/text/alger-archetypes-and-themes.

28. Russell S. Woodbridge, "Prosperity Gospel Born in the USA," Gospel Coalition, June 4, 2015, https://www.thegospelcoalition.org/article/prosperity-gospel-born-in-the-usa/.

29. Megan Garber, "The Perils of Meritocracy," *Atlantic*, June 30, 2017, https://www.theatlantic.com/entertainment/archive/2017/06/the-perils-of-meritocracy/532215/.

30. Melvin J. Lerner, "The Two Forms of Belief in a Just World," in *Responses to Victimizations and Belief in a Just World* (Boston: Springer, 1998), 247–69.
31. Roland Bénabou and Jean Tirole, "Belief in a Just World and Redistributive Politics," *Quarterly Journal of Economics* 121, no. 2, 699–746.
32. "Common Portrayals of Persons with Disabilities," Media Smarts, August 22, 2014, http://mediasmarts.ca/diversity-media/persons-disabilities/common-portrayals-persons-disabilities.
33. "One Last Job," TV Tropes, https://tvtropes.org/pmwiki/pmwiki.php/Main/OneLastJob.
34. Rickey Thompson, Instagram post, May 28, 2019, https://www.instagram.com/p/ByBLnuPl_bE/?utm_source=ig_web_copy_link.
35. Patrick Wright, "When Video Game Streaming Turns from Dream to Nightmare," ABC Life, April 8, 2019, https://www.abc.net.au/life/the-dark-side-of-streaming-games-online/10895630.
36. Dan Camins, "Twitch Streamer Dies Due to Sleep Deprivation during 24-Hour Live-Stream Gaming of 'World of Tanks,'" *University Herald*, February 24, 2017, https://www.universityherald.com/articles/66699/20170224/twitch-streamer-dies-during-24-hour-live-stream-gaming-world.htm.
37. "Bo Burnham's Inspirational Advice: Give Up Now—CONAN on TBS," Team Coco, June 28, 2016, https://www.youtube.com/watch?v=q-JgG0ECp2U.
38. Raymond E. Callahan, *Education and the Cult of Efficiency: A Study of the Social Forces That Have Shaped the Administration of the Public Schools* (Chicago: University of Chicago Press, 1964).
39. Joseph R. Cimpian, Sarah T. Lubienski, Jennifer D. Timmer, Martha B. Makowski, and Emily K. Miller, "Have Gender Gaps in Math Closed? Achievement, Teacher Perceptions, and Learning Behaviors across Two ECLS-K Cohorts," *AERA Open* 2, no. 4 (October 26, 2016), doi:10.1177/2332858416673617.
40. Christina Maslach, "Burnout and Engagement in the Workplace: New Perspectives," *European Health Psychologist* 13, no. 3 (2011): 44–47.

Chapter Two: Rethinking Laziness

1. Devon Price, "Laziness Does Not Exist," Human Parts, Medium, March 23, 2018, https://humanparts.medium.com/laziness-does-not-exist-3af27e312d01.
2. Matthew Stott, "Depression Stigma in University Students: Faculty Differences, and Effects of Written De-Stigmatisation Strategies," master's thesis, Lunds University, 2018.
3. R. Mendel, W. Kissling, T. Reichhart, M. Bühner, and J. Hamann, "Managers' Reactions towards Employees' Disclosure of Psychiatric or Somatic Diagnoses," *Epidemiology and Psychiatric Sciences* 24, no. 2 (April 2015): 146–49.
4. Carly Johnco and Ronald M. Rapee, "Depression Literacy and Stigma Influence: How Parents Perceive and Respond to Adolescent Depressive Symptoms," *Journal of Affective Disorders* 241 (December 1, 2018): 599–607.
5. Shoji Yokoya, Takami Maeno, Naoto Sakamoto, Ryohei Goto, and Tetsuhiro Maeno, "A Brief Survey of Public Knowledge and Stigma towards Depression," *Journal of Clinical Medicine Research* 10, no. 3 (March 2018): 202–9, doi:10.14740/jocmr3282w.
6. Helia Ghanean, Amanda K. Ceniti, and Sidney H. Kennedy, "Fatigue in Patients with Major Depressive Disorder: Prevalence, Burden, and Pharmacological

Approaches to Management," *CNS Drugs* 32 (2018): 65–74, https://doi.org/10.1007/s40263-018-0490-z.

7. Philippe Fossati, Anne-Marie Ergis, and J. F. Allilaire, "Executive Functioning in Unipolar Depression: A Review," *L'Encéphale* 28, no. 2 (November 2001): 97–107.

8. Ibid.

9. Laura A. Rabin, Joshua Fogel, and Kate Eskine, "Academic Procrastination in College Students: The Role of Self-Reported Executive Function," *Journal of Clinical and Experimental Neuropsychology* 33, no. 3 (November 2010): 344–57.

10. Eric D. Deemer, Jessi L. Smith, Ashley N. Carroll, and Jenna P. Carpenter, "Academic Procrastination in STEM: Interactive Effects of Stereotype Threat and Achievement Goals," *Career Development Quarterly* 62, no. 2 (June 2014): 143–55.

11. Gery Beswick, Esther D. Rothblum, and Leon Mann, "Psychological Antecedents of Student Procrastination," *Australian Psychologist* 23, no. 2 (1988): 207–17.

12. Kent Nordby, Catharina Elisabeth Arfwedson Wang, Tove Irene Dahl, and Frode Svartdal, "Intervention to Reduce Procrastination in First-Year Students: Preliminary Results from a Norwegian Study," *Scandinavian Psychologist* 3 (June 25, 2016): e10, https://doi:10.15714/scandpsychol.3.e10.

13. Claudia Iacobacci, "Common and Different Features between Depression and Apathy in Neurocognitive Disorders," *Clinical and Experimental Psychology* 3, no. 3 (2017): 163, doi:10.4172/2471-2701.1000163.

14. Ann Palker-Corell and David K. Marcus, "Partner Abuse, Learned Helplessness, and Trauma Symptoms," *Journal of Social and Clinical Psychology* 23, no. 4 (2004): 445–62.

15. John Dixon and Yuliya Frolova, "Existential Poverty: Welfare Dependency, Learned Helplessness and Psychological Capital," *Poverty & Public Policy* 3, no. 2 (June 2011): 1–20.

16. Arnold B. Bakker, Hetty van Emmerik, and Martin C. Euwema, "Crossover of Burnout and Engagement in Work Teams," *Work and Occupations* 33, no. 4 (November 2006): 464–89.

17. https://theintercept.com/2020/04/09/nonvoters-are-not-privileged-they-are-largely-lower-income-non-white-and-dissatisfied-with-the-two-parties/.

18. Chris Weller, "Forget the 9 to 5—Research Suggests There's a Case for the 3-Hour Workday," *Business Insider*, September 26, 2017, https://www.businessinsider.com/8-hour-workday-may-be-5-hours-too-long-research-suggests-2017-9.

19. Brian Wansink, Collin R. Payne, and Pierre Chandon, "Internal and External Cues of Meal Cessation: The French Paradox Redux?" *Obesity* (Silver Spring, MD) 15, no. 12 (December 2007): 2920–24, doi:10.1038/oby.2007.348.

20. Katherine Dudley, MD, MPH, "Weekend Catch-Up Sleep Won't Fix the Effects of Sleep Deprivation on Your Waistline," Harvard Health Publishing, Harvard Medical School, September 24, 2019, https://www.health.harvard.edu/womens-health/repaying-your-sleep-debt.

21. Shafaat Hussain and Truptimayee Parida, "Exploring Cyberloafing Behavior in South-Central Ethiopia: A Close Look at Madda Walabu University," *Journal of Media and Communication Studies* 9, no. 2 (February 2017): 10–16, http://www.academicjournals.org/journal/JMCS/article-full-text/9A73F0A62800.

22. Heyun Zhang, Huanhuan Zhao, Jingxuan Liu, Yan Xu, and Hui Lu, "The Dampening Effect of Employees' Future Orientation on Cyberloafing Behaviors: The Mediating Role of Self-Control," *Frontiers in Psychology* 6 (September 2015), http://journal.frontiersin.org/article/10.3389/fpsyg.2015.01482/full.

23 Mehlika Saraç and Aydem Çiftçioğlu, "What Do Human Resources Managers Think About the Employee's Internet Usage?" *Anadolu University Journal of Social Sciences* 14, no. 2 (2014): 1–12, https://lopes.idm.oclc.org/login?url=http://search.ebscohost.com/login.aspx?direct=true&db=a9h&AN=97023033&site=eds-live&scope=site.

24. Hussain and Parida, "Exploring Cyberloafing Behavior in South-Central Ethiopia."

25. Farzana Quoquab, Zarina Abdul Salam, and Siti Halimah, "Does Cyberloafing Boost Employee Productivity?" 2015 International Symposium on Technology Management and Emerging Technologies (ISTMET), 119–122, IEEE.

26. Asal Aghaz and Alireza Sheikh, "Cyberloafing and Job Burnout: An Investigation in the Knowledge-Intensive Sector," *Computers in Human Behavior* 62 (September 2016): 51–60, http://www.sciencedirect.com/science/article/pii/S0747563216302424.

27. Alexander Johannes Aloysius Maria van Deursen, Colin L. Bolle, Sabrina M. Hegner, and Petrus A. M. Kommers, "Modeling Habitual and Addictive Smartphone Behavior: The Role of Smartphone Usage Types, Emotional Intelligence, Social Stress, Self-Regulation, Age, and Gender," *Computers in Human Behavior* 45 (2015): 411–20, http://doc.utwente.nl/95319/1/1-s2.0-S0747563214007626-main.pdf.

28. Quoquab, Salam, and Halimah, "Does Cyberloafing Boost Employee Productivity?"

29. Simone M. Ritter and Ap Dijksterhuis, "Creativity—the Unconscious Foundations of the Incubation Period," *Frontiers in Human Neuroscience 8*, no. 1 (April 2014), doi:10.3389/fnhum.2014.00215.

30. Benjamin Baird, Jonathan Smallwood, Michael Mrazek, Julia W. Y. Kam, Michael S. Franklin, and Jonathan Schooler, "Inspired by Distraction: Mind Wandering Facilitates Creative Incubation," *Psychological Science* 23, no. 10 (August 2012): 1117–22.

31. Tom Palmer and Matthew Weiner, "Indian Summer," *Mad Men*, AMC, October 4, 2007.

32. Anna Almendrala, "Lin-Manuel Miranda: It's 'No Accident' *Hamilton* Came to Me on Vacation," Landit, May 26, 2018, https://landit.com/articles/lin-manuel-miranda-its-no-accident-hamilton-came-to-me-on-vacation.

33. Ibid.

34. James W. Pennebaker, "Traumatic Experience and Psychosomatic Disease: Exploring the Roles of Behavioural Inhibition, Obsession, and Confiding," *Canadian Psychology* 26, no. 2 (1985): 82–95.

35. James W. Pennebaker, *Writing to Heal: A Guided Journal for Recovering from Trauma & Emotional Upheaval* (Oakland, CA: New Harbinger Publications, 2004).

36. Stephen J. Lepore, "Expressive Writing Moderates the Relation between Intrusive Thoughts and Depressive Symptoms," *Journal of Personality and Social Psychology* 73, no. 5 (1997): 1030–37.

37. Danielle Arigo and Joshua M. Smyth, "The Benefits of Expressive Writing on Sleep Difficulty and Appearance Concerns for College Women," *Psychology & Health* 27, no. 2 (January 2011): 210–26.

38. Karen A. Baikie and Kay Wilhelm, "Emotional and Physical Health Benefits of Expressive Writing," *Advances in Psychiatric Treatment* 11, no. 5 (September 2005): 338–46.

39. Carolin Mogk, Sebastian Otte, Bettina Reinhold-Hurley, and Birgit Kröner-Herwig, "Health Effects of Expressive Writing on Stressful or Traumatic Experiences: A Meta-Analysis," *Psycho-Social Medicine* 3 (2006): Doc06.

40. Pennebaker, *Writing to Heal.*

41. Eva-Maria Gortner, Stephanie S. Rude, and James W. Pennebaker, "Benefits of Ex-

pressive Writing in Lowering Rumination and Depressive Symptoms," *Behavior Therapy* 37, no. 3 (September 2006): 292–303.

42. James W. Anderson, Chunxu Liu, and Richard J. Kryscio, "Blood Pressure Response to Transcendental Meditation: A Meta-Analysis," *American Journal of Hypertension* 21, no. 3 (March 2008): 310–16.

43. David S. Black and George M. Slavich, "Mindfulness Meditation and the Immune System: A Systematic Review of Randomized Controlled Trials," *Annals of the New York Academy of Sciences* 1373, no. 1 (June 2016): 13–24.

44. Li-Chuan Chu, "The Benefits of Meditation vis-à-vis Emotional Intelligence, Perceived Stress and Negative Mental Health," *Stress and Health: Journal of the International Society for the Investigation of Stress* 26, no. 2 (2010): 169–80.

Chapter Three: You Deserve to Work Less

1. Annette J. Towler, "Effects of Charismatic Influence Training on Attitudes, Behavior, and Performance," *Personnel Psychology* 56, no. 2 (2003): 363–81.

2. Steven C. Currall, Annette J. Towler, Timothy A. Judge, and Laura Kohn, "Pay Satisfaction and Organizational Outcomes," *Personnel Psychology* 58, no. 3 (September 2005): 613–40.

3. Annette J. Towler and Alice F. Stuhlmacher, "Attachment Styles, Relationship Satisfaction, and Well-Being in Working Women," *Journal of Social Psychology* 153, no. 3 (May–June 2013): 279–98.

4. Richard L. Porterfield, "The PERILS of Micromanagement," *Contract Management* 43, no. 2 (February 2003): 20–23.

5. John D. Owen, "Work-Time Reduction in the U.S. and Western Europe," *Monthly Labor Review* 111 (December 1988): 41–45.

6. Vicki Robin and Joe Dominguez, "Humans Once Worked Just 3 Hours a Day. Now We're Always Working, but Why?" Big Think, April 6, 2018, https://bigthink.com /big-think-books/vicki-robin-joe-dominguez-your-money-or-your-life.

7. John Hinshaw and Paul Le Blanc, eds., *U.S. Labor in the Twentieth Century: Studies in Working-Class Struggles and Insurgency* (Amherst, NY: Humanity Books, 2000).

8. Donald M. Fisk, "American Labor in the 20th Century," US Bureau of Labor Statistics, January 30, 2003, https://www.bls.gov/opub/mlr/cwc/american-labor-in -the-20th-century.pdf.

9. Robert Michael Smith, *From Blackjacks to Briefcases: A History of Commercialized Strikebreaking and Unionbusting in the United States* (Athens: Ohio University Press, 2003).

10. Joseph A. McCartin, *Labor's Great War: The Struggle for Industrial Democracy and the Origins of Modern American Labor Relations, 1912–1921* (Chapel Hill: University of North Carolina Press, 1997).

11. Lydia Saad, "The '40-Hour' Workweek Is Actually Longer—by Seven Hours," Gallup, August 29, 2014, https://news.gallup.com/poll/175286/hour-workweek -actually-longer-seven-hours.aspx.

12. Robin and Dominguez, "Humans Once Worked Just 3 Hours a Day."

13. Saad, "The '40-Hour' Workweek Is Actually Longer."

14. "Work and Workplace," Gallup, https://news.gallup.com/poll/1720/work-work -place.aspx.

15. "Survey: U.S. Workplace Not Family-Oriented," Associated Press, May 22, 2007,

http://www.nbcnews.com/id/16907584/ns/business-careers/t/survey-us-work place-not-family-oriented/#.XYEXOShKiUk.

16. US Department of Labor, Wage, and Hour Division, "Overtime Pay," https://www .dol.gov/agencies/whd/overtime#:~:text=Unless%20exempt%2C%20employees %20covered%20by,may%20work%20in%20any%20workweek.

17. "The Productivity-Pay Gap," Economic Policy Institute, July 2019, https://www.epi .org/productivity-pay-gap/.

18. Erik Rauch, "Productivity and the Workweek," 2000, http://groups.csail.mit.edu /mac/users/rauch/worktime/.

19. Victor Lipman, "Workplace Trend: Stress Is on the Rise," *Forbes*, January 9, 2019, https://www.forbes.com/sites/victorlipman/2019/01/09/workplace-trend -stress-is-on-the-rise/#71ceee946e1b.

20. David Blumenthal, MD, "The Decline of Employer-Sponsored Health Insurance," Commonwealth Fund, December 5, 2017, https://www.commonwealthfund.org /blog/2017/decline-employer-sponsored-health-insurance.

21. Lisa Greenwald and Paul Fronstin, PhD, "The State of Employee Benefits: Find- ings from the 2018 Health and Workplace Benefits Survey," Employee Ben- efit Research Institute, January 10, 2019, https://www.ebri.org/content/full /the-state-of-employee-benefits-findings-from-the-2018-health-and-workplace -benefits-survey.

22. Niall McCarthy, "American Workers Get the Short End on Vacation Days," *Forbes*, June 26, 2017, https://www.forbes.com/sites/niallmccarthy/2017/06/26/american -workers-have-a-miserable-vacation-allowance-infographic/#5fbf5035126d.

23. Meghan McCarty Carino, "American Workers Can Suffer Vacation Guilt . . . if They Take Vacations at All," Marketplace, July 12, 2019, https://www.marketplace.org /2019/07/12/american-workers-vacation-guilt/.

24. "Glassdoor Survey Finds American Forfeit Half of Their Earned Vacation/Paid Time Off," Glassdoor, May 24, 2017, https://www.glassdoor.com/about-us/glass door-survey-finds-americans-forfeit-earned-vacationpaid-time/.

25. Austin Frakt, "The High Costs of Not Offering Paid Sick Leave," *New York Times*, October 31, 2016, https://www.nytimes.com/2016/11/01/upshot/the-high-costs -of-not-offering-paid-sick-leave.

26. Kate Gibson, "American Airlines Accused of Punishing Workers Who Use Sick Time," CBS News, July 25, 2019, https://www.cbsnews.com/news/american -airlines-accused-of-punishing-workers-who-use-sick-time/.

27. Diana Boesch, Sarah Jane Glynn, and Shilpa Phadke, "Lack of Paid Leave Risks Public Health during the Coronavirus Outbreak," Center for American Progress, March 12, 2020, https://www.americanprogress.org/issues/women/news/2020 /03/12/481609/lack-paid-leave-risks-public-health-coronavirus-outbreak/.

28. "Paid Sick Days Improve Public Health," National Partnership for Women & Fam- ilies, February 2020, https://www.nationalpartnership.org/our-work/resources /economic-justice/paid-sick-days/paid-sick-days-improve-our-public-health .pdf.

29. Stephen R. Barley, Debra E. Meyerson, and Stine Grodal, "E-Mail as a Source and Symbol of Stress," *Organization Science* 22, no. 4 (July–August 2011): 887–906, doi:10.1287/orsc.1100.0573.

30. Daantje Derks, Desiree van Duin, Maria Tims, and Arnold B. Bakker, "Smart- phone Use and Work-Home Interference: The Moderating Role of Social Norms

and Employee Work Engagement," *Journal of Occupational and Organizational Psychology* 88, no. 1 (March 2015): 155–77.

31. "Work and Workplace," Gallup.
32. Kristine M. Kuhn, "The Rise of the 'Gig Economy' and Implications for Understanding Work and Workers," *Industrial and Organizational Psychology* 9, no. 1 (March 2016): 157–62.
33. Jessica Greene, "Is 40 Hours a Week Too Much? Here's What History and Science Say," askSpoke, https://www.askspoke.com/blog/hr/40-hour-work-week/.
34. John Pencavel, "The Productivity of Working Hours," Institute for the Study of Labor (Germany), April 2014, http://ftp.iza.org/dp8129.pdf.
35. "How Many Productive Hours in a Work Day? Just 2 Hours, 23 Minutes . . . ," Voucher Cloud.com, https://www.vouchercloud.com/resources/office-worker-productivity.
36. Geoffrey James, "New Research: Most Salaried Employees Only Do About 3 Hours of Real Work Each Day," *Inc.*, July 19, 2018, https://www.inc.com/geoffrey-james /new-research-most-salaried-employees-only-do-about-3-hours-of-real-work -each-day.html.
37. Deborah Dillon McDonald, Marjorie Wiczorek, and Cheryl Walker, "Factors Affecting Learning during Health Education Sessions," *Clinical Nursing Research* 13, no. 2 (May 2004): 156–67.
38. Donald A. Bligh, *What's the Use of Lectures?* (New York: Josey-Bass, 2000).
39. "How Long Should Training Videos Be?" Panopto, February 21, 2020, https://www .panopto.com/blog/how-long-should-training-videos-be/.
40. Catherine J. P. Oswald, Sébastien Tremblay, and Dylan Marc Jones, "Disruption of Comprehension by Meaning of Irrelevant Sound," *Memory* 8, no. 5 (October 2000): 345–50.
41. Harry Haroutioun Haladjian and Carlos Montemayor, "On the Evolution of Conscious Attention," *Psychonomic Bulletin & Review* 22, no. 3 (June 2015): 595–613.
42. R. W. Kentridge, C. A. Heywood, and L. Weiskrantz, "Attention Without Awareness in Blindsight," *Proceedings of the Royal Society B: Biological Sciences* 266, no. 1430 (September 1999): 1805–11.
43. Eyal Ophir, Clifford Nass, and Anthony D. Wagner, "Cognitive Control in Media Multitaskers," *Proceedings of the National Academy of Sciences of the United States of America* 106, no. 37 (September 2009): 15583–87.
44. Lori Sideman Goldberg and Alicia A. Grandey, "Display Rules versus Display Autonomy: Emotion Regulation, Emotional Exhaustion, and Task Performance in a Call Center Simulation," *Journal of Occupational Health Psychology* 12, no. 3 (July 2007): 301–18.
45. Jelle T. Prins, F. M. M. A. van der Heijden, Josette Hoekstra-Weebers, A. B. Bakker, Harry B. M. van de Wiel, B. Jacobs, and S. M. Gazendam-Donofrio, "Burnout, Engagement and Resident Physicians' Self-Reported Errors," *Psychology Health and Medicine* 14, no. 6 (December 2009): 654–66.
46. Hengchen Dai, Katherine L. Milkman, David A. Hofmann, and Bradley R. Staats, "The Impact of Time at Work and Time Off from Work on Rule Compliance: The Case of Hand Hygiene in Health Care," *Journal of Applied Psychology* 100, no. 3 (2015): 846–62.
47. Stephen Deery, Roderick Iverson, and Janet Walsh, "Work Relationships in Telephone Call Centres: Understanding Emotional Exhaustion and Employee Withdrawal," *Journal of Management Studies* 39, no. 4 (June 2002): 471–96.

NOTES

48. Ken J. Gilhooly, George Georgiou, and Ultan Devery, "Incubation and Creativity: Do Something Different," *Thinking & Reasoning* 19, no. 2 (2013): 137–49.

49. Renzo Bianchi, Eric Laurent, Irvin Sam Schonfeld, Lucas M. Bietti, and Eric Mayor, "Memory Bias toward Emotional Information in Burnout and Depression," *Journal of Health Psychology* (March 2018), doi:10.1177/1359105318765621.

50. Renzo Bianchi, Eric Laurent, Irvin Sam Schonfeld, Jay Verkuilen, and Chantal Berna, "Interpretation Bias toward Ambiguous Information in Burnout and Depression," *Personality and Individual Differences* 135 (2018): 216–21.

51. Christina Maslach and Susan E. Jackson, "Burnout in Organizational Settings," *Applied Social Psychology Annual* 5 (1984): 133–53.

52. Christina Maslach and Susan E. Jackson, "The Measurement of Experienced Burnout," *Journal of Organizational Behavior* 2, no. 2 (April 1981): 99–113.

53. Maslach and Jackson, "Burnout in Organizational Settings."

54. Maslach and Jackson, "The Measurement of Experienced Burnout."

55. Arnold B. Bakker, Pascale M. Le Blanc, and Wilmar B. Schaufeli, "Burnout Contagion among Intensive Care Nurses," *Journal of Advanced Nursing* 51, no. 3 (August 2005): 276–87.

56. Maslach and Jackson, "The Measurement of Experienced Burnout."

57. Carolyn S. Dewa, Desmond Loong, Sarah Bonato, Nguyen Xuan Thanh, and Philip Jacobs, "How Does Burnout Affect Physician Productivity? A Systematic Literature Review," *BMC Health Services Research* 14, no. 1 (July 2014): 325.

58. Ingo Angermeier, Benjamin B. Dunford, Alan D. Boss, and R. Wayne Boss, "The Impact of Participative Management Perceptions on Customer Service, Medical Errors, Burnout, and Turnover Intentions," *Journal of Healthcare Management* 54, no. 2 (March–April 2009): 127–40.

59. Krystyna Golonka, Justyna Mojsa-Kaja, Katarzyna Popiel, Tadeusz Marek, and Magda Gawlowska, "Neurophysiological Markers of Emotion Processing in Burnout Syndrome," *Frontiers in Psychology* 8 (2017): 2155, doi:10.3389/fpsyg.2017.02155.

60. Sarah Green Carmichael, "Working Long Hours Makes Us Drink More," *Harvard Business Review*, April 10, 2015, https://hbr.org/2015/04/working-long-hours-makes-us-drink-more.

61. Charles A. Morgan III, Bartlett Russell, Jeff McNeil, Jeff Maxwell, Peter J. Snyder, Steven M. Southwick, and Robert H. Pietrzak, "Baseline Burnout Symptoms Predict Visuospatial Executive Function during Survival School Training in Special Operations Military Personnel," *Journal of the International Neuropsychological Society* 17, no. 3 (May 2011): 494–501, doi:10.1017/S1355617711000221.

62. Tom Redman, Peter Hamilton, Hedley Malloch, and Birgit Kleymann, "Working Here Makes Me Sick! The Consequences of Sick Building Syndrome," *Human Resource Management Journal* 21, no. 1 (December 2010): 14–27.

63. Christina Maslach, "What Have We Learned about Burnout and Health?" *Psychology and Health* 16, no. 5 (September 2001): 607–11.

64. Eva Blix, Aleksander Perski, Hans Berglund, and Ivanka Savic, "Long-Term Occupational Stress Is Associated with Regional Reductions in Brain Tissue Volumes," *PLoS One* 8, no. 6 (2013): e64065, doi:10.1371/journal.pone.0064065.

65. Kaitlin Smith, "Some Thoughts on Lifestyle Design for Wild Minds," Wild Mind Collective, August 30, 2017, https://www.wildmindcollective.com/483-2/.

66. Elnar M. Skaalvik and Sidsel Skaalvik, "Teacher Self-Efficacy and Perceived

Autonomy: Relations with Teacher Engagement, Job Satisfaction, and Emotional Exhaustion," *Psychological Reports* 114, no. 1 (February 2014): 68–77.

67. Anders Dysvik and Bård Kuvaas, "Intrinsic Motivation as a Moderator on the Relationship between Perceived Job Autonomy and Work Performance," *European Journal of Work and Organizational Psychology* 20, no. 3 (June 2011): 367–87.

68. Wenqin Zhang, Steve M. Jex, Yisheng Peng, and Dongdong Wang, "Exploring the Effects of Job Autonomy on Engagement and Creativity: The Moderating Role of Performance Pressure and Learning Goal Orientation," *Journal of Business and Psychology* 32, no. 3 (June 2016): 235–51.

69. "About CQ Net—Management Skills for Everyone!" CQ Net, https://www.ckju.net/en/about-cq-net-management-skills-for-everyone/37034.

70. Mark R. Lepper, David Greene, and Richard E. Nisbett, "Undermining Children's Intrinsic Interest with Extrinsic Reward: A Test of the 'Overjustification' Hypothesis," *Journal of Personality and Social Psychology* 28, no. 1 (1973): 129–37, doi:10.1037/h0035519.

71. Barry Gerhart, Sara L. Rynes, and Ingrid Smithey Fulmer, "Pay and Performance: Individuals, Groups, and Executives," *Academy of Management Annals* 3, no. 1 (January 2009): 251–315, doi:10.1080/19416520903047269.

72. Trish A. Petak and Gabbie S. Miller, "Increasing Employee Motivation and Organization Productivity by Implementing Flex-Time," *ASBBS Proceedings* 26 (2019): 409–23.

73. Evangelia Demerouti, Arnold B. Bakker, and Josette M. P. Gevers, "Job Crafting and Extra-Role Behavior: The Role of Work Engagement and Flourishing," *Journal of Vocational Behavior* 91 (December 2015): 87–96.

Chapter Four: Your Achievements Are Not Your Worth

1. Andrew Tobias, *The Best Little Boy in the World* (New York: Ballantine Books, 1973).

2. Christopher D. DeSante, "Working Twice as Hard to Get Half as Far: Race, Work Ethic, and America's Deserving Poor," *American Journal of Political Science* 57, no. 2 (April 2013): 342–56, http://www.jstor.org/stable/23496601.

3. Brent Barnhart, "How the Facebook Algorithm Works and Ways to Outsmart It," Sprout Social, May 31, 2019, https://sproutsocial.com/insights/facebook-algorithm/.

4. Jillian Warren, "This Is How the Instagram Algorithm Works in 2020," Later, February 3, 2020, https://later.com/blog/how-instagram-algorithm-works/.

5. Josh Constine, "Now Facebook Says It May Remove Like Counts," TechCrunch, September 2, 2019, https://techcrunch.com/2019/09/02/facebook-hidden-likes/.

6. Fred B. Bryant and Joseph Veroff, *Savoring: A New Model of Positive Experience* (Mahwah, NJ: Lawrence Erlbaum Associates, 2007).

7. HaeEun Helen Chun, Kristin Diehl, and Deborah J. Macinnis, "Savoring an Upcoming Experience Affects Ongoing and Remembered Consumption Enjoyment," *Journal of Marketing* 81, no. 3 (January 2017): 96–110.

8. Daniel B. Hurley and Paul Kwon, "Savoring Helps Most When You Have Little: Interaction between Savoring the Moment and Uplifts on Positive Affect and Satisfaction with Life," *Journal of Happiness Studies* 14, no. 4 (September 2012): 1261–71.

9. Fred B. Bryant, Colette M. Smart, and Scott P. King, "Using the Past to Enhance the Present: Boosting Happiness through Positive Reminiscence," *Journal of Happiness Studies* 6, no. 3 (2005): 227–60.

10. Hurley and Kwon, "Savoring Helps Most When You Have Little."

11. Jennifer L. Smith and Linda Hollinger-Smith, "Savoring, Resilience, and Psychological Well-Being in Older Adults," *Aging & Mental Health* 19, no. 3 (2015): 192–200.

12. Paul Grossman, Ludger Niemann, Stefan Schmidt, and Harald Walach, "Mindfulness-Based Stress Reduction and Health Benefits: A Meta-Analysis," *Journal of Psychosomatic Research* 57, no. 1 (July 2004): 35–43.

13. Anthony D. Ong, Daniel K. Mroczek, and Catherine Riffin, "The Health Significance of Positive Emotions in Adulthood and Later Life," *Social and Personality Psychology Compass* 5, no. 8 (August 2011): 538–51.

14. Jordi Quoidbach, Elizabeth V. Berry, Michel Hansenne, and Moïra Mikolajczak, "Positive Emotion Regulation and Well-Being: Comparing the Impact of Eight Savoring and Dampening Strategies," *Personality and Individual Differences* 49, no. 5 (October 2010): 368–73.

15. Ibid.

16. Jeff Haden, "Science Says Time Really Does Seem to Fly as We Get Older. This Is the Best Way to Slow It Back Down," *Inc.*, October 16, 2017, https://www.inc.com /jeff-haden/science-says-time-really-does-seem-to-fly-as-we-get-older-this-is -best-way-to-slow-it-back-down.html.

17. Melanie Rudd, Kathleen Vohs, and Jennifer Aaker, "Awe Expands People's Perception of Time, Alters Decision Making, and Enhances Well-Being," *Psychological Science* 23, no. 10 (August 2012): 1130–36.

18. Quoidbach, Berry, Hansenne, and Mikolajczak, "Positive Emotion Regulation and Well-Being."

19. Jan Kornelis Dijkstra, Antonius H. N. Cillessen, Siegwart Lindenberg, and René Veenstra, "Basking in Reflected Glory and Its Limits: Why Adolescents Hang Out with Popular Peers," *Journal of Research on Adolescence* 20, no. 4 (December 2010): 942–58.

20. Alice Chirico and David Bryce Yaden, "Awe: A Self-Transcendent and Sometimes Transformative Emotion," in Heather C. Lench, ed., *The Function of Emotions* (New York: Springer, 2018), 221–33.

21. Christina Maslach and Michael P. Leiter, "Reversing Burnout: How to Rekindle Your Passion for Your Work," *Stanford Social Innovation Review*, Winter 2005, 43–49.

22. Christina M. Puchalski and Margaret Guenther, "Restoration and Re-Creation: Spirituality in the Lives of Healthcare Professionals," *Current Opinion in Supportive and Palliative Care* 6, no. 2 (June 2012): 254–58.

23. Mary L. White, Rosalind Peters, and Stephanie Myers Schim, "Spirituality and Spiritual Self-Care: Expanding Self-Care Deficit Nursing Theory," *Nursing Science Quarterly* 24, no. 1 (January 2011): 48–56.

24. Joe Palca, "Why the Trip Home Seems to Go by Faster," NPR, September 5, 2011, https://www.npr.org/2011/09/05/140159009/why-the-trip-home-seems-to-go -by-faster.

25. Judith Halberstam, *The Queer Art of Failure* (Durham, NC: Duke University Press, 2011).

26. Ibid., 88.

27. Thuy Ong, "Apple Says It Will Introduce New Features to Help Parents Protect Children," *Verge*, January 9, 2018, https://www.theverge.com/2018/1/9/16867330 / apple-response-smartphone-addiction-youth.

28. Amanda Christine Egan, "The Psychological Impact of Smartphones: The Effect of Access to One's Smartphone on Psychological Power, Risk Taking, Cheating, and Moral Orientation," PhD dissertation, Loyola University Chicago, 2016.

29. "Do You Think You Could Go One Day a Week for Three Months Without Digital Technology?" Digital Sabbath, https://digitalsabbath.io/.

30. Marcello Russo, Massimo Bergami, and Gabriele Morandin, "Surviving a Day Without Smartphones," *MIT Sloan Management Review*, Winter 2018, https://sloanreview.mit.edu/article/surviving-a-day-without-smartphones/.

31. Kostadin Kushlev, Jason D. E. Proulx, and Elizabeth Dunn, "'Silence Your Phones': Smartphone Notifications Increase Inattention and Hyperactivity Symptoms," *Proceedings of the 2016 CHI Conference on Human Factors in Computing Systems*, 1011–20.

32. Jon D. Elhai, Robert D. Dvorak, Jason C. Levine, and Brian J. Hall, "Problematic Smartphone Use: A Conceptual Overview and Systematic Review of Relations with Anxiety and Depression Psychopathology," *Journal of Affective Disorders* 207 (January 2017): 251–59.

33. Amy Kosterlitz, "The Four Traits of Confidence: Growth Mindset, Courage, Grit, and Self-Compassion," *Woman Advocate* 21, no. 1 (November 2015): 12–17.

Chapter Five: You Don't Have to Be an Expert in Everything

1. "The Academic Major," in James W. Guthrie, ed., *Encyclopedia of Education*, 2nd edition, vol. 1 (New York: Macmillan Reference USA, 2006), 19–23.

2. Lydia Dishman, "How the Master's Degree Became the New Bachelor's in the Hiring World," Fast Company, March 17, 2016, https://www.fastcompany.com/3057941/how-the-masters-degree-became-the-new-bachelors-in-the-hiring-world.

3. Laura Pappano, "The Master's as the New Bachelor's," *New York Times*, July 22, 2011, https://www.nytimes.com/2011/07/24/education/edlife/edl-24masters-t.html.

4. Jon Marcus, "Graduate Programs Have Become a Cash Cow for Struggling Colleges. What Does That Mean for Students?" PBS News Hour, September 18, 2017, https://www.pbs.org/newshour/education/graduate-programs-become-cash-cow-struggling-colleges-mean-students.

5. J. Steven Perry, "What Is Big Data? More Than Volume, Velocity and Variety . . ." *developerWorks* (blog), IBM.com, May 22, 2017.

6. IMB Marketing Cloud, "10 Key Marketing Trends for 2017," original retrieved from: https://public.dhe.ibm.com/common/ssi/ecm/wr/en/wrl12345usen/watson-customer-engagement-watson-marketing-wr-other-papers-and-reports-wrl12345usen-20170719.pdf.

7. "Welcome to the Information Age: 174 Newspapers a Day," *Telegraph*, https://www.telegraph.co.uk/news/science/science-news/8316534/Welcome-to-the-information-age-174-newspapers-a-day.html.

8. And that's to say nothing of how traumatic working as a social media moderator can be; see Casey Newton, "The Trauma Floor: The Secret Lives of Facebook Moderators in America," *Verge*, February 25, 2019, https://www.theverge.com/2019/2/25/18229714/cognizant-facebook-content-moderator-interviews-trauma-working-conditions-arizona.

9. "APA *Stress in America* Survey: US at 'Lowest Point We Can Remember'; Future of Nation Most Commonly Reported Source of Stress," American Psychological Association, November 1, 2017, https://www.apa.org/news/press/releases/2017/11/lowest-point.

10. Ibid.

11. Grace Ferrari Levine, "Learned Helplessness in Local TV News," *Journalism & Mass Communication Quarterly* 63, no. 1 (March 1986): 12–18.

12. Grace Ferrari Levine, "'Learned Helplessness' and the Evening News," *Journal of Communication* 27, no. 4 (December 1977): 100–105.

13. Ted Chiricos, Kathy Padgett, and Marc Gertz, "Fear, TV News, and the Reality of Crime," *Criminology* 38, no. 3 (August 2000): 755–86.

14. Mirka Smolej and Janne Kivivuori, "The Relation between Crime News and Fear of Violence," *Journal of Scandinavian Studies in Criminology and Crime Prevention* 7, no. 2 (2006): 211–27.

15. F. Arendt and T. Northup, "Effects of Long-Term Exposure to News Stereotypes on Implicit and Explicit Attitudes," *International Journal of Communication* 9 (January 2015): 21.

16. Robin L. Nabi and Abby Prestin, "Unrealistic Hope and Unnecessary Fear: Exploring How Sensationalistic News Stories Influence Health Behavior Motivation," *Health Communication* 31, no. 9 (September 2016): 1115–26.

17. Jeff Niederdeppe, Erika Franklin Fowler, Kenneth Goldstein, and James Pribble, "Does Local Television News Coverage Cultivate Fatalistic Beliefs about Cancer Prevention?" *Journal of Communication* 60, no. 2 (June 2010): 230–53.

18. Erika Salomon, Jesse Preston, and Melanie B. Tannenbaum, "Climate Change Helplessness and the (De)moralization of Individual Energy Behavior," *Journal of Experimental Psychology: Applied* 23, no. 1 (2017): 15–28.

19. Adam Gorlick, "Media Multitaskers Pay Mental Price, Stanford Study Shows," Stanford News, August 24, 2009, https://news.stanford.edu/news/2009/august24/multitask-research-study-082409.html.

20. On Amir, "Tough Choices: How Making Decisions Tires Your Brain," *Scientific American*, July 22, 2008, https://www.scientificamerican.com/article/tough-choices-how-making/.

21. Ibid.

22. Mary Atamaniuk, "Phishing: What Is Phishing and What to Do about It," Clario, February 7, 2020, https://stopad.io/blog/phishing-spearphishing-security.

23. Marc-André Reinhard, "Need for Cognition and the Process of Lie Detection," *Journal of Experimental Social Psychology* 46, no. 6 (November 2010): 961–71.

24. John B. Horrigan, "Information Overload," Pew Research Center, December 7, 2016, https://www.pewinternet.org/2016/12/07/information-overload/.

25. Rose Zimering, PhD, and Suzy Bird Gulliver, PhD, "Secondary Traumatization in Mental Health Care Providers," *Psychiatric Times*, April 1, 2003, https://www.psychiatrictimes.com/ptsd/secondary-traumatization-mental-health-care-providers.

26. James Hale, "'Sadblock' Google Chrome Extension Helps You Avoid Sad, Triggering, or Just Plain Annoying News," Bustle, December 1, 2017, https://www.bustle.com/p/sadblock-google-chrome-extension-helps-you-avoid-sad-triggering-just-plain-annoying-news-6748012.

27. CustomBlocker, Google Chrome Web Store, https://chrome.google.com/webstore/detail/customblocker/elnfhbjabfcepfnaeoehffgmifcfjlha?hl=en.

28. Natalie Jomini Stroud, Emily Van Duyn, and Cynthia Peacock, "News Commenters and News Comment Readers," Engaging News Project, 1–21.

29. Isabelle Krebs and Juliane A. Lischka, "Is Audience Engagement Worth the Buzz? The Value of Audience Engagement, Comment Reading, and Content for Online News Brands," *Journalism* 20, no. 2 (January 2017): 714–32.

30. Stroud, Van Duyn, and Peacock, "News Commenters and News Comment Readers."

NOTES

31. Ricky Romero, "Shut Up: Comment Blocker," Firefox Browser Add-Ons, https://addons.mozilla.org/en-US/firefox/addon/shut-up-comment-blocker/.

32. M. Bodas, M. Siman-Tov, K. Peleg, and Z. Solomo, "Anxiety-inducing media: the effect of constant news broadcasting on the well-being of Israeli television viewers,"*Psychiatry* 78, no. 3 (2015): 265–76.

33. S. P. Roche, J. T. Pickett, and M. Gertz, "The scary world of online news? Internet news exposure and public attitudes toward crime and justice," *Journal of Quantitative Criminology* 32, no. 2 (2016): 215–36.

34. Dr. Bruce Weinstein, "Stop Watching the News (for Awhile)," *Huffpost*, December 6, 2017.

35. Richard E. Petty and John T. Cacioppo, "The Elaboration Likelihood Model of Persuasion," in *Communication and Persuasion: Central and Peripheral Routes to Attitude Change* (New York: Springer, 1986), 1–24.

36. Ibid.

37. Andreu Vigil-Colet, Pere Joan Ferrando, and Pueyo Atanio Andrés, "Initial Stages of Information Processing and Inspection Time: Electrophysiological Correlates," *Personality and Individual Differences* 14, no. 5 (May 1993): 733–38, doi:10.1016/0191-8869(93)90121-i.

38. D. S. McNamara, R. Best, and C. Castellano, "Learning from Text: Facilitating and Enhancing Comprehension," SpeechPathology.com, 2004, www.speechpathology.com.

39. Keith N. Hampton, Inyoung Shin, and Weixu Lu, "Social Media and Political Discussion: When Online Presence Silences Offline Conversation," *Information, Communication & Society* 20, no. 7 (2017): 1090–107.

40. Michael J. Mallen, Susan X. Day, and Melinda A. Green, "Online versus Face-to-Face Conversation: An Examination of Relational and Discourse Variables," *Psychotherapy: Theory, Research, Practice, Training* 40, nos. 1–2 (2003): 155–63.

41. Devon Price, "Comment Culture Must Be Stopped," Medium, May 22, 2019, https://medium.com/@devonprice/comment-culture-must-be-stopped-6355d894b0a6.

Chapter Six: Your Relationships Should Not Leave You Exhausted

1. Lindsay C. Gibson, *Adult Children of Emotionally Immature Parents: How to Heal from Distant, Rejecting, or Self-Involved Parents* (Oakland, CA: New Harbinger Publications, 2015), chapter 1.

2. Arlie Hochschild and Anne Machung, *The Second Shift: Working Families and the Revolution at Home* (New York: Penguin, 2012).

3. Theodore N. Greenstein, "Gender Ideology and Perceptions of the Fairness of the Division of Household Labor: Effects on Marital Quality," *Social Forces* 74, no. 3 (March 1996): 1029–42.

4. Emma, "You Should've Asked," EmmaCLit.com, May 20, 2017, https://english.emmaclit.com/2017/05/20/you-shouldve-asked/.

5. Colleen Flaherty, "Relying on Women, Not Rewarding Them," Inside Higher Ed, April 12, 2017, https://www.insidehighered.com/news/2017/04/12/study-finds-female-professors-outperform-men-service-their-possible-professional.

6. Manya Whitaker, "The Unseen Labor of Mentoring," *Chronicle of Higher Education*, June 12, 2017, https://chroniclevitae.com/news/1825-the-unseen-labor-of-mentoring.

7. Marlese Durr and Adia M. Harvey Wingfield, "Keep Your 'N' in Check: African

American Women and the Interactive Effects of Etiquette and Emotional Labor," *Critical Sociology* 37, no. 5 (March 2011): 557–71.

8. Social Sciences Feminist Network Research Interest Group, "The Burden of Invisible Work in Academia: Social Inequalities and Time Use in Five University Departments," *Humboldt Journal of Social Relations* 39, no. 39 (2017): 228–45, http://www.jstor.org/stable/90007882.

9. "Values Clarification," Therapist Aid, https://www.therapistaid.com/therapy-worksheet/values-clarification.

10. Miriam Liss, Holly H. Schiffrin, and Kathryn M. Rizzo, "Maternal Guilt and Shame: The Role of Self-Discrepancy and Negative Evaluation," *Journal of Child and Family Studies* 22 (2013): 1112–19, doi:10.1007/s10826-012-9673-2.

11. John B. Watson, *Psychological Care of Infant and Child* (New York: W. W. Norton & Co., 1928).

12. William Sears, MD, and Martha Sears, RN, *The Attachment Parenting Book: A Commonsense Guide to Understanding and Nurturing Your Baby* (Boston: Little, Brown and Company, 2001), 2f, 5, 8–10, 110.

13. Foster Cline, MD, and Jim Fay, *Parenting with Love and Logic: Teaching Children Responsibility* (Colorado Springs, CO: Piñon Press, 1990), 23–25.

14. Kathryn M. Rizzo, Holly H. Schiffrin, and Miriam Liss, "Insight into the Parenthood Paradox: Mental Health Outcomes of Intensive Mothering," *Journal of Child and Family Studies* 22, no. 5 (2013): 614–20, doi:10.1007/s10826-012-9615-z.

15. Baylor College of Medicine, "How to Deal with Online Mom-Shaming," Medical Xpress, July 13, 2018, https://medicalxpress.com/news/2018-07-online-mom-shaming.html.

16. In the original literature (and even in some contemporary writing), this was referred to as the "good-enough mother." I'm using the gender-neutral "parent" here, because a loving, present, supportive parent of any gender can be more than good enough.

17. D. W. Winnicott, *The Child, the Family, and the Outside World* (New York: Penguin, 1973), 173.

18. Carla Naumburg, "The Gift of the Good Enough Mother," Seleni, March 14, 2018, https://www.seleni.org/advice-support/2018/3/14/the-gift-of-the-good-enough-mother.

19. Peter Gray, PhD, "The Good Enough Parent Is the Best Parent," *Psychology Today*, December 22, 2015, https://www.psychologytoday.com/us/blog/freedom-learn/201512/the-good-enough-parent-is-the-best-parent.

20. Jonathan Stern, "Why Spending Time Alone Is the Key to Keeping Your Family Together," Fatherly, May 23, 2016, https://www.fatherly.com/love-money/relationships/how-to-have-a-life-outside-parenting/.

21. Michael Torrice, "Want Passionate Kids? Leave 'Em Alone," Live Science, February 9, 2010, https://www.livescience.com/6085-passionate-kids-leave-em.html.

22. Albert J. Bernstein, *How to Deal with Emotionally Explosive People* (New York: McGraw Hill Professional, 2002), 41.

23. Ibid., 17–20. Tips adapted from advice provided in the book, but edited, paired with unproductive behaviors, and placed in a table by me.

Chapter Seven: Shrugging Off Society's "Shoulds"

1. "Mad Style: Man with a Plan," TomandLorenzo.com, May 15, 2013, https://tomandlorenzo.com/2013/05/mad-style-man-with-a-plan/.

2. Denise Martin, "*Mad Men*'s Teyonah Parris on Dawn's Surprise Promotion, Don vs. Lou, and Doing Improv with Amy Poehler," *Vulture*, April 21, 2014, https://www.vulture.com/2014/04/teyonah-parris-dawn-mad-men-chat.html.

3. "Mad Men: Ending Explained," The Take, https://www.youtube.com/watch?v=mDHxXY6FL_8.

4. Melungeon is a complex racial identity, and its relationship to whiteness is complicated. See A. Puckett, "The Melungeon identity movement and the construction of Appalachian whiteness," *Journal of Linguistic Anthropology* 11, no. 1 (2001): 131–46 and M. Schrift, *Becoming Melungeon: Making an Ethnic Identity in the Appalachian South.* (Lincoln, NE: Univ. of Nebraska Press, 2013).

5. Siraad Dirshe, "Black Women Speak Up about Their Struggles Wearing Natural Hair in the Workplace," *Essence*, February 7, 2018, https://www.essence.com/hair/black-women-natural-hair-discrimination-workplace/.

6. Gemn Jewelery, "A Guide to Wear Jewellery in the Workplace," Medium, December 16, 2016, https://medium.com/@gemnjewelery1/a-guide-to-wear-jewellery-in-the-workplace-29744e543266.

7. Jacob Tobia, "Why I'm Genderqueer, Professional, and Unafraid," *HuffPost*, December 6, 2017, https://www.huffpost.com/entry/genderqueer-professional-_b_5476239.

8. "The $72 Billion Weight Loss & Diet Control Market in the United States, 2019–2023," BusinessWire, February 25, 2019, https://www.businesswire.com/news/home/20190225005455/en/72-Billion-Weight-Loss-Diet-Control-Market.

9. John LaRosa, "Top 9 Things to Know about the Weight Loss Industry," MarketResearch.com, March 6, 2019, https://blog.marketresearch.com/u.s.-weight-loss-industry-grows-to-72-billion.

10. Your Fate Friend, "The Bizarre and Racist History of the BMI," Medium, October 15, 2019, https://elemental.medium.com/the-bizarre-and-racist-history-of-the-bmi-7d8dc2aa33bb.

11. Kelly Crowe, "Obesity Research Confirms Long-Term Weight Loss Almost Impossible," CBC News, June 4, 2014, https://www.cbc.ca/news/health/obesity-research-confirms-long-term-weight-loss-almost-impossible-1.2663585.

12. Harriet Brown, "The Weight of the Evidence," *Slate*, March 24, 2015, https://slate.com/technology/2015/03/diets-do-not-work-the-thin-evidence-that-losing-weight-makes-you-healthier.html.

13. Crowe, "Obesity Research Confirms Long-Term Weight Loss Almost Impossible."

14. A. Janet Tomiyama, Britt Ahlstrom, and Traci Mann, "Long-Term Effects of Dieting: Is Weight Loss Related to Health?" *Social and Personality Psychology Compass* 7, no. 12 (2013): 861–77, http://www.dishlab.org/pubs/2013%20Compass.pdf.

15. "kellybellyohio," Instagram, https://www.instagram.com/kellybellyohio/.

16. J. Gerard Power, Sheila T. Murphy, and Gail Coover, "Priming Prejudice: How Stereotypes and Counter-Stereotypes Influence Attribution of Responsibility and Credibility among Ingroups and Outgroups," *Human Communication Research* 23, no. 1 (September 1996): 36–58.

17. Jamie L. Dunaev, Paula M. Brochu, and Charlotte H. Markey, "Imagine That! The Effect of Counterstereotypic Imagined Intergroup Contact on Weight Bias," *Health Psychology* 37, no. 1 (January 2018): 81–88.

18. Russell B. Clayton, Jessica L. Ridgway, and Joshua Hendrickse, "Is Plus Size Equal? The Positive Impact of Average and Plus-Sized Media Fashion Models

on Women's Cognitive Resource Allocation, Social Comparisons, and Body Satisfaction," *Communication Monographs* 84, no. 3 (2017): 406–22, doi:10.1080 /03637751.2017.1332770.

19. Rachel Andrew, Marika Tiggemann, and Levina Clark, "The Protective Role of Body Appreciation against Media-Induced Body Dissatisfaction," *Body Image* 15 (August 2015): 98–104.

20. Peter Strelan and Duane Hargreaves, "Reasons for Exercise and Body Esteem: Men's Responses to Self-Objectification," *Sex Roles* 53, nos. 7–8 (2005): 495–503.

21. B. L. Fredrickson, T. A. Roberts, S. M. Noll, D. M. Quinn, and J. M. Twenge, "That Swimsuit Becomes You: Sex Differences in Self-Objectification, Restrained Eating, and Math Performance," *Journal of Personality and Social Psychology* 75, no. 1 (July 1998): 269–84.

22. Brit Harper and Marika Tiggemann, "The Effect of Thin Ideal Media Images on Women's Self-Objectification, Mood, and Body Image," *Sex Roles* 58, nos. 9–10 (2008): 649–57.

23. Tracy L. Tylka and Casey L. Augustus-Horvath, "Fighting Self-Objectification in Prevention and Intervention Contexts," in Rachel M. Calogero, Stacey Tantleff-Dunn, and J. Kevin Thompson, eds., *Self-Objectification in Women: Causes, Consequences, and Counteractions* (Washington, DC: American Psychological Association, 2011), 187–214.

24. Jessie E. Menzel and Michael P. Levine, "Embodying Experiences and the Promotion of Positive Body Image: The Example of Competitive Athletics," in Calogero, Tantleff-Dunn, and Thompson, eds., *Self-Objectification in Women*.

25. Elle Hunt, "Essena O'Neill Quits Instagram Claiming Social Media 'Is Not Real Life,'" *Guardian*, November 3, 2015, https://www.theguardian.com/media/2015 /nov/03/instagram-star-essena-oneill-quits-2d-life-to-reveal-true-story-behind -images.

26. Kristina Rodulfo, "100 Shots, One Day of Not Eating: What Happens When You Say What Really Goes into the Perfect Bikini Selfie?" *Elle*, November 2, 2015, https:// www.elle.com/culture/news/a31635/essena-oneill-instagram-social-media-is -not-real-life/.

27. Ged, "18-Year-Old Model Edits Her Instagram Posts to Reveal the Truth behind the Photos," Bored Panda, https://www.boredpanda.com/truth-behind-insta gram-social-media-not-real-life-essena-oneill/?utm_source=google&utm_me dium=organic&utm_campaign=organic.

28. Maria Fischer, "These Honest Photos Show Why You Should Never Compare Your Body to Bloggers," Revelist, June 21, 2017, https://www.revelist.com/internet /bloggers-photoshopped-body-photos/8165/following-goodheads-lead-more -and-more-youtubers-bloggers-and-social-media-influencers-have-committed -themselves-to-the-fight-against-photoshop/2.

29. Erin A. Vogel, Jason P. Rose, Lindsay Roberts, and Katheryn Eckles, "Social Comparison, Social Media, and Self-Esteem," *Psychology of Popular Media Culture* 3, no. 4 (2014): 206–22.

30. Jacqueline Nesi and Mitchell J. Prinstein, "Using Social Media for Social Comparison and Feedback-Seeking: Gender and Popularity Moderate Associations with Depressive Symptoms," *Journal of Abnormal Child Psychology* 43, no. 8 (November 2015): 1427–38, doi:10.1007/s10802-015-0020-0.

31. Jiyoung Chae, "Virtual Makeover: Selfie-Taking and Social Media Use Increase

Selfie-Editing Frequency through Social Comparison," *Computers in Human Behavior* 66 (January 2017): 370–76.

32. Siân A. McLean, Susan J. Paxton, Eleanor H. Wertheim, and Jennifer Masters, "Photoshopping the Selfie: Self Photo Editing and Photo Investment Are Associated with Body Dissatisfaction in Adolescent Girls," *International Journal of Eating Disorders* 48, no. 8 (December 2015): 1132–40.

33. Erin A. Vogel, Jason P. Rose, Bradley M. Okdie, Katheryn Eckles, and Brittany Franz, "Who Compares and Despairs? The Effect of Social Comparison Orientation on Social Media Use and Its Outcomes," *Personality and Individual Differences* 86 (November 2015): 249–56.

34. Jonathan R. B. Halbesleben and M. Ronald Buckley, "Social Comparison and Burnout: The Role of Relative Burnout and Received Social Support," *Anxiety, Stress & Coping* 19, no. 3 (2006): 259–78.

35. Chiara Rollero, "'I Know You Are Not Real': Salience of Photo Retouching Reduces the Negative Effects of Media Exposure via Internalization," *Studia Psychologica* 57, no. 3 (2015): 195–202.

36. Pieternel Dijkstra, Frederick X. Gibbons, and Abraham P. Buunk, "Social Comparison Theory," in James E. Maddux and June Price Tangney, eds., *Social Psychological Foundations of Clinical Psychology* (New York: Guilford Press, 2011), 195–207 [italics mine].

37. Susan Clayton Whitmore-Williams, Christie Manning, Kirra Krygsman, and Meighen Speiser, "Mental Health and Our Changing Climate: Impacts, Implications, and Guidance," American Psychological Association, March 2017, https://www.apa.org/news/press/releases/2017/03/mental-health-climate.pdf.

38. Anthony Leiserowitz, Edward Maibach, Connie Roser-Renouf, Seth Rosenthal, Matthew Cutler, and John Kotcher, "Climate Change in the American Mind: March 2018," Yale Program on Climate Change Communication, April 17, 2018, https://climatecommunication.yale.edu/publications/climate-change-american-mind-march-2018/2/.

39. Whitmore-Williams, Manning, Krygsman, and Speiser, "Mental Health and Our Changing Climate."

40. "Planting for the Future in a Changing Climate," Chicago Botanic Garden, https://www.chicagobotanic.org/education/symposia_professional_programs/future planting.

41. "First Nations Community Garden," American Indian Center, https://www.aicchicago.org/first-nations-community-garden.

Conclusion: Compassion Kills the Laziness Lie

1. Galen V. Bodenhausen, Andrew R. Todd, and Jennifer A. Richeson, "Controlling Prejudice and Stereotyping: Antecedents, Mechanisms, and Contexts," in Todd D. Nelson, ed., *Handbook of Prejudice, Stereotyping, and Discrimination* (New York: Psychology Press, 2009), 111–35.

2. Amy D. Waterman, James D. Reid, Lauren D. Garfield, and Sandra J. Hoy, "From Curiosity to Care: Heterosexual Student Interest in Sexual Diversity Courses," *Teaching of Psychology* 28, no. 1 (2001): 21–26.

3. Corey Robin, "Who Really Said That?" *Chronicle of Higher Education*, September 16, 2013, https://www.chronicle.com/article/Who-Really-Said-That-/141559.

4. Edmund Burke quote, Bartleby, https://www.bartleby.com/73/560.html.

Index

INDEX

INDEX

Instagram, 29, 33, 113, 114, 117, 153, 173, 192, 193, 196, 203, 210
instincts, 10
interference loop: between work and private life, 79–80, 94, 101–3
Internet
  and active reading, 151
  and comment-section culture, 147–48, 151, 153
  and information overload, 131–39, 143, 144, 145, 147–48, 151–52, 153, 156
  junk data on, 137
  and limiting of information, 144, 145, 156
  and online scams, 143
  popularity of, 141
  and real-time conversations, 151–52
  redundancy of information on, 138
  sharing on, 153
isolation: and information overload, 141

J
Jackson, Susan, 90
James: procrastination by, 42–44, 45, 47, 48–49, 89
Jason (therapist), 64–66, 69, 70, 101
Jenner, Kylie, 29
Joan: as documenting her life, 124–26, 129
jobs/workplace. *See* hard work; unemployed people; work/jobs; workday/workweek
Julie
  as overextended, 37–41, 50
  and "shoulds," 187, 196–97

K
Kaitlin: and "shoulds," 185, 187
Kardashian, Kim, 29
"keeping up with the Joneses," 192, 194
Kim (friend)
  disability of, 198
  as homeless, 12
  and saving the world, 197–98, 203
Knope, Leslie, 107–8, 110

L
labeling, 209, 210
labor movement, 76, 81
Labriola, Kathy
  and relationships, 161–62, 163, 164, 165, 168–69, 177, 178, 179–80
  and saving the world, 198
  "shoulds" and, 198
Lavery, Danny M., 179

laziness
  as basic human need, 36
  as beneficial, 42, 64
  characteristics of, 3–5, 42
  definition of, 12, 49
  demonization of, 57
  and future of individual, 4–5
  listening to, 57–64
  popular concepts about, 1–2
  rethinking, 37–71
  as self-preservation instinct, 10
  as warning system, 49–57, 75, 96
  See also specific topic
Laziness Lie
  avoiding pressures of, 93–94
  and big picture, 208–10
  and binary thinking, 142
  compassion as killing, 205–14
  fighting/resisting the, 15, 187, 205–14
  history/origins of, 23–25, 214
  indoctrination of, 15, 118, 206, 212
  influence/prevalence of, 9–10, 11–15, 16, 22–23, 24, 25, 26, 27–33, 36, 210, 214
  and judging laziness, 11–15
  and reasons for feeling lazy, 33–36
  tenets of, 15–23, 214
  unlearning the, 205–14
  and warning signs, 20–21
  what is the, 9, 15–23
  and why you feel lazy, 33–36
  See also specific topic
learned helplessness, 49
Leo
  as overextended, 50–52, 54–56
  and "shoulds," 196–97
Leslie (friend): activism of, 199–200
letting go, 61–64, 71
Levine, Grace: and communications research, 141
life
  documenting your, 124–30
  gamification of your, 110–14, 126, 129
  living your own, 175–76
  as messy, 192–96
  work and private, 40, 78–80, 94, 96, 101–3
life expectancy, 91
lifestyle
  comparisons of, 194–96
  and "shoulds," 192–96
limitations
  and achievements, 128
  benefits of, 145
  importance of, 10

INDEX

TikTok, 33
time
 how you spend your, 168–69
 See also cyberloafing
Tobia, Jacob, 186
Tobias, Andrew, 105–6
Tom (Riley's husband): and relationships,
 165–67, 171–72
Towler, Annette, 56, 73–74, 78, 82, 85–86,
 94, 96, 103
transgender people, 109, 137, 168, 186
TV shows: and influence/prevalence of
 Laziness Lie, 28–29
Twitter, 113, 118, 125, 129, 136, 144, 145,
 147, 153

U
unemployed people, 13
Upswing Advocates, 62–63

V
vacations, 64, 212
values
 clarification of, 169–71
 definition of, 169
 and origins of Laziness Lie, 23
 ranking of, 170
 and relationships, 169–71, 182
Van Bavel, Jay, 84
veterans: healing of, 68
visual arts: and why you feel lazy, 33–35

W
warning signs/system
 ignoring of, 20–21
 and influence/prevalence of Laziness
 Lie, 36
 and rethinking laziness, 49–57
 and tenets of Laziness Lie, 20–21
 and working less, 75, 96
 See also specific sign
wasting time. *See* cyberloafing
Watson, John B., 172
wealth, 29, 30
Weil, Andrew, 148–49
Weiner, Matthew, 184
welfare, 26
what matters: and rethinking laziness,
 61–64
white supremacy, 26
Wick, John, 3, 27
Wild Mind Collective, 92, 93, 185
willpower, 15, 20

withdrawal: and working less, 87
women, 165–67, 209. See *also* feminism;
 sex/sexism; *specific person*
WordPress, 137
work/jobs
 absenteeism from, 82
 advocating at, 59–61, 94, 95–99, 103
 as center of life, 9
 coffee in, 93
 conformity in, 184, 186
 cyberloafing in, 52–54
 definition of people by, 16–19
 doing poor, 171–72
 gig economy and, 76, 80–81
 and judging laziness, 16–19
 and laziness as warning, 52–54, 56
 Laziness Lie and, 9, 75, 78, 93–94, 102, 103
 and listening to laziness, 59–61
 as meaningless, 87–90
 pensions/benefits from, 77
 petty misbehavior against employers
  in, 89
 and priorities, 92, 93, 95, 97, 98
 and private life, 40, 78–80, 94, 96, 101–3
 quality of, 85–86, 90–91, 96, 99–101, 212
 quitting, 98, 102–3, 210
 remote, 79–80, 97–98
 and rethinking laziness, 52–54, 56, 59–61
 sick days from, 78–79
 success in, 184
 trusting employees in, 96
 as unrewarding, 88
 vacations from, 78
 and working less, 73–104
 working more in, 75–81
 See also hard work; overextended;
  productivity; workday/workweek
workday/workweek
 average, 76, 77
 forty-hour, 49–50
 increase in, 75–83
 and laziness as warning, 49–50
 productivity and, 81–83
 quality of, 94, 99–101
 and rethinking laziness, 49–50
 standard, 82
 and technology, 76
 unrealistic, 82–83
 wasted time during, 83
 and working less, 94, 99–101

Y
YouTube, 29, 30, 192, 214

About the Author

Dr. Devon Price is an Assistant Clinical Professor of Applied Psychology and Data Science at Loyola University Chicago's School of Continuing & Professional Studies. Their research on intellectual humility and political open-mindedness has been published in *The Journal of Experimental Social Psychology*, *Personality and Social Psychology Bulletin*, and *The Journal of Positive Psychology*. Devon's work has been featured on the front page of Reddit and on National Public Radio, and they have been interviewed by outlets such as *Sex Out Loud with Tristan Taormino*, *Chicago Tonight*, and KPCC's *Airtalk*.

Devon's essay "Laziness Does Not Exist," originally published to Medium in March 2018, has reached an audience of more than 2.5 million people, has been translated into Spanish, Portuguese, Arabic, German, Turkish, Mandarin Chinese, and Japanese, and has introduced people throughout the world to the idea that when we judge a person for being "lazy," we're overlooking the immense barriers and challenges they're facing that we cannot see.

Devon's writing has appeared in *Slate*, *The Rumpus*, *The Toast*, *Chicago Reader*, *The Huffington Post*, *Human Parts*, and *Elemental*, and is regularly featured on Medium's front page.

Devon lives in Chicago with their partner, Nick, and their chinchilla, Dump Truck.